OLD GRAHAM THE HUNTER.

See page 61

THE

Early Days of California:

EMBRACING

WHAT I SAW AND HEARD THERE, WITH SCENES IN THE PACIFIC.

BY J. T. FARNHAM, ESQ.

AUTHOR OF "TRAVELS IN THE GREAT WESTERN PRAIRIES," ETC. ETC.

Illustrated.

PHILADELPHIA:
PUBLISHED BY JOHN E. POTTER,
No. 617 SANSOM STREET.
1859.

PREFACE.

CALIFORNIA is my theme. She is now an integral portion of this great Republic. A mighty population from all parts of the world has congregated on her shores, and with giant strides she marches on to power and greatness. Her mineral wealth seems inexhaustible, vast sums of gold being annually exported to the Atlantic States and elsewhere.

But a few short years and her condition was widely different. With but a sparse white population; with a government hardly existing other than in name, deeds of wrong, of violence, and of blood were of constant occurrence. Of this interesting portion of her history comparatively little is known; and it is of this period that I propose to write. To what I saw and heard while in the country has been added authentic information from every known source.

We may learn much from the pulseless solitudes—from the desert untrodden by the foot of living thing—from the frozen world of mountains, whose chasms and cliffs never echoed to aught but the thunder-tempests girding their frozen peaks—from old Nature, piled, rocky, bladeless, toneless—if we will allow its lessons of awe to reach the mind, and impress it with the fresh and holy images which they were made to inspire.

And now, dear reader, my task is done. Should you laugh and weep, suffer and rejoice, with the actors in the wayfarings before you, and send your fancy in after-times over those rose-clad realms where they will lead you, and feel the dews of a pleasant remembrance falling on your life, I shall receive a full reward for my toil.

Adieu.

THE AUTHOR.

CONTENTS.

CHAPTER I.

The great Pacific—A Storm at Sea—Our Crew and Company—Various Yarns—Old Ocean in a Rage—How we turned in,........ 5

CHAPTER II.

Pictures of Woe—The Sack of Bones—His Experiences in California—The Black Cook and Scotch Mate—Land, ho!—Various Emotions produced—Honolulu and the Professor of Psalmody,........ 22

CHAPTER III.

The First Visitors to the Hawaiian Islands—What Civilization and Christianity has done—On the Sea again—Our Crew and Passengers—A Squall—Land ahead—California forever!........ 37

CHAPTER IV.

Brief Whispers of a Revolution—California Officials—Famishing in Prison—Isaac Graham and his Men—Alvarado in Power—Base Treachery,........ 52

CHAPTER V.

What the Prisoners Said—John Warner's Story—The Spectral Fleet—The Hardy American Trappers—The Mock Trial—The brave Tennesseean in Despair—A California Festa,........ 70

CHAPTER VI.

Vale of San Carmelo—A California Lawyer—Long Tom Sassafras—The Coast—El Mission De Santa Barbara—The Prisoners again—A Friend in Need,........ 98

CHAPTER VII.

California as it was—The Search for Gold—Wreck and Horrible Sufferings of Cortes' People—The Excitement at its Height—The Star of Cortes wanes,........ 117

CHAPTER VIII.

Spanish Adventurers again — Their Fortunes and Misfortunes—Indian Courtesy—A Terrible Disease—Officers all Sick—A Sovereign Balm and an Affecting Scene,......... 127

CHAPTER IX.

Brilliant Hopes and Small Results—An Intended Massacre—A Holy Voyage Commenced—Trouble with the Indians—The Padres Triumphant—Last Days of Father Kino,...... 149

CHAPTER X.

The Holy Voyagers at their Work—A Famine—The First Execution in California—What one Musket did—Poison and Death,.. 168

CHAPTER XI.

The Padres and the Indians—Hope on, Hope ever—The Good Father Salva Tierra—His Sufferings and Death—Great Mourning—Thirty Thousand People in Prayer,........... 189

CHAPTER XII.

The Wealth of Exhaustless Energy—Triumph of the Cross—Zeal of the Padres — Frightful Tempests and a Water Spout,... 201

CHAPTER XIII.

How Father Napoli Discomfited the Indians—A Band of Depredators—A Terrible Storm—An Indian Force and a Victory—A Voyage of Discovery—Another Jonah and an Enormous Shark,...................................... 221

CHAPTER XIV.

Troubles Thicken—The Indians in Revolt—Brutal Murder of Father Carranco—Infernal Orgies—Another Murder—The Indians to the Rescue—A Victory of Love—California Shrouded in Gloom,.................................. 237

CHAPTER XV.

Life and Light again for California—Thieves and a Fight—Death of Father Junipero—What California was—Masterly Inactivity of Alvarado—Captain Jose Castro, his Intrepid Ally,.. 261

CHAPTER XVI.

War with the United States—Heroism of the Americans—Various Battles—Conquest—Discovery of Gold—On the Pacific again—Long Tom finishes his Yarn—Poor Graham and the last of the Prisoners—Home again,............... 299

CHAPTER I.

A Reminiscence—A Spectacle—Oregon—Landward and Seaward—The Great South Sea—Magic Palace—Taking in Studding-sails—Caverns—Storm in Full Blast—Professor of Psalmody—Fur Hunter—A British Tar—An Author—A Seaboat—A Corkscrew—A Flagon—A Conversation about Life in the Northwest—Its Dogs—Logs—Food—Surface—Lords of the North—Frozen Mountains—Moss—Flowers—Potatoes, Oats and Barley—Indian Wives and Sheep—The Arctic Shore—Suicide of a Brave Man—A Solo—Eel Pond—Ghost in the Shrouds—Tumult in Upper and Lower Ocean—Minor Key—War-cry—Special Pleading—The Sea—Wine and Song—To Bed.

In a work entitled "Travels in the Great Western Prairies," &c., to which the following pages are a sequel, I left my readers off the mouth of Columbia river, in sight of the green coast of Oregon. Lower Oregon! A verdant belt of wild loveliness!—A great park of flowering shrubs, of forest pines, and clear streams! The old unchanged home of the Indian; where he has hunted the moose and deer; drawn the trout from the lake, and danced, sung, loved, and warred away a thousand generations. I cannot desire for myself any remembrances of the Past which shall bring me more genuine wealth of pleasurable emotions than those which came to me from that fourth sunset of December, 1840, when I was leaning over the bulwarks of the ship Vancouver, looking back on Oregon, and seaward over the great Pacific! A spectacle of true grandeur! The cones of eternal snow which dot the green heights of the President's range of mountains, rose on the dark outline of the distant land, and hung glittering on the sky, like islands of precious stones; so brightly did they shine in the setting sun, and so completely did the soft clouds around their bases seem to separate them from the world below!

The shores of Lower Oregon! They rise so boldly from the sea! Themselves mountains sparsely clad with lofty pines, spruce and cedar trees, nodding over the deep!

And then the ground under water! No flats, no mud banks there. The cliffs are piled up from the bottom of the ocean The old Pacific, with his dark depths, lies within one hundred yards of them! And the surges that run in from the fury of the tempests, roll with unbroken force to the towering rocks, and breaking with all their momentum at once, making the land tremble, and send far seaward a mighty chorus to the shouting storm!

The Pacific! the Great South Sea! It was heaving at our bows! steadily, wave on wave came and went and following each other in ceaseless march pressed onward; like the world's hosts in marshaled files, they hastened past us, as if intent to reach the solid shores, where some resistance would broach their hidden strength and pour their fury out!

Behold the sea! Its troubled wastes are bending and toppling with a wild, plashing, friendly sound; a deep, blue, uncertain vastness; itself cold and passive; but under the lash of the tempest, full of terrific life! Our ship stood staunch upon the palpitating mass, and seemed to love it.

Mizen and mizen-top, main and main-top, fore and fore-topsails, and the lower weather studding-sails were out. The breeze from the land which had carried us over the bar still held, every thread of canvass drew, every cord was tight, and as we looked up through the rigging to the sky, the sails, cordage and masts swayed under the clouds like the roofing of some magic palace of olden tales. All hands were on deck; both watches sat about the windlass; while the second officer and mate looked at the horizon over the weather-bow, and pointed out a line of clouds crowding ominously up the southwestern sky. The captain stood

Sailing of the Vancouver from the Shores of Oregon.—Page 6.

upon the companion-way, looking at the barometer. In a little time officers and passengers gathered in a knot on the larboard quarter.

"I ken there's a storm comin' up frae the soo'est," said the Scotch mate.

"The clouds loom fast, sir, in that quarter," said Mr. Newell, the American second-mate. "I reckon it will be upon us soon."

Captain Duncan needed no information in regard to the weather on these shores. He was everywhere an accomplished seaman. On the quarter deck—with his quadrant—on the spars—and at the halyards; but especially in that prophetic knowledge of the weather, which gives the sons of Neptune their control over the elements, he had no superiors.

"Take in the studding-sails and make all fast on deck," is the order, issued with quietness and obeyed with alacrity. Water casks, long-boat, and caboose are lashed; ropes coiled up and hung on the pins in the bulwarks, and the hatches put down in storm rig. The wind before which we were running abated, and the horizon along the line of departing light began to lift a rough undulating edge.

"Take in the mainsail!" "Go aloft and take a reef in the maintop!" "In with the fore-main, and let the trysail run!" followed each other in haste, as the sailors moved to the cheering music of their songs in the work of preparing the ship to wrestle with a southwester. Everything being made snug, we waited its coming.

The rough water which appeared a mere speck when the wind came upon the circle of vision, had widened till its extreme points lay over the bows. On it came, widening and elevating itself more and more! The billows had previously been smooth, or at least ruffled sufficient only to give their gentle heaving sides a furzy aspect, while the tops occasionally rose in transparent combs, which immediately crumbled by their own weight, into foam down their leeward acclivities. But now a stronger spirit had laid his arm on these ocean coursers. The wind came on, steadily increasing its might from moment to moment! At first it tore the tops of the waves into ragged lines, then rent the whole surface into fragments of every conceivable form, which rose, appeared and vanished, with the rapidity of thought, dancing like sprites among the lurid moving caverns of the sea! A struggling vastness! constantly broken by the flail of the tempest, and as often reunited, to be cleft still farther by a redoubled blast.

The darkness thickened as the storm increased; and when the lanthorn was lighted in the binnacle, and the night-watch set, the captain and passengers went below to their wine and anecdotes. Our company consisted of four persons. One was a singing-master, from Connecticut, Texas, New Orleans, and St. Louis. He was such an animal as one would wish to find if he were making up a human menagerie; so positive was he of step, so lofty in the neck, and dignified in the absurd blunders wherewith he perpetually corrected the opinions and assertions of others.

Another was a Mr. Simpson, a young Scotchman, of respectable family, a clerk in the service of the Hudson's Bay Company. This was a fine fellow, twenty-five years of age, full of energy and good feeling, well-informed on general topics, and like most other British subjects abroad, troubled with an irrepressible anxiety at the growing power of the States, and an overwhelming loyalty toward the mother country and its Sovereign skirts. The other personages were the commander, Duncan, and the author.

The Captain was an old British tar, with a heart full of generosity for his friends, and a fist full of bones for his enemies. A glass of cheer with a messmate, and a rope's end for a disobedient sailor, were with him impromptu productions, for which he had capacity and judgment; a hearty five foot nine inch, burly, stout-chested Englishman, whom it was always pleasant to see and hear.

This little company gathered around the cabin table, and all as one listened a moment to the beatings of the tempest,

A surge—another—and a third still heavier, beat upon the noble ship, and sent a thrill through every timber. On they rolled, and dashed, and groaned. But her iron heart only seemed to gather strength from the conflict, and inspire us with a feeling of perfect safety.

"A fine sea-boat is the Vancouver, gentlemen," said Captain Duncan, "she rides the storm like a petrel:" and with this comfortable assurance we seated ourselves at the table.

I had nearly forgotten Tom, the cabin-boy; a mere mouse of a lad; who knew the rock of a ship and the turn of a corkscrew as well as any one; and as he was spry, had a short name, a quick ear, and bore the keys to the sideboard and some things elsewhere, all well-bred stomachs would not fail to blast my quill, if I omitted to write his name and draw his portrait.

Well, Tom was one of those sons of old England, who are born to the inheritance of poverty, and a brave heart for the seas. Like many thousand children of the Fatherland, when the soil refused him bread, he was apprenticed for the term of seven years to seamanship. And there he was, an English sailor-boy, submitting to the most rigorous discipline, serving the first part of his time in learning to keep his cabin in order, and wait at the table, that when, as he was taught to expect, he should have a ship of his own, he might know how to be served like a gentleman. This part of his apprenticeship he performed admirably. And when he shall leave the cork-screw and the locker for the quarter-deck, I doubt not he will scream at a storm, and utter his commands with sufficient imperiousness to entitle him to have a Tom of his own.

"Tom," said Captain Duncan, "bring out a flagon of Jamaica, and set on the glasses, lad. This storm, gentlemen, calls for cheers. When Neptune labors at this pace, he loves his dram. Fill, gentlemen, to absent wives." This compliment to the sacred ascendency of the domestic affections was timely given. The storm howled hideously, for our lives, our families were far distant over seas and mountains, the heart was pressed with sadness: we drank in silence and with swimming eyes.

A pleasant conversation followed this toast, in which each one of our little band exhibited himself in his own way. The Captain was a hearty old Saxon, who had inherited from a thousand generations, a love for home, its hearth and blazing evening fire, its old oaken table, its family arm-chair, and the wife who presided over that temple of holy affections. In him, therefore, we had the genuine spirit of those good old times when man used his physical and mental powers, to build about his heart the structures of positive happiness, instead of the artificial semblances of these, which fashion and affectation draw around the modern home.

Our professor of psalmody was the opposite of this. He had, when the red blood of youth warmed his heart in the ways of honest nature, spoken sweet things to a lovely girl, won her affections, promised marriage, and as his beard grew became a gentleman; that is, jilted her. He, therefore, was fond of freedom, could not be confined to so plain and quiet a business as the love of one woman, and the care of a family of children. "It was quite horrid, indeed it was, for a man who had any music in his soul; the mere idea was concentrated *picra* to his moral stomach; the thought, bah! that a gentleman could ever think of being a daddy, and trotting on his paternal knee a semi-yearling baby."

Mr. Simpson was from the braes of Scotland. For many years he had lived an isolated and roving life, among the nows, morasses, and lakes of the wilderness, which lies west and north-west of Hudson's Bay. He had been taught his catechism at kirk, and also a proper respect for the ties of the domestic sentiments. But the peculiar idea of manliness which grows up in those winter realms of danger, privation, and loneliness, had gradually habituated him to speak of these relations as desirable mainly when the body had expended its energy in striding mountains, in descending rocky torrents with boats laden with furs, and in the other bold enterprises of these daring traders.

From him we obtained a description of some portions of that vast country occupied by the Hudson's Bay Company; and some information on other topics connected with it. Life in the Company's service was briefly described. Their traveling is performed in various ways at different seasons of the year and in different latitudes. In Oregon their journeys are chiefly made in Mackinaw boats and Indian canoes. With these they ascend and descend the various streams, bearing their cargoes, and often their boats, from the head-waters of one to those of another. In this manner they pass up the Cowelitz and descend the Chihilis with their furs and other goods; thus do they reach the head-waters of the northern fork of the Columbia, pass over the Rocky Mountains, and run down the rivers and lakes to Canada. Farther north on the east side of the Rocky Mountain range, they travel much on foot in summer, and in winter (which is there the greatest part of the year) on sledges drawn by dogs. Ten or twelve of these animals are attached to a light sledge, in which the man sits wrapped in furs and surrounded by meat for his carnivorous steeds and provisions for himself. Thus rigged, the train starts on the hard snow crust, and make eighty or one hundred miles before the dogs tire. When the time for rest comes, they are unharnessed, fed, tied to the bushes or shrubs, and the traveler enveloped in furs, addresses himself to sleep under the lea of a snow-bank or precipitous rock. When nature is recruited, the train is again harnessed and put on route. The Aurora Borealis, which flames over the skies of those latitudes, illuminates the country so well, that the absence of the sun during the winter months offers no obstacles to these journeyings. Drawn by dogs over mountain and plain, under heavens filled with electric crackling light, the traveler feels that his situation harmonizes well with the sublime desolation of that wintry zone. In this manner these adventurous men travel from the mouth of Mackenzie's river to York on Hudson's Bay and to Canada.

Their dwellings are usually constructed of logs in the form of our frontier cabins. They are generally surrounded by pickets, and in other respects arranged so as to resist any attack which the neighboring savages may make upon them. They are usually manned by an officer of the Company and a few Canadian Frenchmen. In these rude castles, rising in the midst of the frozen north, live the active and fearless gentlemen of the Hudson Bay Company. The frosts of the poles can neither freeze the blood nor the energy of men who spring from the little Island of Britain. The torrid, the temperate, and the frozen zones alike hear the language and acknowledge the power of that wonderful race.

The food of these traders is as rude as their mode of life. At most of the Forts they live almost exclusively on the white and other kinds of fish; no vegetables of any description are obtainable; an occasional deer or woods buffalo or musk ox is procured; but seldom is their fare changed from the produce of the lakes and streams. At a few of their stations not even these can be had; and the company is obliged to supply them with *pemican*. This is buffalo meat dried, finely pulverized, mixed with fat and service berries, and secured in leathern sacks. They transport this from latitudes forty-eight and nine to different places on Mackenzie's river, and other parts of the extreme north. Wild fowls, geese and ducks afford another means of subsistence. At York and other posts in the neighborhood of lakes, large numbers of these fowl are taken in the summer season, and salted for winter use. But with all their painstaking, these gentlemen live but poorly; on a diet of flesh alone, and that of an indifferent quality. Hardy men are these lords of the snow. Their realm embraces one-ninth of the earth. This immense territory Mr. Simpson informed us has a great variety of surface.

On the north-eastern portion lie extensive tracts of perpetually frozen mountains, cut by narrow valleys filled with fallen cliffs, among which dash and roar numerous rivers on their way to the frozen sea. Scarcely any timber or other vegetation grows in these wastes. A lonely evergreen or a stunted white birch takes root here and there, and during the few weeks of summer, mosses and linchens present a few verdant spots in the damp recesses of the rocks. But cold winds, laden with hail and sleet, howl over the budding of every green thing! The flowers can scarcely show their petals and set their seeds, before winter with its cracking ices and falling snow embraces them!

The section of country which lies about Mackensie's river, differs from that described, in having dense forests skirting portions of the valleys, and large plains of moss and linchen, on which feed the deer, buffalo, musk-ox and moose. The river itself is, in summer months, navigable for batteaux several hundred miles. It is well stored with trout, salmon, white and other fish. But the winters there also scarcely end, before they begin again their work of freezing land, stream, and sea.

The extensive country lying on the head waters of the streams which run northward into the Frozen Ocean, eastward into Hudson's Bay, and southward into the Canadian waters, is composed of swamps, broken at intervals with piles of boulders and minor mountains, and dotted with clumps of bushes, plots of hassocks, and fields of wild rice. The waters of these table-lands form many lakes and lofty cascades on the way to their several destinations. The roar of these on the dreadful frozen barrenness around, Mr. Simpson represented to be awful in the extreme; so wild, hoarse, and ringing are their echoes.

We are informed that there are considerable tracts of arable land on the western side of Hudson's Bay, occupied by several settlements of Scotch: that these people cultivate nothing but potatoes, oats, barley, and some few garden vegetables; and are altogether in a very undesirable condition. He also informed us of a tract of tillable land, lying some hundreds of miles north-east of Lake Superior, on which Lord Selkirk had founded a colony; that this settlement contains about three thousand people composed chiefly of gentlemen and servants, who have retired from the Company's service with their Indian wives and half-breed children. They cultivate considerable tracts of land, have cattle and horses, schools and churches, a Catholic Bishop and a Protestant preacher of the English Church. Some years since, a Mr. McLeod, from this settlement, went to Indiana and purchased a very large drove of sheep for its use. But in driving them a thousand miles over the prairies, their fleeces became so matted with poisonous burrs, that most of them died before reaching their place of destination.

Mr. Simpson related a few incidents of an exploring expedition, which the Company had despatched to the northern coast of America. The unsatisfactory results of those fitted out by the home government, under Parry, Franklin, Ross, and Back, which had been partially furnished with men and means by the Company, led it at length to undertake one alone. To this end it despatched, in 1838, one of its officers, accompanied by our friend Simpson's brother, well furnished with men, instruments, and provisions, on this hazardous enterprise. I have since been informed, that this Mr. Simpson was a man of great energy and talent—the one indeed on whom the Company relied for the success of the undertaking. From his brother I learned only that the unexplored part of the coast was surveyed, that the waters of Davis' Strait were found to flow with a strong current westward, and enter the Pacific through Behring's Strait; and that Greenland consequently is an island or continent by itself! The Mr. Simpson of this expedition is now known to the civilized world to have trodden the ices and snows, and breathed the frozen air of that horrid shore; and by so doing to have added these great facts to the catalogue of human knowledge; and having become deranged in consequence of his incredible sufferings, to have blown out his own brains on the field of his glorious deeds. Our companion, poor fellow, was happily ignorant of that sad event, and spoke of the expedition only as one of great hardship, yet such as he would have gladly shared. His brave kinsman was then dead!

When Mr. Simpson paused in these interesting narrations, our professor of psalmody, who had been beating the table with a tuning-fork, opened a solo upon Texas. He had been in that country, and was, in his own estimation, as familiar with its rivers, plains, forests and destiny, as with the paths across his father's sheep pasture. Galveston was a London in embryo: Sam Houston had inherited the knee-buckles and shoe-knots of Washington's patriotism: the whole country was an Eden in which he had obtained the best sight for a grist-mill and the finest pond for eels! In short, we were informed in a tone of self-consequence, at least an octave above *mi*, on any known scale of conceit, that himself and a brace of fellow blades, on hearing that the government had offered a bounty of land to emigrants, went thither, remained long enough to perfect their title to a share of the public domain, and were then obliged by pressing business to return to the States and leave others to fight and die for freedom.

He had a belief that the Californias would make a respectable abode for man, if it were conquered by a bold arm, a little music, and made into a Republic by a man, he did not mention his own name, whose character for bravery, intelligence and taste for the fine arts, he did not say psalmody, would draw around him the unemployed intellect and courage of the States. In conclusion he modestly remarked, that he himself was destined to the Californias, but did not say that he intended to open there a revolutionary singing-school.

While this conversation was going on, the good old ship was struggling with the tempest. She headed north-westerly, and as the storm and swells came from the south-west, she at one time lay in the trough of the sea, and then, as the wave bore down upon her, swayed to the leeward a moment, rocked upon its summit, and as the surge passed on, reeled to the windward and slid into the trough again. This is the bitterest motion of a ship at sea, whether he whom it staggers be a "land lubber" or "salt." The latter finds it difficult to take his watch-walk from the windlass to the fore-stays, and swears that such a lullaby is as unworthy of the ocean god as it is unseemly for a decent sailor, to stand, at one instant with one leg clewed up and the other out, and the next clewed the other way, and be compelled, at each change, to brace himself back in the attitude of being frightened to death by a ghost in the shrouds.

The landsman, may perhaps feel too much awe to swear at the great deep, employed in its sublime labors; or if he dare profane thus the majesty of his Maker's movements, his noble self is usually the object of so much solicitude as to deny him any adequate opportunity of doing so. His stomach will demand much of the attention which he would fain bestow upon other objects; and it will scarcely be refused what it requires. We sat at the table till eight bells. A delightful chit-chat we had; such a variety of wisdom, such splendor of reminiscence, such bolts of reason rending and laying bare all the mines of thought were there!

But this and all that we had in expectancy that night ended not in smoke; that would have been land-like; but in a stealthy withdrawal of our company, one at a time, to pay their tribute to *Padre* Neptune. The singing master struck *minor key* first; the fur hunter followed with his war-cry; the Green Mountain lawyer came to the encounter with a throat full of special pleading; and after a hot melée each surrendered, on such terms as he could procure, all claim to the inborn rights of a quiet stomach and clean nose; and turned in. The night was passed by us in the cabin in clinging to our berths. The seamen on deck struck the bells, changed the watch, and stood out like iron men on the tide of that terrible tempest! Their thrilling "O he oe" occasionally cut sharply and cheeringly into the hoarse cadences of the storm! Every other sound of living thing was buried in the clangor of the elements.

The next morning opened with gloomy grandeur. The clouds brightened by the first rays of the sun in detached spots only, appearing and disappearing in rapid succession, intimated that the whole mass of ærial fluid was fleeing at a fearful pace before the unabated tempest. As the light increased into full day, the canopy hung so dark and densely down the heavens, that night appeared to have retained the half of its dominion. It need not touch the water as fogs do; but the massive heavy fold left between itself and the surface of the ocean, a space apparently three hundred yards in depth. That was a sight to wonder at. I could conceive of nothing in nature so far beyond the power of words to portray. Does the simile of a boundless tomb, vaulted with mourning crape, shaken by fierce winds, half lighted, filled with death-screams, represent it? I cannot tell: but such an idea rose as I looked out upon the scene.

Old Ocean, too, was in a glorious mood. I have often seen the Atlantic lay with his mighty bosom heaving to the sky, calm and peaceful like a benevolent giant slumbering on a world of lesser things; or, to use no figure, I had seen it slightly agitated, every particle tremulous under a soft breeze, every drop sending back the sunshine, or multiplying indefinitely the stars of a clear June night. I had seen it when the swells were torn by a "dry squall," or an hour's "blow," and heard its icebergs crack and plunge; and seen its fearful waterspouts marching so near me that I could hear their awful roar! But I had not seen it raised and rent, in the height of its tumult and power. All this was now before me in the great Pacific.

At ten o'clock the storm had gained its utmost strength. The ship was laid to. The waves were dashing over her bulwarks. The Captain was standing braced upon the weather quarter, dressed in a long pea-jacket, stout sea-pants and boots, an oil-cloth cap covering head and shoulders. The watch on duty were huddled under the weather bow and lashed to the stays to prevent being washed overboard. The second mate stood midship, holding fast to the rigging. All were looking at the storm. The ship herself lay like a lost water bird, rising, falling, buried and mounting again, among the overwhelming waves.

The appearance of the sea!—Who can describe it? Like the land, it had its valleys, and mountains, and streams. But its vales, instead of flowers and grasses, were covered with wisps of torn water; the mountains instead of snowy peaks, were billows, crested with combs of light blue water, tipped with foam, perpetually tumbling down and forming again, as the floods rushed on, lashing one another. And the streams were not such as flow through meadows and woodlands among creeping flower vines; but swift eddies, whirling through the heaving caverns of the sea.

Its voice! Its loud bass notes!—What is like it? Not the voice of the storms which assemble with lightning, thunder and wind, and pour devastating hail and fire on the upper heights and vales of the Rocky Mountains. Nor is it like the deep monitory groan that booms down the Great Prairie Wilderness at midnight, growing louder as it draws near, until the accumulated electricity ignites in one awful explosion, rending the clouds and tearing up the shaken ground! Nor is it like the voice of Niagara. That great cataract of the earth has a majestic stave, a bold sound, as it leaps from the poised brink to the whirling depths below! And when the ancient woods, with all their leafy canopies and ringing crags, stood up around it, and neither the hammer of the smith, nor other din of cultivated life, cast its vexing discords among the echoes, the sounds of Niagara must have resembled this sublime duett of the sea and storm; but never equalled it! It was a single note of nature's lofty hymns. To the ear of the Indian who stood upon the shelving rocks and heard it; who saw the floods come coursing down the rapids, bend upon the brink, and plunge

plunge with quickened speed into the vexed caldron, sending their peals to the rainbowed heaven, they must have borne an anthem as grand as his wild mind could compass—greater even. His bow must have dropped, and himself and the unharmed deer stood together, in mute wonder at Niagara chanting to the shades and silence of the old American Wilderness!

But the song of the sea! Is it not more than this? Miles in depth; hundreds of leagues in breadth; an immensity drop on drop and mass on mass in motion! The tempest piles up the surface into lofty ridges, every inch of which emits a peculiar liquid sound, which, mingling sweetly with each other far and wide, pulsates through the surrounding air and water! Sweet and boundless melodies of the seas! We know that the incumbent air takes up a part of them, while another part goes down into the still and motionless depths below; the sublime unbroken darkness of the sea! It was unpleasant to feel that the screaming cordage of our ships and the quarreling of the hull and the waves, should deprive us of hearing the tones of the Pacific waters, during the strength of a hurricane, unmarred by any other sound. Can it ever be given man to hear it? It is the Creator's great choir! Ocean tuned by His own hand, and swept by the fingers of his tempest!

Our good ship, carrying barely sail enough to make her obey the helm, beat from the southeast to the northwest. On the outward tack we generally made a few miles on our course, a part of which we lost on the other. It was vexatious to be buffetted thus to no purpose; to have our stomachs in a tumult; our jaws grinding down our teeth instead of eating; but withal it was very amusing. I had always thought men in a tolerable state of misery, possessed increased capacities to render themselves ridiculous. A number of common-place things proved this idea to be true. Turning-in was one of these. This is a process of going to bed; extraordinary in nothing else than the novel manner in which it is performed at sea in a gale.

The reader will pardon me. Please step into the cabin of the Vancouver, and be seated by the nice little grate, filled with blazing coals from the mines of Paget's Sound. You will perhaps amuse one eye with Tam O'Shanter, while with the other you explore. The six foot lawyer is gathering toward his berth. It is the lower one on the larboard side of the cabin. His countenance, you will observe, is a miniature tempest. The ship rolls suddenly, his feet slip from under him, and he slides under the table, accompanied by a bag of apples, a scuttle of coal, Tom, the cabin-boy, and a hot poker! Coal, apples, and the law, strown in indiscriminate confusion! As one might expect, the lawyer extricates himself from his difficulty, enters a "*nolle prosequi*" against further proceedings in that direction, and stretches himself in his berth, without attempting to persuade his wardrobe to take separate lodgings.

The fur-trader seems determined to undress. Accordingly, when the ship, in her rollings, is nearly right side up, he attempts to take off his coat; unfortunately, however, when he has thrown it so far back as to confine his arms, the ship lurches heavily, and piles him up in a corner of the cabin! Odds-blood! how his Scotch under-jaw smites the upper! It appears that wrath usually fights its battles in that part of mortality to a greater or less extent. On this occasion, our friend's teeth seem to have been ignited and his eyes set blazing by the concussion! As, however, there is nothing in particular to fight but the sea, and Xerxes has used up the glory of that warfare, the fur-dealer takes to his berth, without further demonstration of himself than to say that he thinks "the devil's tail is whisking in the storm," and that "his oxfoot majesty and the fin-tailed god must be quarreling stoutly about the naiads."

But the professor of psalmody is not to be prevented by these failures from unrobing himself for the embraces of Somnus; not he. "And if the planks of the ship will float me long enough it shall be done." He does not say that he is on his way to the conquest of the Californias; and that he will strip himself of his blue roundabout, as he will that beautiful country of its ill-fitting tyranny. His berth is on the starboard side. The ship is pitching and dodging like a spent top. How his bravery will end under such circumstances is a question of no little interest But that something will soon be done, you perceive becomes evident; for now as the starboard side lowers on the retreating wave, he seizes his outer garment with both hands, and with a whistle and jump that would do credit to a steam-car off the track, wrenches himself out of it just in time to seize the edge of his berth as the next surge strikes the ship and throws it suddenly on the other side. His vest comes off with more ease and less danger. Boots, too, are drawn without accident. But the pants! they are tight! He loosens the buttons; slides them down; with one hand he holds fast to the berth; pulls off the left leg with the other, and is about extricating the right foot, but, alas! that sudden jerk of the ship scatters his half-clad person, bravery, pants and all, among the trembling trunks, stools, table-legs, &c., to the manifest detriment of the outer bark of his limbs! At this moment Mr. Simpson is in the midst of his favorite passage—

"Ah Tam, ah Tam, thou 'll get thy fairin',
In hell they 'll roast thee like a herin'."

The professor of psalmody, after some search, finds himself again, and with courage unimpeached, lies down in silence.

CHAPTER II.

The next Morning—Eating—Mermaids—Cupid—A Sack of Bones on its Legs—Love—A Grandsire—She was a Woman—Chickens—A Black Son o' the De'il—A Crack o' the Claymore—Sublimity—Tropical Sight—Paternal Star—Cook—A Sense—Edge of the Trades—A Night —" On Deck"—A Guess—A Look and Doubt—To be *Dumbfoundered*—A Bird Note—Mouna-Kea—Christmas Eve—Watch-Fires of Angels—Birds—Fish—Homestead—Hawaiians—The Land—Moratai—Mooring —Landing at Honolulu—A Slice of Bull—Poi—The Death Wail—Hospitality—The Lover and his Destination—The Fur Hunter on the Back Track—The Professor of Psalmody.

THE next morning the storm was unabated. The furies seemed abroad. It was a cold sleety day. Both the atmosphere and the ocean looked like maniacs. Not a shred of the visible world seemed at ease with itself! Commotion, perpetual growls, screams and groans, came up from the tempestuous deep! Above were clouds, hurrying as from a falling world! Below was the ocean shaking!

Eating on this day was attended to in a very slight degree. When the dinner bell rang we were all on deck, standing in utter abandonment, to whatever the Fates might have in reserve for us. Not one would have broken a Christmas wish-bone with the prettiest girl living, to decide whether we should go below or be tumbled overboard. Captain Duncan was a skillful diagnostician in all such cases. He urged us below. But the thought of bringing our nasal organs into the full odor of bilge water, the steam of smoking meat, potatoes, and bean soup, arrested our steps. The good Cap tain, however, pressed us with renewed kindness, and we dragged ourselves down to the table. Ye Mermaids, how could ye ever learn to eat at sea! How could ye, rocked to sleep in infancy by the billows, educated in the school of the tempest, learn to hold your heads still enough to comb your glistening tresses! and much more get food within your pearly grinders!

Pictures of woe were we, starving, yet loathing food; thirsting, yet unable to drink; wishing for a mote of the stable world to look upon, yet having nothing but the unstable water and air; imprisoned on the rolling deck, with no foothold, or any odor of flower or earth around. I am reminded here how interesting to the antiquarian would be the inquiry, whether or not Cupid was ever at sea in a storm. If he were, he would have crowned Hogarth's immortality with its richest wreath, if transferred to canvass, in the act of running from the dinner-table, throwing his quiver behind him, and tipping his roguish face, bloated with the effort of a retching stomach, over the taffrail. Poor fellow, it makes one quiver to think if there ever were a Cupid, and he ever took passage from the Columbia river to the Hawaiian islands, and ever did attempt to eat, and while doing so were obliged to conform to the etiquette of sea sickness, how sadly he must have suffered, and how unlovely the arrow-god must have become!

This sea-sickness, however, is a farce of some consequence. Like the tooth-ache, fever and ague, and other kindred follies of the body it has its origin in——the faculty will please answer what. But seriously. It is an effort of our nature to assimilate its physical condition to the desires of the mind. Man's natural home as an animal is on land. As an intellectual being he seeks to pass this bound, and resorting to his capacity to press the powers of external nature into the service of his desires, he spikes planks to timbers, commits himself to the waves, rocks on their crests, habituates head and foot to new duties, and, girded with the armor of his immortal part, that wealth of Heaven, goes forth, the image and representative of his Maker, to see, to know, and to enjoy all things. But a truce to philosophy. We are on the sea. The elements have raved twelve days and are at rest again. Quiet and variable breezes from the north push us pleasantly along; appetites return; we shave our chins, comb our hair, and begin once more to wear the general aspect of men.

On the nineteenth of December our group of characters was honored by the appearance of a fine honest fellow from the steerage. He had suffered so much from sea-sickness, that he appeared a mere sack of bones. He was a native of one of the Southern States; but the Yankee spirit must have been born in him: for he had been to the Californias with a chest of carpenter's tools, in search of wealth! Unfortunate man! He had built the Commandante-General a house, and never was paid for it; he had built other houses with like consequences to his purse; had made many thousands of red cedar shingles for large prices and no pay; and last and worst of all, had made love, for two years, to a Spanish brunette, obtained her plighted faith for marriage, and did not marry her. It was no fault of his. During the last year of his wooing, a Californian Cavaliero, that is, a pair of mustachios on horseback, had been in the habit of eating a social dish of fried beans occasionally with the father of the girl, and by the way of reciprocating his hospitality, he advanced the old gentleman to the dignity of a grandsire.

This want of fidelity in his betrothed wrought sad havoc in our countryman's affections. He had looked with confiding tenderness on her person, returned her smile, and given her one by one his soul's best emotions. Such affections, when they go forth and not lost, leave a void to which they never return. He was alone again without trust, with nothing on earth, or rather, on the sea, to love but his carpenter's tools. The object of his regard had disgraced herself and him. To avoid the scene of his misery, he had invested in horses the little money he had accumulated; accompanied the Hudson's Bay Trading Company to Oregon, and having cultivated land a year or two in the valley of the Willamette, had sold his stock and property, and shipped for home, with every tooth strung with curses against the Californian Spaniards.

California itself, not including the bodies or souls of the people, he thought to be a desirable country. The very atmosphere was so delicious that the people went half-naked to enjoy it. Hard to abandon was that air, and the great plains and mountains covered with horses, black Spanish cattle, and wild game. The fried beans, too, the mussels of the shores, and the fleas even, were all objects of pleasure, utility or industry, of which he entertained a vivid recollection. But that loved one! she was beautiful, she was kind, alas! too kind. He loved her, she was wayward; but was still the unworthy keeper of his heart; still a golden remembrance on the wastes of the past—lovely, but corroded and defiled. His opinion was that she was a woman!

The weather became sensibly milder each day as we moved on our course; the water warmer, the fish and fowl more abundant. The latter presented themselves in considerable variety. The white and grey albatross, with their long narrow wings, and hoarse unmusical cry, cut through the air like uneasy spirits, searching the surrounding void for a place of rest, and finding none! Our cook contracted a paternal regard for these birds; the basis of which was, that whenever he threw overboard the refuse of the table, they alighted in the wake of the ship, and ate the potatoe peelings, bits of meat, &c., with a keen appetite. "Ah," said he of the spit, "it is a pleasure to cook for gentlemen in feathers even, when they eat as if they loved it." But he was still more partial to Mother Carey's chickens. In a fair morning these beautiful birds sat on the quiet sea in flocks of thousands, billing and frollicking in great apparent happiness.

"There's your poultry, gentlemen," cried his curly pate, peering from the galley. "Handsome flocks these about the stacks of water; plumper and fatter, I'll warrant ye, than any that ever squawked from the back of a Yorkshire Donkey. No need of cramming there to keep life agoin'.

They finds themselves and never dies with pip or dyspepsy."

"Hout wi' yer blaguard pratin', ye black son of the De'il; and mind ye's no burn the broo' agen. Ye're speerin' at yer ugly nose, an' ne'er ken the eend o' ye whilk is upward. Ye sonsie villain; when I'se need o' yer clatter I'se fetch ye wi' a rope's-end. And now gang in and see yer dinner is fit for Christian mooths."

This salutation from our Scotch mate, drove in the head of our poultry man, and we heard no more dissertations on sea-fowl during the voyage. At dinner the mate congratulated the company on the excellence of the pea-soup, remarking that it "smacked muir o' the plaid than usual," because he "had gi'en the cook a crack o' the claymore on his bagpipe; a keekin, as he war, at things wi'out when he should ha' been o' stirrin' his meal." Trifling incidents like this occasionally broke the monotony of our weary life. Our latitude and longitude were taken daily at twelve M., and the report of these and the distance from the islands always gave rise to some prophetic announcements of the day and hour when we should anchor in the dominions of Kamehameha. The evenings also furnished a few diversions and pleasant objects of contemplation. Bathing was one of the former. After the shadows of night had set in, we used to present ourselves at the mainstays, and receive as much of the Ocean as our love of the sublime by the gallon, or our notions of cleanliness demanded. And when the hooting, leaping, and laughing of the ceremony were silenced, the cool comfort of the body left the mind in listless quietude, or to its wanderings among the glories of a tropical sky.

It was the 24th of December; the mid-winter hour. But the space over us was as mild and soft a blue as ever covered a September night in the States. The stars sent down a delicate sprinkling light on the waters. The air itself presented some peculiar aspects. It was more nearly transparent than any I had ever breathed; and there seemed to be woven into all its thousand eddies a tissue of golden and trembling mist, streaming down from the depths of heaven! There was a single sad spot on the scene. The north star, so high and brilliant in the latitude where I had spent my previous years, was gradually sinking into the haze about the horizon. I had in very early life looked with greater interest upon that than any other star. The little house which my deceased father had built on the shore of a beautiful lake among the green woods of Vermont, stood "north and south" upon the authority of that star. And after he had died at that humble outpost of the settlements, leaving me a boy of nine years, his death-bed, the little house, and the star which had guided my parent's hand in laying the foundation on the brow of the deep wilderness, came to be objects of the tenderest recollection. I was sorry to see it obscured; for it always burned brightly in our woodland home; and was the only thing which, as years rolled on, remained associated with paternal love.

I remember, too, another class of emotions that gave occupation to my heart in those beautiful nights. We thought and talked of Cook. He had ploughed those seas long before us; had discovered the group of islands to which our voyage tended; had met a fearful death at the hands of the inhabitants; and some of his bones yet lay, scraped and prepared for the gods, in the deep caverns of Hawaii! The waters rippling at our ship's side, had borne him; had rushed in tempests, and lain in great beauty around him; had greeted the discovery flag of the brave old Fatherland, and heard its cannon boom! We were sailing under the same flag. It was not, indeed, the same identical bunting which floated in 1789; but it was the emblem of the same social organization, of the same broad intelligence; the insignia of the same Power, whose military embattlements, grain fields and homes, gird the Earth! I was glad to approach the Hawaiian Islands on the track of Cook, under the old British flag.

Is there a human sense which derives its nutriment from

the things which are gone? Is there a holy-flower which springs up among the withered tendrils of buried beauty? a strong and vigorous joy, which, like the Aloe, blooms a moment on the cold midnight of heavy sorrow? Is there an elevation of the whole being into a higher condition, when we wander among the trees, the ruins and the graves of former times? It may be so. For surely he who treads the dust of Rome and stands on the ruins of Thebes, has a species of previous existence wrapped about him. He sees in the one case armies thronging the Appian-way, hears the multitude surging in the forum under the enthusiasm kindled by Cicero, and feels that the eagle of freedom is throwing the pinions of his protection over the energies of man.

In the other case he hears the voice of the mighty chieftain summoning his millions of subservient hands. The hammer and the chisel, from the beginning to the end of day, send up their vast din to the passing hours. The mountain columns of Thebes stand up in the presence of the pyramids! And a subject land bows in servitude to a great and controlling intellect. We are there, and form an integral wave in the sea of vitality that flowed forty ages ago! We venerate the broken tomb of the past. We knock gently at its gate, and find our bodies and minds grow vigorous and happy in those sublime imaginings, which carry our entire selves back to see and converse with those men, the mere ruins of whose deeds still astonish mankind!

We retired to rest this evening in unusually fine spirits, for, with the aid of the good breeze piping down from the northwest, we expected sight of land by the next sunset. Our sleep, however, was not remarkably deep, for I recollect that the wind freshened during the night, as it generally does in the edge of the trades, and compelled the morning-watch to take in sail. The noise occasioned by this movement was construed, by the wakeful ear of our desires, into a shortening canvass to prevent running on land; and we turned out to see it. But it was yet beyond view. The night, however, was worth beholding. It was one o'clock; the sky overhead was clear and starry; around the north-western horizon hung a cluster of swollen clouds, like Moorish towers, faintly tipped with the dim light. In the southwest lay another mass, piled in silent grandeur, dark battlement-like, as if it were the citadel of the seas! The waters were in an easy mood. The ship moved through them evenly, save that she cut the long smooth swells more deeply than the space between them, and occasionally started from his slumber a porpoise or a whale.

We turned-in again and slept till the breakfast dishes clattered on the table, and Tom informed us that Mr. Newell supposed he had seen at sunrise the looming of the land in the southeast! That announcement brought us to our feet; sleep gave place to the most active efforts at hauling on and buttoning up the various articles of our wardrobe. "On deck! on deck! where away the land?" and we tasked our eyes with their utmost effort to scan the nature of the dark embankment on which the mate had founded his auguries. The excitement at length drew all the passengers and officers to the starboard-quarter; each man looked and expressed himself in his own way. To guess, was the Yankee's part; to look and doubt, was John Bull's pleasure; to wuss it might be true, was the Scotch contribution; and to reckon awhile and commend himself to be *dumbfoundered* if anything could be known about it, was the Carolinian carpenter's clincher. The matter left standing thus, we obeyed Tom's summons to breakfast.

While engaged in filling our countenances with the realities of life, we were startled with a bird's note from the deck! It proved to come from one of those winged songsters of the islands, which often greet the toiling ship far at sea, and with their sweet voices recall to the soul, weary with the rough monotony of an unnatural life, the remembrance and anticipation of the land; the green and beautiful land; where the glorious light brightens the flowers; where the flowers shed their perfume on the air, and the fruits of trees, and shrubs, and plants, are poured into the lap of the ripened year.

Who does not love the birds? who is not made better and happier by hearing them sing among the buds and leaves, when the streams begins to babble, and the mosses to peer above the retiring snows? when the violet opens, and meadows and forests change the brown garb of winter for the green mantle of the young year? No one who loves nature and can sympathize with it.

But this one—perched in the rigging of the ship in which we had been imprisoned for weeks—a messenger from the glens and hills sweetly chanting our welcome to them, was an object of the tenderest interest. It had the cordial greeting of our hearts; and while talking about it, we could not forbear reaching our hands towards it, and grieving that we had no intelligible language wherewith to convey our salutations, and ask the tidings from its beautiful home. The captain consulted his reckoning, and found that we lay about one hundred miles northwest-by-north from the island of Hawaii.

The breeze, instead of decreasing with the ascent of the sun, as it had done for a number of days past, held on; and with all the weather studding-sails out, we made about ten knots during most of the morning. About ten o'clock, Mr. Newell, who had been watching that embankment of cloud in the southwest, which had excited our hopes at sunrise, touched his hat to Captain Duncan and remarked, "That cloud retains its bearing and shape very much like the looming of land, sir. We must be in sight of some of the islands: we made ten knots by the log, sir, during my watch."

The Captain had expressed his belief that he could sail his ship under that cloud without lead line, or copper bottom; and it was still his opinion that an English commander like himself, an old salt of thirty years' standing, would be as likely to know the complexion of the land as any gentleman with less experienced optics. However, he sent Tom for his glass and peered into it with the keenest search. It was delightful, meantime, to us land-lubbers, to watch the workings of his face. There was a gleam of triumph creeping over it as he first brought his glass to bear upon the object. But as the highest part of the pile came into the field of vision, his cheeks dropped an instant, then curled into the well-known lineaments of chagrin, and then into those of rage, as if he would rather all the land were sunk, than he be found mistaken in a matter so purely professional.

"Damn the land!" he at length exclaimed; "I suppose it must be Mauna-Kea," and gave the glass to a passenger.

The breeze piped up and we moved on merrily. Merrily flew the gladdening waters from the prow; steadily as the masts stood out the canvass on the clear blue sky; and brightly beamed the warm and mellow day on the sea. The Scotch mate, who swore by any dozen of things that his memory happened to seize, affirmed by his blood and the whisky that had been buried seven comfortable years at his auld aunt's homestead, that he would see the lassies of Honolula before he was a day older; the professor of psalmody sung, "Here's a health to thee, Tom Moore;" the Hawaiian Island servants of the Hudson's Bay Company began to count their money preparatory to the purchase of *poi;* the crew began to tell yarns about "sprees" they had enjoyed in Chili, New Holland, Liverpool, Vera Cruz, St. Petersburgh and Montevideo; the six foot bootswain began to whistle; Tom began to grin; a former cabin-boy began to think of his mother, whom he expected to meet in the islands; the visitor bird chirped in the rigging; and all for joy! For now the lofty peaks of Hawaii loomed above the clouds, the sea-weed gathered on the prow, and the odor of the land puffed over us.

At five o'clock the breeze slackened again, and until nightfall the ship barely moved enough to obey her helm. Near ten in the evening it freshened, but as we were in the neighborhood of a lee-shore, the captain thought it prudent to keep good sea-room, and accordingly shortened sail and lay off a part of the night.

This was Christmas eve, that nucleus of so much social and religious joy throughout the Christian world, and a merry one it was to us. Not so in the ordinary sense of the trencher and cup, the music, dance, and the embrace of kindred ; nor rendered such by the pealing anthem or the solemn prayer, swelling up through the lofty arches hung with boughs of ever-green and the prophetic star of Bethlehem! But nature herself seemed worshipping! The heavens were unmarred by a single breath of mist, except what rested upon the heights of Hawaii; and on all its vault the stars shone, not as brightly as in the frosty skies of the temperate zones, but with a quiet subdued lustre, as if they were the watch-fires of angels assembled to celebrate the earth's great jubilee.

The Pacific, too, lent the scene its most charming condition. Wide and gently curved swells rolled down from the north, smooth, and noiseless, except when they dashed upon our noble ship, or were broken by the dolphin coursing through and dotting them with phosphorescent light! The sea-birds were hailing each other a merry Christmas. The grey and mottled albatross, flying from billow to billow, occasionally clipped the waves with his sword-shaped wings, and shouted gladly to the elements ! The gulls and other birds sat in countless flocks in every direction, sinking, rising and chattering on the panting sea ? And schools of tiny fish with bright golden backs swam by the side of the ship, as children, after long absence, gather with cherished remembrances around the old homestead on this blessed night.

At dawn on the 25th one of the islands lay six mile distant in the southeast. The sky was clear ; the sea smooth ; the porpoises blowing about us ; a right whale was spouting a hundred rods astern ; and our Hawaiians, looking from the mainstays at the land, were uttering their beautiful language of vowels with great volubility. *Poi* (the name of their national dish), *wyhini* (woman), and *iri* (chief), were the only words I then understood; and these occurred very often in their animated dialogues. Poor fellows! they had been five years absent from their *poi;* five years separated from the brown beauties of their native isles; five years away from their venerated sovereign. No wonder, therefore, they were charmed with the dim outline of their native land! A mass of vapor hung along its heights and concealed them from view, save here and there a volcanic spire which stood out on the sky, overlooking cloud, mountain, and sea. As the light increased to full day, this cloudy mass was fringed on the edge nearest us with delicate golden hues; but underneath it and inward toward the cliffs, the undisturbed darkness reached far eastward, a line of night belting the mountains mid-heaven. Downward from this line to the sea, sloped red mountains of old lava, on which no vegetable life appeared. On a few little plains near the beach the cocoa-tree sent up its bare shaft; and as the clouds broke away we discerned clumps of rich foliage on the heights. But generally the aspect was that of a dreary broken desert.

We sailed past the western cape of Moratai, and laid our course for the southeastern part of Oahu. At two o'clock our good old ship lay becalmed under the lofty piles of extinct craters, six miles northeast of Honolulu. At four the breeze freshened, and bore us down abreast of the town. Soon after a boat came rapidly from the shore with a pilot on board by the name of Reynolds; a generous, jolly old American gentleman, of long residence in the islands. He greeted his countrymen with great kindness, and having brought the ship to anchor outside the reef, invited us to go ashore in his boat. It was manned with islanders. They rowed to the entrance of the channel, rested on their oars while the angry swells lifted us at one instant on the summit of the waters and at another dropped us into the chasm between them, till the third and largest came, when, by a quick and energetic movement, they threw the boat upon the land side of it, and shot us into the harbor with the rapidity of the wind! We passed the American whalers which crowded the anchorage; ran under the guns of the fort; struck the landing at the pier; leaped ashore among crowds of natives, besprinkled with an occasional European face: followed an overgrown son of John Bull to another man's house, took a glass of wine, and scattered ourselves in various quarters for the night.

Thus terminated our voyage from the Columbia river to the Kingdom of Hawaii. The distance between Oregon and these islands is about three thousand miles. We had sailed it in twenty-one days.

The next morning the Vancouver entered the harbor with the land-breeze, and anchored near the pier. The "steerage" and the Hawaiians now came on shore. The former settled his hat over his eyes and sought a barber's shop; the latter repaired to the town with their friends. I followed them. Whenever they met an old acquaintance they immediately embraced him, and pressed noses together at the sides. After many salutations of this kind they arrived at the market-place; made a purchase of *poi* (a fermented paste of boiled *taro*), and seated themselves with their friends around it. The *poi* was contained in large calabashes or gourdshells. With these in the midst they began to eat and recall the incidents of pleasure which had sweetened their early years.

Their mode of conveying the *poi* to their mouths was quite primitive. The fore and middle fingers served instead of a spoon. These they inserted to the depth of the knuckles, and having raised as much as would lie upon them, and by a very dexterous whirl brought it into a globular shape upon the tips, they thrust it into their mouths, and licked their fingers clean for another essay. They had been seated but a short time when others joined them, who brought sad news. One of their former friends had recen died! On hearing this their hands dropped, and the dreadful wail *ewai* burst from every mouth, as they rose and went towards the hut in which the dead body lay. It was situated a short distance from the hotel; and during the night I heard that wail ring through the silent town! A more painful expression of sorrow I hope never to hear. The next morning I went to the burial. The wail was suspended during the ceremonies; but for several succeeding nights it continued to break my slumbers. A few days afterward I saw them gathered again near the market-place employed with their *poi*. The wages of five years' service was nearly exhausted. They had given a large portion to the chief of their district, and spent the rest in feasting and clothing their poor relatives. They were poor when I lost sight of them. But those whom they had fed were sharing their pittance with them. The most affectionate and hospitable people on earth are these Hawaiians.

Our Carolinian remained a few days at Honolulu, and took passage in one of P. J. Farnham & Co.'s ships for New York. He insisted to the very last of my intercourse with him, that his Californian brunette was a woman!

Mr. Simpson took lodgings with that distinguished slice of a John Bull to which I have already referred. He employed himself with much industry upon his duties of settling accounts with his host, who, as the agent of the Company, had sold the lumber, fish, &c., exported from Oregon to these islands. After tarrying a month at Honolulu, he returned in the Vancouver to Columbia River. He was a fine fellow, full of anecdote and social feeling, talented and modest; and I doubt not will eventually rise to the highest rank in the Company's service.

The professor of psalmody stopped at the hotel and prepared to exhibit himself. His first essay was to deliver to the American Missionaries and others, certain letters which he had obtained in Oregon. His next was to awaken the genius of music. For this purpose he attended a number of singing parties, at which he attempted to make himself useful to three young Americans, who sang with masterly taste. In the opinion of the professor they "needed a little burnishing," which he volunteered to give them. Unfortunately for the art, however, they were vain enough to suppose they had learned music before his arrival; and did not therefore value his suggestions so highly as he himself did. But the professor persevered. His forbearance knew no limit towards the deluded tyros. On all public occasions he never failed to throw out many invaluable hints as to movement, ascent, and style generally. He even encouraged them to hope that, with all their imperfections, they might attain a respectable degree of excellence if they would attend to his instructions. Whether or not his exertions were ever properly appreciated by these gentlemen is a question whch remains unsettled to this day. But the most interesting event which occurred to the professor in Honolulu was his interview with the sister of the young lady whom he had forsaken. She was the wife of a Missionary, a zealous servant of her Master. He called on her and was invited to remain to tea. I was present. Everything was sad as the grave! The mercies of Heaven were implored upon his blighted conscience! He left, little happier for the reminiscences awakened by the visit, and soon after sailed for California. I heard of him as an ingenious man in mending a watch on shipboard, but never as one of moral integrity or as the Napoleon of the Californias!

The Missionary's Wife:—**P: 36**

CHAPTER III.

Hawaiian Islands—Spaniards first visited them—Hooт ili Wyhini—Account of Cook's visit—A god—A Robber and his Death—Vancouver's Visit—Kamehameha I.—A Treaty—Cattle—Origin of the Islands—Poetry, and another Book—Legends—*Tabu*—Philosophy of Civilization—A Way to the End—What is Taught—Gratitude—Departure from the Islands—Lava and Cauldrons—Goats and Men—Passengers—Captain, Mates and Crew—A Human Managerie—Northing—Variables—Ten days Out—Too nauseous for Music—Uncombed Hair—Exhilarated—Lovely—Growing Fat—Ten Knots—Ten more days out—An Ocean Don--American and English Tars—A Squall—A new mode ot taking Eels—Land ho—Mission—Wrath—Monterey.

THIS group of islands was first visited by a Spanish ship, during the early explorations of the northwest coast of America, by Admiral Otondo, Viscaiyno, and others. The traditions of the natives say, that a small vessel was driven ashore on the southern coast of Hawaii, that two of the crew only escaped death among the breakers, and that these intermarried with the natives and left children. I saw some descendants of these men. Their European features and the use of a few corrupted Spanish words, satisfied me of the truth of the legend and the ship's nationality.

Captain Cook next visited them in 1779. The circumstances of his visit and massacre, as given me by a very aged chieftainess, Hoopili Wyhini, will interest the reader.

"Captain Cook's men were allowed to steal a canoe belonging to our people. Our chiefs asked that it might be returned; but Captain Cook had made us believe that he was a god, and thought to take what he pleased. Our traditions asserted that gods would not rob, and we told him so. But the canoe was not restored. Our people thought, therefore, that if Cook would steal from them, it would be right to steal from him; so in the night time, they swam under water a long distance to the ships, loosened the boat from one of them, and having brought it ashore, broke it in pieces for the nails. Cook was very much enraged at the loss of his boat, and threatened us with destruction if it were not returned. But it could not be; it was destroyed.

"A number of days passed in very angry intercourse between our people and the foreigners, during which a chief suggested that so unjust a being could not be a god. But all others said he was the great Kono. This was in our days of darkness. Why do you press me to remember such unpleasant things?"

I explained that I was anxious to know the truth of the matter, and she continued:

"At length Cook came on shore with an armed force, and went to the king's house to persuade him to go on board his ship. The chiefs interfered and prevented him. Cook was angry, and the people were in a great rage. He went down to the shore where his boat lay. The people gathered around him. The chief who did not believe him a god, tried to kill Cook, but Cook killed him; and then the people who belonged to that chief, killed Cook. It thus became clear that Cook was no god; for we thought our old gods could not die. These were our years of sin, before the Pono (Gospel) came among us; and it is not pleasant to speak of them."

This venerable chieftainess was advanced in womanhood at the time of Vancouver's visit, in 1779. She gave the following account of it:

"When Vancouver arrived at Hawaii, Kamehameha was the chief of three districts on that island. These were Kona, Kohala, and Hamakua. That year he fought against the reigning king, and conquered the whole island. Kamehameha did not see Vancouver at Kona, where he first ar

Shipwreck of the Spanish Vessel on the coast of Hawaii.—P. 38.

chored. But a little after the time of our national holidays, which occurred in the latter part of the Christians' December, he came to Kealukekua Bay. There I first saw him. Kamehameha also visited him at that place. The flag-ship, brig and store-ship, appeared to be under the general command of a man whom we called Pukéki; the captain of the store-ship we called Hapilinu.

" While this squadron remained in the bay, myself and thirteen others went aboard. They were Kamehameha, his three brothers and one sister, myself, my aunt, and two other women. The remainder were chief men. After being at sea four days, we anchored in Kealukekua Bay in which Cook was killed.

" Kamehameha was very friendly to Vancouver—according to our old rules of hospitality, he furnished him with a concubine. He gave me to him. I passed nine days on board his ship. Kamehameha presented to him a great many hogs and bananas, and received trifling presents of old iron in return. At the end of nine days I left the ship, in company with some other chiefs, to visit my sick brother, and did not return.

" On another occasion, Kamehameha, his chiefs, and two Englishmen who had been adopted by some old chiefs and made a part of the king's counsel, named John Young and Isaac Davis, were passing the day on board the flag-ship, when Kamehameha addressed to Vancouver these words: 'E nana mai ea u, eia ka aina,' which being interpreted, means, 'Look after us, and if we are injured, protect us.' To this Vancouver assented. An instrument in writing, which he said would bind his sovereign to keep the promise he had made, was framed and presented to the king. I do not know whether Kamehameha understood what was written; nor do I know whether or not the king signed it. But until the French captain, La Place, came, and abused us, we thought the English would protect us; because Vancouver promised to do so. Kamehameha always said the English were our friends—that the islands were his, and these friends would keep off all danger from abroad. It is not clear to me that they have been faithful to the words of Vancouver.

"Vancouver built a tent and high tower on shore. In the former he sometimes slept. In the latter his learned men pointed bright instruments at the moon and stars. A doctor, whom we called Makaua, visited the volcano. He had sore lips when he returned. He brought down some sulphur, saltpetre, and lava.

"Vancouver gave me two fathoms of red broadcloth. To the king and chiefs he also gave some of the same. He said the king of England sent it to us. I had two husbands at this time. The one was Kalanimamahu, the son of Keona, and the other Hoopili, the late governor of Maui. The first was the father of Queen Auhea; the latter is buried among the people near the church. Those were days of darkness.

"Vancouver gave to Kamehameha four cattle, three cows and one bull. He said to Kamehameha, 'feed them five years, and then begin to kill and eat.' They were shut up in a field several years, but broke out one after another, and went to the mountains. Very few were killed for thirty years. During the last ten, many have been slaughtered for their hides and tallow. Vancouver killed one of the calves before he left us. They were brought from California.

"Vancouver had an interpreter whom our people called Lehua; and another who was a native chief in the island of Taui. This latter had made a voyage in an English whale-ship, during which he had learned the language of that nation. By means of these men, he asked questions, and received answers in regard to our old ways. Once he asked 'whence came these islands?' and our chiefs replied—'Hawaii is the child of the gods Papa and Wakea, and the other islands are the children of Hawaii.'

"The chief priests then said Hawaii was in a very soft state immediately after birth, but a god descended from the skies and called—'E Hawaii Ea, O Hawaii Oh,' and the god

Hawaii came forth, communicated to the pulpy land a gyratory motion, made it come around him, and assume a permanent form. Vancouver replied, 'right.'

"I am sixty-five years old and must die soon."

I was exceedingly interested in these conversations with this remarkable woman. She had been one of the wives of Kamehameha the First; had commanded his navy of war canoes, during his conquests, and was at the time of my interview with her the acting executive of Maui, and a scholar in the Missionary Sabbath school!

I remained three months in these beautiful islands, enjoying the revelations of these chronicler of old and curious times. The king, chiefs, foreign residents and Missionaries, perceiving my avidity in gathering information respecting the country and its people, rendered me every aid in their power to facilitate my inquiries. Nor do I ever expect again to find a richer field of the strange, the beautiful, the wonderful and the sublime, than was there presented to me.

The legends of a thousand generations of men, living apart from the rest of mankind, among the girding depths of the Pacific seas; the stories of their gods and goddesses; the tales of their wars; the fate of bad princes whom their deities reprimanded from the skies; the beatification of the good on whom their divinities scattered blessings; their forms of government; their religious ceremonies; their genealogies; their poetry, more of it than Greece ever had, and still sung by bards travelling from village to village, their dances; their rejoicings at a birth; their wailings over the dead, and, the solemn ceremonies of their burials; are a few of the interesting subjects investigated.

The intense interest, as well as the amount of writing required to exhibit these matters, will furnish my best apology for passing them in this place. They may hereafter appear in a separate volume. But I cannot allow my readers to pass from the Hawaiian kingdom, without presenting to their ce the interesting fact, that a hundred and seven thousand savages have been brought within the pale of civilization and Christianity through the instrumentality of the Americans.

Twenty-five years ago a nation occupied the kingdom of Hawaii which sought its happiness from a systematic violation of the fundamental laws of Creation. Their food was under the *tabu*, or ban; so that the powerful in civil and religious affairs appointed the best edibles for their own use, and made death the penalty to their wives, daughters and inferiors, if they tasted them. The fire kindled to cook the food of the men was *tabued;* it was death for woman to kindle hers from it, or cook or light a pipe at it. The person of the king was *tabued.* It was death to touch him, or any article which he had used, or to step on his shadow, or the shadow of his house. And at the hour of midnight human victims were slaughtered, and piled on scaffolds with dogs and hogs, around the temples which they would consecrate to their deities!!

Here human nature had been forced from its true appetencies to the material and spiritual Universe. Its misery followed as an inevitable consequent. But the Hawaiians were thinkers. The violated ordinances of the world recoiling on them at every tread of life, forced on them the thought of obedience and its blessings. And they rose in their power; ate from the full hand of Heaven; prostrated their ancient temples; burned their hideous gods; made the civil power subservient to the common good; and restored themselves, after immemorial ages of degradation, to the quiet reign of the natural laws. It is most remarkable that the American missionaries were on their voyage to the islands while these things were being done!

The law of relationship between these people and their Maker had been lost among the crude follies of idol-worship and civil tyranny. These they had broken down by a mighty blow. The fragments of their temples, altars and gods, were strewn over the land. An entire nation looked on the flowers, the stars, the rivulet, the ocean, the birds and themselves,

Cocoa Tree of Hawaii.—P. 42.

and believed in no God!! The vessel which brought to them the Christian faith anchored at Honolulu! The event, which shook the hill, darkened the sun and opened the graves of Judea, was proclaimed, and gave its hopes of Heaven to a hundred thousand people! A nation thus entered the world as its loved homestead became obedient to its organization; called back the wandering religious sympathies to the worship of the true God; opened to every faculty the sphere of its legitimate enjoyments; and made human nature again a component part of creation, existing in harmony with it and its Author.

Man must incorporate himself into that great chain of relationship and sympathy which runs from inorganized matter to the first feeble manifestation of vegetable life, and thence upward through bud, leaf and blossom, and upward still along the great range of animal existence to the thinking and feeling principle, and thence to God. It is in this manner alone, that he can feed his faculties with their own aliment. And it is his ignorance of the dependence of each portion of his body and mind, on each and every external existence, which makes thorns for his feet and keeps up a perpetual warfare between himself and the immutable conditions of his true happiness.

I am sincerely persuaded that the regulating principle of human culture, is to sympathize with every form of creation within our knowledge; to enter the world as our home; to seat ourselves at its hearth; to eat its viands and drink its blessings; to slumber in its arms; to hear the floods of harmonious sounds which come up to us from the matter and life about us; and to yield our being to the great dependent chain of relationship which binds God's material empire, His realms of mind and Himself, in one sympathizing whole!

The universal requirement is, that man's nature shall be brought into harmony with creation and its Author. This is the whole law of our being. Obedience to it is the unalterable condition of happiness; the only true test of civilization; the only state in which our powers, physical and mental, will operate harmoniously; the only position of our existence which looks forward on the path of our destiny, with any certainty that thought, feeling, and act, will lead to results pleasureable to ourselves and in harmony with the rest of the world.

It is a want of proper reflection on this matter which has rendered abortive so many efforts to civilize different portions of the race. In India, in the forests of the west, in every other place, except the Hawaiian Islands, where the societies of Protestantism have made efforts to ameliorate the condition of the barbarian, nearly the whole acting force has been brought to bear on the cultivation of the religious sentiments. The theory has been, make them Christians, and everything else will follow as a promised favor of Heaven.

No error has cost the church more money and life than this. The savage has been taught the doctrines of salvation, and his direct relations to the Deity. Thus far, well. But there was no corresponding teaching to the rest of his nature. His physical wants and the mode of supplying them, remained unchanged. All his relations to the external world continued the same. And the largest number of the strongest desires of the mind being thus left, to contend with those which the missionaries attempted to excite and purify, it is no wonder that so little has been accomplished.

In the Hawaiian Islands the missionaries found a people living in villages, having a property in the soil, and depend ing chiefly upon its culture for their subsistence. They also found them destitute of every kind of religion, and desirous of receiving one: they were a talented people and anxious for new ideas. This was a remarkable state of things. Their physical adaptation to the natural world was so far in advance of the mental, that the latter only required to be placed on an equal footing with the former, to produce the civilization and moral rectitude which they now possess.

The result of missionary efforts in these islands, if well

understood, may lead to some valuable changes in the mode of operating elsewhere. It will be learned that while the physical wants and the mode of supplying them, are opposed to the ordained condition, it is vain to expect the Christianized state.

We may, meanwhile, rejoice at this single result. It is one of the great events of the age. Twenty thousand Hawaiians are members of Christian churches. Seventy thousand read and write. The whole people are better taught, more intelligent, and farther advanced in civilization than are the citizens of the Mexican Republic. Their Government is more paternal, and administered more kindly than any other known to civilized man. But I must hasten homeward.

The hospitality of countrymen during my tarry in these islands, the kindness of countrymen, bestowed on me, a stranger, fleeing from my grave, and sad—away from those on whose hearts I had a right to lean—how can I ever forget them! While those beautiful islands have a place in my memory, they will be associated with some of the most grateful recollections of my life. It is painful to think that I may never again grasp the hands of some noble spirits, whom I saw and loved in the kingdom of Hawaii!

To the sea! on board the bark Don Quixote, Paty, master, bound for Upper California! We left the harbor of Honolulu, under a sweet land breeze from the forests crowning the volcanic hills in the rear of the city, and bore away to the westward along the coast. The mountains of decomposing lava rose from the water side in sharp curving ridges, which, elevating themselves as they swept inland, lay in the interior piled above the clouds. Some of them were covered with the dense green foliage of the tropics; and others were as destitute of vegetation as when they were poured, a liquid burning mass, from the cauldron of the volcanoes. Many valleys dotted with the hay-thatched huts of the natives, their fields of *taro*, and orchards of bread-fruit, cocoa and plantain, lay along the shore. The lower hills were covered with frolicking goats, and here and there on the projecting cliffs, stood a group of stalwart figures, brown as the rocks, shouting their pleasure at seeing our ship, with all sails steadily drawing, push through the waves. Having rounded the southwestern cape, we laid our course through the channel between Oahu and Taui, with the intention of availing ourselves of the northern "variables" to carry us to the American coast.

In the cabin we had seven passengers; Mr. Chamberlain the fiscal agent of the American Missions at the islands—a man of a fine mind and unpretending goodness, who had undertaken the voyage for the benefit of his health—Mr. Cobb, the mate of a whaler, a plain honest man, going home to die of an injury from the falling of a spar on shipboard; a spendthrift of Philadelphia, returning from a two or three years' spree in the Pacific; and a brace of Charlestown boys, who were on their way homeward for goods and sweethearts. One of these was an excellent little fellow, with a soul full of music and justice; the other a singer of bass and an acting agent general, in the same department. The only representative of the fair sex we could boast of was a half-breed Hawaiian lass, going to visit the "Major," her father, an old mountaineer from New England, who was keeping a small shop at Santa Barbara, in Upper California.

Captain Paty was a little man, with a quiet spirit, and a generous heart; a New England man who always kept his eye to the windward, and gave his sails to the stoutest breeze without fear of clew lines or stays. The mate, a lusty English tar of the Greenwich school, was a jolly old boy, whose face was always charged with a smile, ready to be let off on the least occasion of conferring happiness. Our second mate was an Italian, who had left his country for doubtful reasons, married an American girl in the city of New York, buried her, and was now roaming the seas in the double capacity of second mate and ship's carpenter, for the means of educating his only child.

Our crew was a collection of odd-fellows. The first in

weight and importance was "Yankee Tom;" the second a pair of English renegadoes, from the royal navy or elsewhere; next came a number of old tars, who hailed from the earth generally; then several Hawaiians, and last of all, the cook; as dark a piece of flesh as ever wore wool, and as independent a gentleman as ever wrestled with a soup pot. Thus we were all manned fore and aft. The extremes of cursing and prayer, of authority and subserviency, law, divinity, and merchandize, were there.

Indeed, we had a piece of everything in the way of thought, feeling, taste and form, requisite to furnish a very respectable human menagerie. And if the shade of our friend Cuvier had leisure on his hands to look in upon us, and observe the paws of our lions, the teeth of our tigers, the grins of our apes, the wool of our lambs, and the mental and physical qualities of each species, I doubt not he was satisfied with the diversity of their powers and the completeness of the collection.

When leaving the latitude of the islands, we had a distant view of the Taui. It was studded with mountains of moderate elevation, clothed with evergreen forests. It appeared beautiful enough to be the island of Indian Mythology under the setting sun, where the good will find eternal hunting, fishing, and women of unfading beauty. But our ship stood away under a strong breeze, and we soon lost sight of the island in the mist and shades of night.

While making our northing we experienced a great variety of weather. On the first two or three degrees it was comparatively mild, and the generous breezes appeared to push us on with a right good will. But on reaching the latitude beyond the Trades, the winds from the northwest overtook us. These currents of air in the winter and spring are exceedingly rough, gusty and cold; and being often alternated with the warm breezes from the torrid zone, produce conditions of the atmosphere, which, in more senses than one, may be termed "variables." The balmy breath of one day contrasts strongly with the frozen blasts of another; the soft bright clouds from the south, with the harsh dark shadows from the north, and the rippling sea when the former fans it, with the ragged waves which roll under the latter.

Ten days out; latitude thirty-eight; wind fresh from the northwest; Mr. Chamberlain quite ill, but able to be on deck with his thermometer; the Charlestown boys too sick to make music; the Philadelphia blade's hair uncombed; Mr. Cobb very much exhilarated with the bold movement of the ship; the half-breed Hawaiian lass as lovely as circumstances permitted; the crew growing fat on salt beef; the ship, making her ten knots, headed towards Cape Mendocino, and everything else in some sort of condition; thus stood the affairs of our floating home.

Ten days more passed on, and little change in these things occurred, for better or worse; save that, when we arrived within a hundred miles of the coast, the northerly winds became less violent, and their temperature higher. Our old bark was as brave a Don among the waters as one would wish to see. He was of American origin, a fine model of an ocean cavalier, and did battle with the floods as fearlessly as any ship that ever doubled the Cape. Our time on board, therefore, went off rather agreeably; for the speed of a landsman's passage at sea is the absorbing element of its pleasures.

The officers and crew had employment enough to occupy them, and were usually in that agreeable mood of body and mind which produces a good appetite, hearty joking and sound sleeping. When the winds were stiff, they busied themselves in keeping sails, ropes, spars and masts at their appropriate duties; and when a warm sun and steady breeze came, the sailors overhauled the wormy biscuits, repaired old sails, picked oakum, put the spun-yarn wheel in motion, while the Italian carpenter drove jack-plain, and the English mate gave us a specimen of rope-splicing and bending sails according to the rules at Greenwich.

I noticed on board the Don Quixote, and elsewhere during

my wanderings, a difference between British and American seamen, which I believe to be quite general. It is this. The Briton is better acquainted with the things to be done on deck and among the rigging than the American is. He splices a rope better; he knows better how to make a ship look trim and comely. But he knows comparatively nothing about the hull of his craft. His seven years apprenticeship has been devoted to learning the best mode of sailing a vessel and keeping her in good condition. He learns nothing more. The American, on the other hand, begins at the keel, and reads up through every timber, plank and spike, to the bulwarks. And although he does all the minor labor of the fair-day deck work with less neatness and durability, yet he will do it so well, and throw his canvass on the winds with such skill and daring, as to outsail, as well as outmanage his very clever rival. The Fatherland should be proud of Jonathan. He is a rough, hard-featured lad; and in right of primogeniture, as well as other indisputable relations, he must succeed to the paternal power over the seas.

At meridian, on the 16th of April, we ascertained ourselves to be about seventy-five miles from the American coast. All were weary of the voyage. It had been exceedingly monotonous; not even a storm to break its tedium.

At two o'clock of this day, however, we had an incident in the shape of a squall, from the northwest. It was attended with chilling winds which fell upon us like a shower of freezing arrows, and drove everybody, except officers and seamen, below. The blowing, the raining, the clatter of quick feet upon deck, the cry of the sailors, "heave-a-hoy!" as they shorten sail and brace up the yards; the heavy swells, beating the ship like ponderous battering-rams; the air, that upper ocean, running its flood most furiously upon that which lies beneath; our vessel riding the one as if escaping from the wrath of the other; the upper surface of the airy seas, crowded with fleets of thunder-clouds chasing each other madly, and sending out the fire and noise of terrible conflict.

These are the features of that squall. Our good ship reeled and trembled under the shock of the waters and winds, as if her planks and timbers were separating.

Below at such a time was doubtless our safest berth, but that was far from being peculiarly comfortable! About half of the passengers were on each side of the cabin, holding at the berths; and when the ship rose on a billow and careened, it straightened those on the larboad side like lamprey-eels hanging to rocks; while, as the surge passed on, the ship careened the othey way, making eels of those on the starboad side! The furniture tumbled, the steward giving chase fell in the midst of it; the Hawaiian lass attempted to gain her berth and fell; and tumult, danger, sublimity, and the ridiculous, united to provoke alternatively our laughter, fear and admiration. It cleared up in an hour, however, and we went on again pleasantly, under a three-knot breeze.

On the evening of the 17th, we heard right gladly the cry of "Land ho!" Where away?" "A little on the starboard bow!" I was in the cabin at the time. Any other word spoken with a greater volume of voice would have passed unheard. But land! land! the solid land! with its odor of earth and flower, is a word which, if uttered in a whisper, has deep music for one who has for twenty odd days been stunned by contentious waves; a sweetness and vigor of meaning to the weary wayfarer on the seas, which must be heard,—"Land ahead."

Its winged messengers already twittered in the rigging! The shores loomed on the edge of the horizon! The white cliffs on the north side of Monterey Bay, in Upper California, were in sight! We kept our course towards them till daylight-down, and then beat off and on till the dawn of the following morning.

April 18th. The land, the glorious old land, is near us on our left—five miles away! The cattle of the Mission Santa Cruz are grazing on the hill! The matin bells are ringing from its tower, and the arrowy light is routing the darkness

Sailing of the Don Quixotte from Honolulu.—P. 50.

from the Californian mountains! A morning of the blooming spring poured down from Heaven on this Italy of America! A sunrise on the land; and the conquered night where it very properly may be, running wild over the seas!

A breeze from the west drove us slowly down the bay, so near the shore that we had a clear view of it. At the northeast corner of the bay is a green gorge, down which flows a small stream of pure water. Near its mouth, on a snug little plain, stands the mission of Santa Cruz, with its chapel and adobie Indian huts. Around it are some fields, on which the Indians raise grains, vegetables and grapes. Beyond this, to the northward, the country swells away into lofty hills, covered with grass and sprinkled with copses of pine and oak.

From Santa Cruz down to Monterey, the land is broken by low hills, too rough for general cultivation, upon which grow a few trees of a soft and worthless character. But the greenness of the whole surface in the spring of the year, and the absence of any abode of man, make it very appropriate pasture-ground for the wild horses, cattle, mules, and the grisly bears, lions and elk, that herd upon it.

About five o'clock we round to, under the Castle of Monterey. The boat is lowered, the captain and part of the passengers get aboard of her, and shove off for the landing. The ship meanwhile lies off and on within hail. When a hundred fathoms from the shore we are hailed by the custom-house barge, and ordered back to the ship! Whereupon a parley takes place, during which we are informed that California is in a state of revolution, and that no foreigners can enter the country.

I was emaciated with sea-sickness, enfeebled for want of fresh food, and altogether so miserable at the idea of not dining that day upon Californian beans and beef, that I made a desperate effort to express in Spanish the honest rage of my heart at such treatment. But having uttered French instead of Spanish wrath, I was about correcting myself, when a lean villainous physiognomy, supported a lank, long-armed and long-shinned carcass, in lieutenant's epaulettes, replied in French, "*Ah, mon frère Français,*" and immediately gave orders for us to land. The boat therefore ran through the surf, grazed upon the rocks, and lay dry on the beach.

CHAPTER IV.

Mother Earth—Revolution—Americans and British in Prison—A Guard—A Governor—An Interview—An Alcalde—A Passport—A running Salute—Cries for Air and Water—Despair—A Horrid Night—Starvation—Dungeons—A Demand—Signals—A course adopted—A Leaf of History—General Echuanda and his Deeds—A Tennessean Hunter and a Clerk—A Camp Formed—A League—A March—An Attack—A Banishment—Independence—An old Method of Rewarding Friends—A Notification—A Junto—Wagers and Senoritas—A Stratagem and its Consequences—Names of Prisoners.

On the land! The human frame derives its vital elements from the generous land! The earth is our mother, and she seems to rejoice when her children tread her threshold and ask her for bread and happiness.

We inquired the cause of the reported tumult in the country, and were answered in brief whispers! The speakers looked cautiously around them for listening ears and Spanish rapiers. It was difficult to find a man with an English tongue and a white skin, who dared converse alone with us on any subject. Indeed, it was impossible to do so. For whenever the attempt was made, some Spaniard drew stealthily near to listen! And when the gentleman from the ship left the landing for the town, in company with some American and British residents, the government officers mingled among them, and changed the conversation as often as it turned upon what they termed "the revolution." Men of stout hearts even spoke little. Life appeared to hang upon a breath in Monterey! We entered the house of an American merchant by the name of Larkin, and sat down to tea. We did not eat alone! An officer of the government sat with us! Conversation ran on general topics. The cause of the apparent trepidation was inquired into by an American from the Don Quixote, but nothing could be elicited. The official sat erect, swelled his person into dignity, ate heartily, drank deeply, rose first from the table, an intimation that we might follow his illustrious example; burned his fingers in smoking a paper cigar, and at length rolled his greasy form out of doors.

"Rid of you at last, thank God," said a little Englishman, who had dropped in during supper, "and now for talk inside of ceilings." We soon learned from Mr. Larkin and others, that one hundred and fifty odd Americans and Britons were thirsting and starving in the prisons of the town and destined to be sacrificed to Spanish malignity! The question arose, Can they be saved? It was hoped they might; it was resolved on our lives that they should be; while all in a low voice spoke of the uncertainty of life for an hour in Monterey!

The first duty, on setting foot in California, is to report oneself to the governor, and obtain from him a written permission to remain in the country. This I proceeded to do. Mr. Larkin was obliging enough to accompany me to the governor's residence. We found before it a small number of men, who were usually complimented with the cognomen of "guard." They consisted of five half-breed Indians, and what passed for a white corporal, lounging about the door in the manner of grog-shop savans. Their outer man is worth a description. They wore raw bull's-hide sandals on their feet, leathern breeches, blankets about their shoulders, and anything and everything upon their heads. Of arms, they had nothing which deserved the name. One made pretensions with an old musket without lock; and his four comrades were equally heroic, with kindred pieces, so deeply rusted, that the absence of locks would have been an unportant item in estimating their value.

We passed this valorous body, ascended a flight of stairs, and entered the presence of governor Juan Baptiste Alvarado ; a well-formed, full-blooded, Californian Spaniard, five feet eleven inches in height, with coal-black curly hair, deep black eyes, fiercely black eye-brows, high cheek bones, an aquiline nose, fine white teeth, brown complexion, and the clearly marked mein of a pompous coward, clad in the broad-cloth and whiskers of a gentleman.

When we entered he was sitting behind a kind of writing-desk, at the farther end of the room. He rose as we entered, and received us with the characteristic urbanity of a Spanish body without a soul ; waved us to chairs, when he would have seen us tumbling from the balcony ; smiled graciously at us with one corner of his mouth, while he cursed us with the other ; seated himself, laid up his arms and hands on the upper shelf of his abdomen, and asked if the ship had anchored !

El Goubernador had sundry reasons for making this inquiry concerning the Don Quixote. The chief one, however, was, that he and his officers, like all their predecessors, had been in the habit of looking on the arrival of a ship in the port of Monterey as a discharge of debts and a license for new levies on their credit. Let it not be supposed that I believe a Californian Spaniard is ever so far false to his nature, as to wish his debts paid, while his credit will supply his wants. My investigations into the character of his progenitors both Indian and Spanish, will always preserve me from such an error. Nor would I have it believed, that the transplanted chivalry of the Andalusians does not absolutely boil and bubble, at the bare thought of not being able to plunder from the rest of mankind a gentleman's living. Any such impeachment of the sagacity and scrupulousness of these men would be a wrong against which my sense of justice would most vehemently protest In plain words, then, at the time the

Don Quixote came into the bay, Alvarado and his officers were deeply in debt, and distressed only to select means of paying them, accordant with Californian honor. The arrival of a ship in port furnished just these means. The manner in which it did so may be unworthy of specification.

El Alta California is a department of the Mexican Republic; and by law the moneys collected for port-dues and duties belong to the revenue of the central government. But as the right to life, property, and the pursuit of happiness is, among the Californian Spaniards, construed to authorize both individuals and States to defraud, plunder and murder, if they find it safe and lucrative to do so, the freemen, or rather the Governor of California and his subalterns, were in the habit of commuting a large portion of the port-dues and duties, for certain sums of money and quantities of goods for their own personal use. Their capacity for this kind of plundering formed in part the basis of their credit with foreign merchants and traders, from whom they obtained their supplies.

Hence the anxieties of Sa Excellentissimo about the bark. If she had come to anchor there must necessarily be a small chance for robbery in the tonnage dues; and if richly laden with goods subject to duties, she would be quite a mine, which he already dreamed himself plundering with golden success. As soon as we could turn his attention from these hopes of gain, Mr. Larkin informed him of my wishes, and with much deference suggested the humanity of transferring me from idleness on shipboard to the enjoyment of Castilian industry ashore; to wit, lounging, grinning, sleeping, and smoking rolls of paper tinctured with "the weed."

Sa Excellentissimo found it difficult to comprehend the necessity of the request, inasmuch as the bark might come to anchor for my quiet and health, in which case I would be permitted as seamen were, to be on shore during her stay in port. But being informed that there were no goods on board the bark, that it was not intended to bring her to anchor, and that, consequently, neither bribes nor Mexican tribute would be paid to Don Juan Baptiste Alvarado, El Goubernador del Alta California, he frankly confessed that he saw no necessity, indicated by his interest, why I should ever have existed, and still less made any of my pleasures dependent on him or his Alta California.

This I esteemed, as in all chivalry I was bound to do, an exhibition of the great elevation of character as well as an indication of the height from which Sa Excellentissimo had descended to reach my case! Therefore, I bowed assent to the majesty of such philanthropic and truly civilized opinions. What man in Castilian presence could do otherwise? But a doubt still hung over the eyebrows of the don. He looked at my height, six feet Green Mountain measure; at my wardrobe, consisting of a Hudson Bay Company's frockcoat of blue, a speckled vest from London, pants of English extraction, boots from the lapstones of Lynn; and, shrugging his shoulders like a grisly bear in an effort to be a gentleman, said we could go to the alcalde; then with most sovereign emphasis bowed us out of his presence!

The alcalde was at home, or rather in his adobie den; for there is neither a home nor the semblance of it in all the Spanish world. He was taking his *siesta*, or midday nap, on a bull's hide in the corner of his apartment. The dog, which had barked us into his presence, had awakened him; so that when we entered the room, he was rolling his burly form towards a chair. After being well-seated, and having with some difficulty brought his eyes to bear upon us, he was pleased to remark that, the weather was fine, and that various other things existed in a definite state; as that his dog was very fat; the bean crop gave good promise; the Hawaiian Islands were ten leagues from Monterey!!! the Californians were very brave men; and that the Don Quixote had not come to anchor!! To each of these announcements I gave an unqualified assent.

Having ascertained by these means that I was well-instructed in beasts, beans, men and geography, he immediately took me into favor, expressed great surprise that my friend should have thought that he could refuse my request, and assured me that it gave him infinite pleasure to write me a permission of residence. Here it is. When the reader is informed that it was an impromptu production, he will be able to estimate, in a faint degree indeed, the intelligence and genius of the Californians. Only one hour and a quarter were consumed in bringing it forth!

Mr. Thomas J. Farnham pasagero en la barca Americana Don Quixote habiendama manifesta do el pasporte de su consul y queriendo quidar en tierra a (vertarblesse) en su salud le doy el presente bolito de des en barco en el puerta de Monterey!!

A 18 de Abril de 1840.

ANTONIO MA. ORIO.

A permission this to remain on shore as long as might be necessary for the restoration of my health! Having received it with many demonstrations of regard, we took our leave of the illustrious dignitary under a running salute from his dog, and repaired to el casa del goubernador (the governor's house). The dog accompanied us. He appeared to rejoice in our presence. After he saw us pass into the governor's door he howled piteously, and trotted off toward the prisons.

We obtained from Sa Excellentissimo a written confirmation of the alcalde's document, and returned to the house of Mr. Larkin. There we met a number of Americans and Britons, from whom we learned that their countrymen were famishing unto death in the prisons of the town! A consultation, held in an upper room, in whispers, under the dreadful certainty that death would be the penalty if it became known to the demon government, ended the labors of that day and night! The house of my friend was but a few rods from some of the prisons, and when all was still at midnight, I could hear, between the breaking surges on the beach, the prisoners cry—

"Breathe fast, for God's sake! I must come to the grate soon or I shall suffocate!"

"Give me water, you merciless devils! give me water!" "You infernal sons of the Inquisition, give me drink or fire on me!"

And then another voice at the grate exclaimed, "Give us something to eat! O God, we shall die here! We can't breathe! Half of us can't speak!"

And then another voice, husky and weak, said "Why!" in a tone of despairing agony, which became so low and inarticulate that I could not hear what followed. I had not seen the prisoners, but their cries banished sleep and all desire to rest. I therefore went out upon the balcony and seating myself in a dark nook watched, as well as I was able, the movements in the town.

A portion of the troops were on duty as an armed patrol. The tap of the drum and the challenge, "Quin vive?" with the reply, "Californias;" "Quin jente?" and the response, "Mexicanos," broke in upon their heavy, sounding tramp! About four o'clock the men in the castello, or fort, became alarmed by the cracking of dry brush in the neighboring wood, and the patrol rushed to their rescue. It proved to be the echo of their fears. The patrol soon returned to their posts, and silence again reigned. It was a horrid night! Nature was laughing and bright on earth and in the sky. But fiends had gone forth to mar her beauty. The same spirit which had devastated the virtues and freedom of half the earth was abroad in the wilds of California, as of old in Chili, torturing those whose courage their bravado could not subdue, or their pretension intimidate!

The sun came up next morning most brightly in that clear blue sky of California: but it shone on sadder hearts than I had ever before seen. The flowers were creeping up along the streets; and the grasses, invigorated by the winter rains and the warm days of spring, were growing on the hills; the cattle and wild animals roamed about enjoying the rich liberty which nature gave them. They possessed no qualities which could excite the wakefulness of Spanish malignity! They were lowing and frolicking out their freedom on the kind and beautiful earth. But man was raising the murderous blade against his fellow!

Mr. Larkin made arrangements with the government to-day to furnish the prisoners with food and drink. Their cells were examined and found destitute of floors! The ground within was so wet that the poor fellows sunk into it several inches at every step. On this they stood, sat and slept! From fifty to sixty were crowded into a room eighteen or twenty feet square! They could not all sit at once, even in that vile pool, still less lie down! The cells were so low and tight that the only way of getting air enough to sustain life, was to divide themselves into platoons, each of which in turn stood at the grate awhile to breathe! Most of them had been in prison seven or eight days, with no food except a trifling quantity, clandestinely introduced by a few daring countrymen outside. When I arrived at the prisons some of them were frantic; others in a stupor of exhaustion; one appeared to be dying! An American citizen went to the governor with a statement of their condition, and demanded that both Americans and Britons should be handsomely treated; that they should have air, food, drink, permission to bathe, and dry hides wherewith to cover the mud in their cells.

Since our arrival the Don Quixote had been lying off and on. She usually ran out one morning and swept into the harbor the next. This circumstance, together with the fact that this American was always on the shore when the vessel passed the anchorage, making signals to her, which neither himself nor those on board understood, created the idea that he was an official of the American Government, and as such, had rights which it would be well to respect. This impression was much strengthened, both by the accidental circumstance of his wearing a cutlass with an eagle upon its hilt, and his holding restraints imposed on his acts as highly insulting and disrespectful! This course of conduct had the effect designed. Those cowardly apologies of men became thoroughly impressed that he bore in his own person the combined powers of the American Republic and the British Empire. Clothed, therefore, with authority so potent, he took measures for the relief of the prisoners.

But, before entering upon the narration of these measures it will be proper to give a history of the events which led to the imprisonment of these men, and their intended immolation.

In 1836, a Mexican General by the name of Echuandra was the Commandant General of Upper California. Some years previous, as will be particularly shown in another place, he had come up from Mexico, with a band of fellow-myrmidons, and having received the submission of the country to the authorities of that Republic, commenced robbing the Government for which he acted, and the several interests which he had been sent to protect. Nothing escaped his mercenary clutches. The people, the missions, and the revenue were robbed indiscriminately, as opportunity offered. A few of the white population of the country participated in these acts. But generally the Californians were the sufferers; and, as is always the case with unhonored rogues, raised a perpetual storm of indignation about the dishonest deeds of those whom they desired to supplant, for the purpose of enacting the same things. An occurrence of this kind was the immediate cause of the Revolution in 1836.

A vessel had cast anchor in the harbor of Monterey. General Echuandra, not having that honorable confidence in the immaculate integrity of the custom-house officers, which thieves are accustomed to have in one another, placed a guard on board the craft, to prevent them from receiving bribes for their own exclusive benefit. To this the officers demurred; and in order to free their territory from the creatures of one whose conscience would compel him to receive bribes for his own pocket instead of theirs, they sent their own clerk, a young rascal of the country, by the name of Juan Baptiste Alvarado, to inform the general that it was improper to suggest, by putting a guard on board, that the officers of the ship which lay under the fort, either intended or dared attempt to evade the payment of duties!!

The General, however, was too well acquainted with his inalienable rights, to be wheedled out of them in this manner; and manifested his indignation toward the clerk, for attempting to abtrude his plebeian presence on his golden dream, by ordering him to be put in irons. Alvarado, however, escaped. He fled into the country, rallied the farmers, who still loved the descendants of Philip the Second more than *El Presidente*, and formed a camp at the Mission of San Juan, thirty miles eastward from Monterey.

Near this mission lived an old Tennessean by the name of Graham; a stout, sturdy backwoodsman, of a stamp which exists only on the frontiers of the American States—men with the blood of the ancient Normans and Saxons in their veins—with hearts as large as their bodies can hold, beating nothing but kindness till injustice shows its fangs, and then, lion-like, striking for vengeance. This trait of natural character had been fostered in Graham by the life he had led. Early trained to the use of the rifle, he had learned to regard it as his friend and protector; and when the season of manhood arrived, he threw it upon his shoulder and sought the wilderness, where he could enjoy its protection and be fed by its faithful aim. He became a beaver hunter—a cavalier of the wilderness—that noble specimen of brave men who have muscles for riding wild horses and warring with wild beasts, a steady brain and foot for climbing the icy precipice, a strong breast for the mountain torrent, an unrelenting trap for the beaver, a keen eye and a deadly shot for a foe. A man was this Graham, who stood up boldly before his kind, conscious of possessing physical and mental powers adequate to any emergency. He had a strong aversion to the elegant edifices, the furniture, wardrobe, and food of polished life, coupled with a vivid love of mountain sublimity, the beautiful herbage on uncultivated districts, the wild animals and the streams of water roaring down the frozen heights. Even the grey deserts with the hunger and thirst incident to travelling over them, had wild and exciting charms for him. On these his giant frame had obstacles to contend with worthy of its powers; suffering and even old Death himself to take by the throat and vanquish. These and the open air by a projecting rock, with the dry sand or the green sward for a hearth and couch, a crackling pine knot fire blazing against the cliffs, and roasting a buffalo hump or the sirloin of an elk, after the day's hunt had ended, constituted the life he was fitted to enjoy.

He had forced his way over the Rocky Mountains and located himself in Upper California. This country was suited to his tastes. Its climate allowed him to sleep in the open air most of the year; an abundance of native animals covered the hills, and nature was spread out luxuriantly everywhere, in wild and untrodden freshness.

As I have said, this brave man resided near the mission of San Juan. He had erected there a rude dwelling, and a distillery. On the neighboring plans he herded large bands of horses, mules and cattle. To this fine old fellow Alvarado made known his peril and designs; whereupon the foreigners assembled at Graham's summons, elected him their captain, an Englishman by the name of Coppinger, lieutenant, and repaired to San Juan. A council was held between the clerk and the foreigners. The former promised, that if by the aid of the latter he should successfully defend himself against the acting governor, and obtain possession of the country, it should be declared independent of Mexico; and that the law, which incapacitated foreigners from holding real estate, should be abrogated. The foreigners agreed, on these conditions, to aid Alvarado to the utmost of their power. The next morning the united forces, fifty foreigners and twenty-five Californians, marched against Monterey.

They entered the town in the afternoon of the same day, and took up their position in the woods, one hundred rods in the rear of the *castello* or fort. No event of importance occurred till the night came on, when the awe with which darkness sometimes inspires even the bravest minds, fell with such overwhelming power on the valorous garrison, that notwithstanding they were supported by the open mouths of the guns, the barking of their dog, the roar of the surf, and the hooting of an owl on a neighboring tree-top, they were absolutely compelled to forsake the ramparts, for the more certain protection of unmolested flight!

Graham and his men perceiving the discomforture of their enemies, availed themselves of their absence by taking possession of the evacuated fort. Alvarado, meantime, actuated, it is to be presumed, by a desire to save life and a philosophical conviction of the dangers incident to bullets rendered crazy by burning powder, restrained the fiery ardor of his twenty-five Californians, and held his own person beyond the reach of harm, in case some luckless horse or cow straying over hostile ground on that memorable night, should scare the fleeing garrison into an act of defence. The next morning he and his brave men were found peering from their hiding-places in a state of great anxiety and alarm!

A battle had almost been begun in Monterey! The blood of their enemies had almost begun to fatten the soil of California! They themselves had nearly stepped in blood knee deep, among the carcasses of the hated Mexicans; the besom of destruction had shaken itself, and had barely missed commencing the havoc of bone and flesh, which would have crushed every mote of Mexican life within their borders! Thus they gloried among the bushes!!

Old Graham stood at sunrise on the earth embankments of the Castello. A hunting shirt of buckskin, and pants of the same material, covered his giant frame; a slouched broad-brimmed hat hung aroand his head, and half covered his large, quiet, determined face! In his right hand he held his rifle, the tried companion of many fearful strifes among the savages! Four or five of his men sat on a dismounted thirty-two pounder, querying whether they could repair its woodwork so as to bring it to bear on the Presido or government house. Others stood by a bucket of water, swabbing out their rifle barrels, and cleaning and drying the locks. Others of them were cooking beef; others whittling, swearing, and chewing tobacco.

About nine o'clock flags of truce began their onerous duties. Alvarado came from the woods and took part in the councils. The insurgents demanded the surrender of the Government; whereat the cavaliers of the Presido considered themselves immeasurably insulted. Two days were passed in this parleying without advancing the interests of either party. They were days big with the fate of the future; and who could weary under their dreadful burthens? Not such men as Alvarado. He bore himself like the man he was, through all the trying period. He uniformly preferred delay to fighting! He was sustained in this preference by his right hand villain, Captain Jose Castro. Indeed, it was the unanimous choice of the whole Californian division of the insurgent forces, to wit, the twenty-five before mentioned, to massacre time instead of men. For not a single one of them manifested the slightest impatience or insubordination under the delay—a fact which perhaps demonstrates the perfection of military discipline in California! The foreigners differed from their illustrious allies. Graham thought "two days and two nights a waitin' on them baars* was enough." Accordingly, taking the responsibility on himself, after the manner of his distinguished fellow-statesman, he sent a flag to the Presido with notice that two hours only would be given the Governor and his officers to surrender themselves prisoners of war. The demand of the old Tennessean, however, was disregarded. The appointed time passed without the surrender. Forbearance was at an end. The lieutenant of Graham's rifle corps was ordered to level a four pound brass piece at the Presido. A ball was sent through its tiled roof, immediately over the heads of the Mexican magnates!

* Bears.

It is wonderful how small a portion of necessity mingled with human affairs will quicken men's perceptions of duty. No sooner did the broken tiles rattle around the heads of these valiant warriors, than they became suddenly convinced that it would be exceedingly hazardous to continue their resistance against such an overwhelming force; and that the central government at Mexico would not be so unreasonable as to expect four or five hundred troops to hold out against *Los Rifleros Americanos*. This view of the case, taken through the shattered roof of the Presidio, was conclusive. They surrendered at discretion! Alvarado marched into the citadel of government! The Mexican troops laid down their arms! The emblems of office were transferred to the custom-house clerk! When these things had transpired, General Echuandra was pleased to say to Alvarado with the most exalted good sense, "had we known that we were thrice as many as you, we should not have surrendered so soon;" thereby demonstrating to the future historian del Alta California that he and his friends would either have fought the seventy-five with their five hundred or protracted the siege of bravado much longer, had they been able to count the said seventy-five at the distance or five hundred yards, during the lapse of two days! Difficulties in the use of optics often occur in Californian warfare which are not treated of in the books.

The end of this revolution came! The schooner Clarion of New Bedford was purchased, and the Mexican officers shipped to San Blas. Juan Baptiste Alvarado customs' clerk proclaimed El Alta California an independent republic, and himself its govenor. But more of this on a subsequent page. It suffices my present purpose to have shown how far this Alvarado was indebted to the foreigners dying in his prisons for the station and power which he was using for their desruction. He could never have obtained possession of Monterey without them. And had they not slept on their rifles for months after that event, a party in the south under his uncle Don Carlos Carrillo, or another in the north under his uncle Guadaloupe Viejo, would have torn him from his ill-gotten elevation.

Thus upper California became an independent state, and Alvarado its governor. The central government at Mexico was of course much shocked at such unpolished, ungloved impudence; threatened much, and at last in September, 1837, induced Alvarado to buy a ship, send despatches to Mexico, and become *El Goubernador Constitutionel del Alta California*, associated with his uncle Viejo, as *Commandante General.* After this adhesion to the Mexican Government, Alvarado became suspicious of the foreigners who had aided him in the "Revolution," and sought every means of annoying them. They might depose him as they had done Echuandra. And if vengeance were always a certain consequent of injustice, he reasoned well. The vagabond had promised, in the day of his need, to bestow lands on those who had saved his neck and raised him to power. This he found convenient to forget. Like Spaniards of all ages and countries, after having been well served by his friends, he rewarded them with the most heartlsss ingratitude.

Graham in particular was closely watched. A bold open-handed man, never concealing for an instant either his love or hatred, but with the frankness and generosity of those great souls, rough-hewn but majestically honest, who belong to the valley States, he told the Governor his sins from time to time, and demanded in the authorative tone of an elder and affectionate brother, that he should redeem his pledges. The good old man did not remember that a Spaniard would have lost his nationality had he done so. A Spaniard tell the truth! A Spaniard ever grateful for services rendered him! He should have knocked at the tombs of Columbus and Cortes, and every other man who ever served that contemptible race. He would have learned the truth, and gathered wisdom from it. He asked for justice and received what we shall presently see.

Graham loved a horse. He had taken a fine gelding with

him when he emigrated to the country, and trained him for the turf. Every year he had challenged the whole country to the course, and as often won everything wagered against his noble steed. Jose Castro, a villain with a lean body, dark face, black mustachios, pointed nose, flabby cheeks, uneasy eyes, and hands and heart so foul as instinctively to require a Spanish cloak, in all sorts of weather, to cover them, and his Excellentissimo were among Graham's heaviest debtors. Behold the reasons of their enmity.

Another cause of the general feelings against the Americans and Britons in California was the fact that the *Senoritas*, the dear ladies, in the plenitude of their taste and sympathy for foreigners, preferred them as husbands. Hence Jose Castro was heard to declare a little before the arrest of the Americans and Britons, that such indignities could not be borne by Castilian blood; "for a Californian *Cavaliero* cannot woo a *Senorita* if opposed in his suit by an American sailor, and these heretics must be cleared from the land."

Such were the causes operating to arouse the wrath and ripen the patriotism of the Californians. The vengeance of baffled gallantry bit at the ear of Captain Jose Castro; the fear of being brought to justice by Graham, tugged at the liver of Alvarado; and love the keenest, and hate the bitterest, in a soul the smallest that was ever entitled to the breath of life, burnished the little black eyes and inflamed the little thin nose of one Corporal Pinto. These were the worthies who projected the onslaught on the foreigners. Their plan of operation was the shrewdest one ever concocted in California.

Since the "Revolution" of '36 the Californian Spaniards had been convinced that the Americans and Britons were vastly their superiors in courage and skill in war. From the beginning, therefore, it was apparent that if they were to get one or two hundred of these men into their power, it must be done by stratagem. Accordingly, Graham's annual challenge for the spring races in 1840, was conveniently construed into a disguised attempt to gather his friends for the purpose of overthrowing Alvarado's Government. This suggestion was made to the minor leading interests, civil and military, and a Junto was formed for the safety of the State; or in plain truth, for the gratification of the several personal enmities and jealousies of half a dozen scoundrels, who, disregarding the most sacred pledges to their friends, would rob them of their property and sacrifice their lives.

This Junto marshalled their forces at Monterey, and adopted the following plan for accomplishing their fiendish designs:—The soldiers were detailed into corps of two, three and four in number, to which were attached several civilized Indians. These bands were secretly sent to the abodes of the foreigners, with instructions to convey them with dispatch before the Alcaldes of the neighboring missions. This they accomplished. The victims, on receiving information that the Alcaldes desired to see them, repaired to their presence, willingly, and without suspicion of evil intentions against them. As soon, however, as they arrived, they were loaded with irons, and cast into the loathsome cells of these establishments in which the Padres formerly confined their disobedient converts!

Thus, one by one, they succeeded in arresting one hundred and sixty odd Americans and Britons—brave old trappers, mechanics, merchants, whalemen and tars—men who, if embodied under Graham, with their rifles in their hands, could have marched from San Francisco to San Lucas; conquered nine hundred miles of coast, and held the Government of the country in spite of the dastards who were oppressing them. But they were caught in a net skilfully thrown over them, and were helpless. After each man was bolted safely in his dungeon, the harpies proceeded to his house, violated his family, plundered his premises, and drove away his live stock as private booty—the reward of the brave!

Having in this manner collected these unhappy men in the prisons of the several missions, Alvarado and Castro

Monterey, California.—P. 69.

San Francisco, California.—P. 69.

marched their whole disposable force to one mission after another and brought them in heavy irons, a few at a time, to the Government dungeons at Monterey!

The names of some of these men, together with their places of residence in California, which I happened to preserve, are given below.

Those who lived near the mission of San Francisco Bay, were, Lewis Pollock, John Vermillion, William McGlone, Daniel Sill, George Frazer, Nathaniel Spear, Captain McKenley, Jonathan Fuller, Captain Beechay.

Those who resided at El Pueblo San Jose, were William Blirkin, George Fergusson, Thomas Thomas, William Langleys, Jonathan Mirayno, William Weeks, Jonathan Coppinger, William Hauts, Charles Brown, Thomas Tomlison, Richard Westlake, James Peace, Robert McCallister, Thomas Bowen, Elisha Perry, Nathan Daily, Robert Livermore, William Gulenack, Jonathan Marsh, Peter Storm, Job Dye, William Smith, Jonathan Warner, and two Frenchmen.

Those from Santa Cruz, were, William Thompson, James Burnes, F. Eagle, Henry Knight, Jonathan Lucas, George Chapel, Henry Cooper, Jonathan Herven, James Lowyado, Francisco, LaGrace, Michael Lodge, Josiah Whitehouse, Robert King.

From Nativada, Graham's neighborhood, were, Isaac Graham, Daniel Goff, William Burton, Jonathan Smith, and Henry Niel.

Those residents at Selenias, were, William Chard, James O'Brien, William Bronda, William Malthas, Thomas Cole, Thomas Lewis, William Ware, and James Majous.

In Monterey, were, Leonard Carmichael, Edward Watson, Andrew Watson, Henry McVicker, H. Hathaway, Henry Bee, William Trevavan, Jonathan Maynard, William Henderson, James Meadows, Jonathan Higgins, Mark West, George Kenlock, Jeremiah Jones, Jonathan Chamberlain, Daniel ——, Joseph Bowles, James Kelley, James Fairwell, Walter Adams, Mr. Horton, James Atterville, Mr.

Jones, Jonathan Christian, William Chay, William Dickey, Charles Williams, Alvan Willson.

CHAPTER V.

THE PRISONRES.

FORTY-ONE of the prisoners whose names appear on the concluding pages of the last Chapter, furnished me with written accounts of their arrest, and subsequent treatment. Believing that the reader will be more interested in these, than in any abstract that could be made of them, I will transcribe a few which best illustrate this barbarous persecution.

"I, Isaac Graham, a citizen of the United States of America, came across the continent to California, with a passport from the Mexican authorities of Chihuahua, and obtained from the General commanding in Upper California, a license to run a distillery in that country, for the term of eight years; this business I have followed since that time.

"On the sixth of April last (1840) there appeared to be mischief brewing. But what it would prove to be, none of us could tell. The Californian Spaniards travelled usually much about the country; and conversed with the foreigners rather shyly. They had threatened to drive us out of California several times; and we tried to guess whether they were at last preparing to accomplish it. But from what we saw it was impossible to form a satisfactory conclusion.

"On the same day, however, Jose Castro, Bicenta Contrine, Ankel Castro, and a runaway Botany Bay English convict, by the name of Garner, a vile fellow, and an enemy of mine, because the foreigners would not elect him their captain, passed and repassed my house several times, and conversed together in low tones of voice. I stopped Jose Castro, and asked him what was the matter. He replied that he was going to march against the Commandante General Viego, at San Francisco, to depose him from the command of the forces. His two companions made the same assertion. I knew that Alvarado was afraid of Viego, and that Jose Castro was ambitious for his place; and for these reasons, I partly concluded that they spoke the truth.

"A little later in the day, however, the vagabond Garner called at my house, and having drunk freely of whisky became rather boisterous, and said significantly, that the time of some people would be short; that Jose Castro had received orders from the governor to drive the foreigners out of California, or to dispose of them in some other way. He boasted that he himself should have a pleasant participation in the business. I could not persuade him to inform me when or in what manner this was to take place. I had heard the same threat made a number of times within the past year, but it resulted in nothing. Believing, therefore, that Garner's words proceeded from the whisky he had drunk, rather than the truth, I left him in the yard, and in company with my partner, Mr. Niel, went to bed. Messrs. Morris and Barton, as usual, took to their couches in the still-house.

"We slept quietly, until about three o'clock in the morning, when I was awakened by the discharge of a pistol near my head, the ball of which passed through the handkerchief about my neck. I sprang to my feet, and jumped in the direction of the villains, when they discharged six other pistols, so near me that my shirt took fire in several places. Fortunately, the darkness and the trepidation of the cowards prevented their taking good aim; for only one of their shots took effect, and that in my left arm.

"After firing they fell back a few paces and commenced reloading their pieces. I perceive by the light of their pistols that they were too numerous for a single man to contend with, and determined to escape. But I had scarcely got six paces from the door when I was overtaken and assailed with heavy blows from their swords. These I succeeded in parrying off to such an extent that I was not much injured by them. Being incensed at last by my successful resistance, they grappled with me, and threw me down, when an ensign by the name of Joaquin Terres drew his dirk, and saying with an oath that he would let out my life, made a thrust at my heart. God saved me again. The weapon passing between my body and left arm, sunk deep in the ground! and before he had an opportunity of repeating his blow they dragged me up the hill in the rear of my house, where Jose Castro was standing. They called to him, 'Here he is! here he is!' whereupon Castro rode up and struck me with the back of his sword over the head so severely as to bring me to the ground; and then ordered four balls to be put through me. But this was prevented by a faithful Indian in my service, who threw himself on me, declaring that he would receive the balls in his own heart!

"Unwilling to be thwarted, however, in their design to destroy me, they next fastened a rope to one of my arms, and passed it to a man on horseback, who wound it firmly around the horn of his saddle. Then the rest of them, taking hold of the other arm, endeavored to haul my shoulders out of joint! But the rope broke. Thinking the scoundrels bent on killing me in some way, I begged for liberty to commend my soul to God. To this they replied, 'You shall never pray till you kneel over your grave.' They then conducted me to my house and permitted me to put on my pantaloons. While there they asked where Mr. Morris was. I told them I did not know. They then put their lances to my breast and told me to call him or die. I answered that he had made his escape. While I was saying this, Mr. Niel came to the house, pale from loss of blood and vomiting terribly. He had had a lance thrust through his thigh, and a deep wound in his leg, which nearly separated the cord of the heel.

"They next put Mr. Niel and myself in double irons, carried us half a mile into the plain, left us under guard, and returned to plunder the house. After having been absent a short time, they came and conducted us back to our rifled home. As soon as we arrived there, a man by the name of Manuel Larias approached me with a drawn sword, and commanded me to inform him where my money was buried. I told him I had none. He cursed me and turned away. I had some deposited in the ground, but I determined they should never enjoy it. After having robbed me of my books and papers, which were all the evidence I had that these very scoundrels and others were largely indebted to me, and having taken whatever was valuable on my premises, and distributed it among themselves, they proceeded to take an inventory of what was left, as if it were the whole of my property; and then put me on horseback and sent me to this prison. You know the rest. I am chained like a dog, and suffer like one."

Mr. Albert F. Morris, whose name appears in Graham's account of his arrest, gives me some farther particulars. It may be well here to say, that this Morris was a British subject, a descendant of the former Surveyor-General of Nova Scotia or New Brunswick. Having strayed from friends and home, he found himself in California destitute of the means of livelihood. In this state of want he hired himself to Graham as a laborer in his distillery; and was living on his premises in that capacity at the time of the events just related.

"On the night of the sixth of April, 1840, when we were about going to bed, two persons arrived who asked for lodgings. Mr. Graham told them they might find quarters with us in the distillery. They dismounted and took bed with me and Mr. Barton; and Messrs. Graham and his partner Neil took their bed in the house, about thirty yards distant from us.

"Nothing occurred to disturb us until about three o'clock in the morning, when, being awakened by a loud knocking at the distillery door, I sprang out of my bed, and asked who was there? No answer being returned, I repeated the question in a stern voice, when a man outside replied, 'Nicholas Alviso.' He being a near neighbor I answered, 'very well,' and told one of those present to light a candle. But while this was being done, a number of people outside called out, 'Where is Graham? Tear the devil in pieces!' and immediately afterward rushed with great violence against the door. I told them to wait a moment, but they cried out with still greater clamor for Graham, and seemed to rush toward the house where he slept. Quite a number, however, remained at the distillery, beating at the door in a savage manner and threatening death to the inmates. I drew my pistols, and at that instant Nicholas Alviso called aloud for all hands to beat down the door. On they came against it; I fired; and they returned the fire and wounded me in the left side. I then seized my rifle and snapped it at them; they retreated, and I escaped into the swamp in the rear of Graham's house. After concealing myself among the bushes, I saw fifteen or twenty men with drawn swords making most deadly blows at Messrs. Graham and Neil. I heard Ankel Castro give orders to hew them down; Garner urged them to do the same.

"I remained in the swamp till late the next night, when I walked eight miles to the farm of Mr. Littlejohn, where I remained two days. Then, with an Indian to guide me, I rode to the mission of Santa Cruz on the north side of Monterey Bay. Here I called at the houses of Messrs. Dye and Young; told them what had happened, and went up among the hills for safety.

"On the sixteenth, Francisco Young came to me and said, that Captain Burlinen had come after me with a company of riflemen. He assured me that I should not be put to death or manacled if I surrendered myself without resistance. I concluded after some hesitation to do so, and followed him down to Mr. Dye's distillery. There I found Captain Burlinen, with eleven Californians, armed with the rifles which they had taken from the Britons and Americans. After obtaining a promise from the captain that my life should not be taken and that I should not be put in irons or otherwise bound, I delivered my rifle to him and became his prisoner. I was then marched down to the Mission of Santa Cruz between the soldiers, and put under guard until the next morning.

"Soon after sunrise on the seventeenth they began preparations for taking me to Monterey. I had, when escaping from Graham's premises, left most of my clothing, and not knowing in what this affair might end, I desired the captain to take me by that route. To this he consented. But it was of no service to me; for I found both my portmanteaus broken open and all my clothing stolen. Mr. Niel was in the house. He had been badly wounded in the affray of the sixth. A lance had been thrust through his thigh, and a deep sabre cut inflicted upon the leg. He told me that the Botany Bay Garner did it. I saw several balls sticking in the walls of the bedroom in which Mr. Niel lay. The floor was much stained with blood. The premises had been plundered. We stayed at Graham's house an hour, and proceeded towards Monterey.

"I arrived in town the next day. It was occupied by soldiers, and the prisons filled with foreigners. They immediately put me in double-irons, and carried me before a body of men who pretended to act as a court of justice. I desired that Mr. Spence, the alcalde, might be sent for as an interpreter. But they would not allow it. They said I must be content with the one they had provided. His name was Nariago. He was by no means capable of the task. But I was compelled to take him or none, and go into the examination. I was sworn; and then the interpreter said it was well known that I had been writing letters against the government. I asked him to produce the letters, that I might see them. He replied, 'that it is not necessary.' He then said that Mr. Graham was at the head of an attempted revolutionary movement against the government, and that I knew something about it. I replied that I had never heard

Mr. Graham suggest anything of the kind. I said that he had expressed a determination to represent to the governor the shameful treatment of Mr. Higgins; and the outrage upon the foreigners while they were burying their countrymen at Santa Barbara; and particularly the monstrous deed of digging him up after burial, and leaving his corpse naked above ground. I confessed I had offered to go with him to the governor for that purpose.

"The interpreter then asked why I fired on the people at Graham's distillery. I answered that I did it in self-defence. He inquired how that could be. I told him, as it was impossible for me in the night time to see those who made the assault on the distillery, I could not know whether they were the authorized agents of the government, or robbers whom it was my duty to resist. My life was at stake, and I fought for it, as they would have done under like circumstances. It was next asked why I did not seek redress from the government, if I supposed them robbers. I said that I had no time to do so between their attempts to kill me and my own necessary acts to prevent them; and that if I had had opportunity I had no assurance, under the circumstances, that government would protect me. This last answer was translated with some embellishments; and the interpreter informed me it was considered highly insulting to the governor. I answered that no insult was intended, but that I was under oath, and could not vary from the truth. I was then asked why I fled to Santa Cruz. My reply was that I had lost all confidence in the justice of the government, and flew to the wilderness for protection. At this the alcalde was greatly incensed, ordered my answers to be reduced to writing, and commanded me to affix my name to them, together with the additions which their desire for an excuse to destroy me induced them to append. I stated that I did not suppose myself obliged to place my signature to an instrument written in a language which I could not read. I signed it with swords over my head. What the paper contained I never knew.

John Warner leaving the Hope.—Page 77.

They would not allow me to attempt to read it. The examination being ended, they took me to the fort and placed me under a strong guard for the night. The next day, the nineteenth of April, they marched me under escort of a company of infantry into the public green, before the government house, to hear prayers. After which, I have no doubt, they intended to shoot me, but were prevented from doing it through the fear of Mr. ——."

I have other interesting narratives showing the most inhuman conduct in the Governor of Upper California, while arresting these Americans and Britons, which I must pass for want of space. There is one, however, that refers more especially to the causes which brought many of them into a country where they were subject to such merciless usage, that I cannot prevail on myself to omit. It is a saying among seamen that when a ship doubles Cape Horn "the rope's end and shackles are the Old Man's argument." Sailors in those seas are often glad even to escape from a bloody deck to the chances of dungeons and rapiers in the Californias.

"I left the American ship Hope, of Philadelphia, in Manilla, and there being no chance of getting a passage to the United States from that place, I went passenger to Macao, in the ship Rasselas, of Boston, commanded by Captain ******. On my arrival there, all his crew having left him, Captain ****** asked me to ship on board his vessel for a voyage. I and some others agreed to do so on these conditions: that if after serving one month, while the ship lay in that port, we did not like it, we were to be at liberty to leave her. When the month was up we all requested to go on shore. But he said all might go except William Warren, Robert McAlister, and myself. We were accordingly detained on board. No boat from the shore was allowed to come alongside for fear we should escape. After a short time the ship proceeded on her voyage to Kamschatka. And in this way were we forced to go without signing articles, and contrary to our agreement.

One day when my watch was at work on deck the captain came along and said I was not sewing the sail right; and I said I thought I was; when he kicked me over the eye with a large heavy shoe he had on at the time. And when the pain made me start to my feet, with the blood running down my face, he said that I wanted to kill him with a knife, and immediately had me put (hands and feet) in irons. I remained so for half an hour; when the captain, ordering me to be tied up to the main-rigging, and taking his knife from his pocket, cut the shirt off my back, and gave me two dozen lashes with his own hand. After this I was taken down and thrown in the longboat among the hogs, and fed on bread and water for a fortnight. In this situation I suffered very much. For I was ironed hand and foot, the weather was extremely cold, and I was without shirt, shoes and stockings. At the end of the two weeks the ship arrived in port, and I was taken out of the longboat. My feet, too, were stripped of their fetters; they were swelled so much that it was with difficulty I could walk. I was kept manacled at the wrists till the ship had got underway out of the harbor. After she had passed the fort the captain ordered a boat lowered and sent me ashore on a barren place, where it was impossible for me to go to the settlement without a boat, and left me with the irons on my hands. In this situation I spent two days and nights on the beach without food or water, when I was picked up by a man who gave me a passage in a canoe to the settlement. Here I had to work hard for my victuals. After nine months the schooner Clementine, of New York, arrived, and I asked Captain —— to take me out of the country, but he refused. I then went to Ohotsk, thinking to go overland to St. Petersburg; finding a vessel there from the States, however, I wanted to ship in her, but was detained by the Russian government, and forced to work for the Russian American Fur Company the two following years. After having been forced to bear the rigors of two Siberian winters, without much clothing, and to serve as a slave for two and a half years,

I got a passage to Sitka, Northwest America, where, after five months' working for the Russians, I was permitted to go away in the brig Baical and was discharged in San Francisco.

"John Warner, of Scotland."

The next event in this poor fellow's life was his imprisonment in California. His sufferings there were scarcely less than those he had endured elsewhere. The names of his companions at Macao appear in the list of prisoners which was given in the previous chapter.

The 19th was an exciting day. More of my countrymen and others, allied by the blood of a common ancestry, were arriving from the interior in irons. As soon as they came in town they were taken in front of the prisons, pulled violently from their horses by Indians, and frequently much bruised by the fall. Their tormentors then searched them, took forcible possession of their money, knives, flints, steels, and every other little valuable about their persons, and thrust them into prison. About eleven o'clock, A. M., the American called on the governor to learn the cause of this treatment, and was informed that there had been considerable conversation among the prisoners for months past, about "being abused by the government," and that threats had been made about "going to the governor for justice," and other things of that kind, which rendered ti necessary for the peace of the country to get them out of it, or into their graves. The American replied, that the treaty stipulations between the governments of the United States and Mexico required the authorities of each country to treat the citizens of the other with kindness and justice.

His Excellentissimo replied, that the government of the Californias would not be restrained in its action by treaties which the central government might make; and that if the department of the Californias should violate such compact with the United States, that government would seek redress from Mexico; that the Californian government was the mere agent of the Central government, and therefore not responsible to other nations for its administration. The Mexican government alone had a right to complain of its acts.

The American replied, that the department of the Californias being an integral part of the Mexican nation, any injury which its authorities should inflict on the persons and rights of other nations might well be redressed on the persons and property of the Californias. The Governor answered, that he thought not. He was then asked, what he supposed an American or British fleet would do, if one should at that time anchor at Monterey?

This question startled the miserable tyrant. That spectral fleet outside, its reputed commander in his very presence, and the constant plying of the Don Quixote between him and his armament, seemed for a moment to come before him, like a fearful reality. Perceiving the impression made upon him, the American took advantage of the occasion to remark, that it would be necessary for the Californian government to bring the persons then in confinement to a speedy trial for any alleged misdemeanor, or set them at liberty without trial, at a very early day; for the American government and its citizens required him, and would, if necessary, compel him, in this instance at least, to do an act of strict justice.

The quiet and firm tone of this address threw his Excellentissimo into a most sublime rage. He ordered the guards to fire on the American, and strode through his apartment, bellowing fearfully, and raising a very dense cloud of dust! The American, meanwhile, knowing that Californian noise boded little danger, stood quietly awaiting the termination of the tumult. It ceased after a while, and mildly saying to the governor, that he had only to repeat, that the prisoners must be tried and lawfully condemned or set at liberty, and that soon, he walked through the guards and returned to his lodgings. He had not been at home more than an hour when a message arrived from Don Jose Castro, Alvarado's captain advising him not to appear in the streets again, for he feared that his life would be taken by the sub alterns of the insulted government!!

This message was intended to prevent him from appearing before the grates, and encouraging the prisoners to bear their sufferings like men worthy their high extraction; and also to deter him from interfering with the unholy purposes of the Government against their lives. It failed of its object. His reply was, that he did not at that time comprehend the necessity of Captain Castro's anxieties in regard to him, and that as he should have business in the streets about sunset, those who felt disposed would have an opportunity at that time to make any demonstrations congenial with their feelings. At sunset he walked down to the prisons, heard again through the grates the cries of their tenants for air and water, and returned to Mr. Larkin's, to pass a miserable night—a night of unavailing compassion.

The next day he went into two of the cells, took the names and residence of a portion of the prisoners, and learned their general condition. They had nothing on which to sleep or sit except the wet ground; were emaciated, pale and sickly; some of them could scarcely walk to the grate to get fresh air; one could not stand, and his fellows from time to time held him up to breathe! They said in their despair, that they could keep hope alive as long as he dared to walk frequently before the prison, for his presence obtained them better treatment from their enemies, and encouraged the more desponding to expect through him deliverance from their sufferings!

Graham's cell was under a double guard. It could not be approached. People were even forbidden to pass it. I occasionally approached near enough to hear the lion-hearted old man roar out his indignation. A great and brave soul had that man. Its best energies had been bestowed on the ingrate Alvarado. He had made the rascal into a governor; and this was the beginning of his reward.

The afternoon was spent in much perplexity by the officers

of the government. They believed the American to be something more than a Commodore. His precise rank they could not determine. It was evident to them that he had a fleet outside under his command! But he spoke and acted as if he not only had authority on the seas, but the land also, even in Los Californias! He was everywhere present, forbidding one thing and ordering another; rushing into the governor's apartments, upbraiding him for his acts, and threatening to bring destruction upon the town, unless all his capricious wishes in regard to the rebels were gratified. His character was an enigma. If he assumed it, death was too light a punishment. If he were really a high agent of the Republic of North America, his bearing and acts comported with his character, and indicated that great circumspection would be necessary in the course adopted toward the prisoners.

Mr. Larkin was called upon to express his opinion in this vexed matter; but he very properly said that he knew nothing about it, except that this man appeared to be one who understood his duties, whatever they were; and suggested that it might not be well to disregard his opinions, or otherwise treat him with disrespect. The subaltern dignitaries thereupon made their complimentary acknowledgments to the American, and passed a part of the day with him and Mr. Larkin. It pleased them to say many handsome things of the bravery and intelligence of the citizens of the States. They were told in reply that the United States expected the prisoners to be released from unjust and tyrannical imprisonment. The Señors bowed assent; but mentioned as a difficulty in the way of this proceeding, that to release them would be an act of great disrespect to the governor, Juan Baptiste Alvarado. To this it was replied that such disrespect would not be very alarming—not quite so serious as the Paixhan guns of an American or British man-of-war.

Another night of suffering in the prisons. "Heat, heat! Air! for God's sake give us air! air! You brown devils, give us air!" were heard at intervals, till the noise of opening day drowned these agonizing entreaties.

On the morning of the twenty-first, the American was refused any intercourse with the prisoners. During the forenoon, therefore, he walked many times past the grates of the several buildings; stopped often and encouraged the inmates by his mien to hope on still. Mr. Larkin had fed them liberally in the morning, and furnished every cell with an abundant supply of water. Yet they suffered greatly! They looked on damp prison walls, and dragged chains at their wrists and ancles! They stood or sat or lay on poached mud! They saw in the future every image of coming evil! Suffocation, the pangs of death one at a time, coming slowly by day and among the sleepless moments of the long and hot night—life pendent on the mercy of a Californian Spaniard. These constituted heir condition.

About noon of the 21st, a half-breed Spaniard rode into town at full speed and held a hurried conversation with the guard around the prison, and then entered the house of the Governor. A few moments having elapsed he reappeared and went to the quarters of Jose Castro. A moment more Castro came upon the green, issued a hasty order to Corporal Pinto, and repaired to the Governor. The horseman, meantime, galloped rapidly to the Castello. Immediately his Excellentissimo appeared on the balcony, and ordered the drums to beat to arms! Soon there was hot haste in every dwelling. Women ran to the windows and doors; children pulled at their mothers' skirts, and asked what had happened. The men ran to the public green, took their stations in the ranks, and looked alternately towards the hills and the prisons. The dogs barked and trotted about in apparent wonder; the goats bleated and stamped their feet; and the horses neighed and ran to the sea-side, and the cattle raised head and tail and ran together! In fact, such a time of locomotion had not for many a day been seen in Monterey. In order to explain this phenomenon, it will be necessary for me to show its cause.

A law of the Republic of Mexico requires the citizens of other nations, who would hunt, trap, or trade for furs on any portion of her dominions, to obtain from the proper authorities written licenses to that effect. Three, four, and six months, are the usual terms of time specified in them, and the rights conveyed by them vary, from the mere privilege of trapping, to all the several franchises of a general trader. With these stowed away in deer-skin pouches, enveloped in the bladders of the buffalo so saturated with grease that neither the storms nor streams can penetrate them, they load their mules with traps and goods and go forth into the wilderness. The territories over which they more commonly travel are those which lie on the rivers Jila, the Colorado of the West, the San Joaquin, and Sacramento, countries inhabited by Indians only, among which the citizens of the *Indio-Spanio-Bravo-Furioso-Militario-Despotico-Republica-Americana*, dare not enter. Into these wastes the daring Americans fight their way through the savage tribes; trap the beaver among flying poisoned arrows; guard each other while they take in turn their hurried sleep; eat the flesh of wild animals and beaten grass seed; or, as is often the case, loose themselves and die of hunger, thirst, or the prostrating effects of the poisonous waters in the sandy solitudes over which they attempt to travel.

If, however, they survive the hardships of these journeyings, collect large quantities of furs, and return to the borders of civilization, satisfied that their toil, however hazardous it may have been, has resulted in an adequate reward, it is still uncertain whether they have labored for their own or another's benefit. The authorities who have sold them their licenses employ various means to rob them of what they have so dearly acquired. The more common of these is to raise questions in regard to the validity of the licenses. To this end the hunter and his furs are seized and carried before the Alcalde, on the assumption that they have been obtained without lawful permission. The court is opened, and the possession and seizure is proven—the hunter offers in evidence of his right of pro

American Fur Traders.—P. 84.

perty, his carefully preserved license. It is examined by the court and if found to have been granted by the political party then in power, it is declared sufficient, and the hunter and his furs are released. But if it unfortunately proceeded from the antagonist political sect, the court, with a wisdom by no means peculiar to themselves, pronounce that act of their predecessors of no effect, and declare the furs forfeited to the government. Nor is the hunter rendered secure from depredation by the adjudged legality of his acquisition. Numerous instances have occurred in which the officials of New Mexico, after they have rendered judgment in his favor, have hired the partially civilized Indians to follow the poor hunter, on his way over the plains towards his home, and rob him of every skin he has taken, even his wardrobe, food, animals, rifle, and left him to perish or return to the cold hospitality of those whose creatures have ruined him.

Instances of another manner of committing these robberies have occurred. An American hunter obtained his license in Chihuahua, went to Upper California, and after a very successful hunt among the Tulares' lakes in the valley of the San Joaquin, went down to Monterey for rest and supplies. On his arrival he was summoned before the Alcalde to show by what right he had entered the country and trapped the beaver He had lost some of his animals while fording a mountain torrent, and with them his passport and license. He therefore, could show no authority for his presence, nor cause why the furs in his possession should not be declared contraband. He was not permitted to send to Chihuahua for evidence. The loss of some three thousand dollars' worth of furs, and seven years imprisonment, at Monterey, was the result.

Another American by the name of Young, who appears in in the narrative of my travels across the continent, was, by means like these robbed of some thousands of beaver-skins, the avails of many years' toil. But this iniquitous plundering has not been confined to the whites. The civilized Indians on our western frontier, who make frequent excursions over the Rocky Mountains in search of furs, have from time to time been subjected to losses and the most degrading personal treatment from the Californian and New Mexican authorities. Whites and Indians having been injured in this manner, without personal resistance, until all hope of retribution from the federal government, and every prospect of better morals on the part of the robbers, had forsaken them, have taken the club into their own hands: and the ruined Indian and white man put on the red paint of battle, band together, make incursions among the covyards of Santa Fé, and even cross the mountains, and lay tribute upon the mules and horses of the Californians. Such were the Indians whose presence created the alarm at Monterey. They numbered about fifty. And the vagabond government well knew that those fifty rifles if brought upon the town at that time would send every poltroon of them to their last rest. No wonder, then, that there was quaking at Monterey. Old scores and later ones would have been balanced, if those men had dreamed that Americans and Britons were in the prisons of Monterey.

It was suggested by several persons that the prisoners would be shot during the week without trial. Acting upon this hint the American intimated to some of the more prudent and intelligent among them, his willingness to aid them in breaking prison, taking the town, and disposing of the authorities at rope's end, if they did not give them a fair trial within three days thereafter. These propositions inspired them with such new life, or rather so kindled into action the little that was left in them, that those who had strength enough to make themselves heard, struck up "Hail Columbia," and "Rule Britannia," with a fervor that at intervals choked their utterance!

I never before felt the force of these national songs. The night was still! Scarcely a sound was heard save the heavy surf beating on the rocks of Puentos Pinos. I walked around the prisons till eleven o'clock, to the peril of life, indeed, but in the enjoyment of feelings dearer than life itself.

"Hail Columbia!" I wish my readers could conceive something of the stirring might of those words sung by parched lips within the prisons of California! Dying Americans sang them! The unconquerable sons of the Republic sang them, though strength was sinking and the blood flowed feebly through her children's veins!

"Rule Britannia!" The battle anthem of the fatherland! Sturdy Britons were there to sing. Their voices seemed weak when they began it; but as their feelings seized more perfectly the inspiration of poetry and music, the floating walls of the Island Empire seemed to heave in view. "Rule Britannia!" It came ringing through the grates during the latter part of the evening with a broken, wild shout, as if the breath of those who uttered it came fresh from Trafalgar!

Pinto, the captain of the guard, inquired the purport of their songs, and was told by a Scotchman at the grates that they were "the war-cries of Britain and America, and that the Californians, Mexicans, and the rest of the Spanish creation, had better vote themselves asses and devils before those nations forced the idea into them from the muzzles of their rifles!"

This Pinto was a small pattern even of a coward, but what there was of him one could not doubt was the genuine article. He had a small narrow head, very black stiff hair, a long thin nose with a sharp pendant point; small snakish eyes, very near neighbors, and always peering out at the corners of the sockets; a very slender sharp chin, with a villanous tuft of bristles on the under lip; a dark swarthy complexion burnished with the grin of an idiotic hyena. Who would not expect such an animal to be frightened at the carnage songs of the parent of nations and her firstborn child! He did fear, the miniature scoundrel! He had been one of the principle instigators of this barbarity, and if he believed in the recupe rative energies of prostrated justice he had reason to tremble.

In his trepidation he sought the quarters of Jose Castro. This man was his monster superior. With the general outlines of the human frame, he united every lineament of a thoroughbred ourang-outang: as, very long arms, very large brawny hands, a very heavy body, and a very contemptible face, wrinkled and drawn into a broad concentrated scowl of unsatisfied selfishness.

This dignitary made the rounds of the guard and retired to his couch, satisfied that he was really what he modestly called himself—the Napoleon of Western America! Pinto took up his position with great resolution in the shade of an adobie wall, at a safe distance from the prisons; and when I left the ground he was employing his knees in knocking each other into a stiff stand against unmanly fear. Nothing else worthy of note occurred during the night.

On the morning of the 22d the governor sent again for the American. He would not see the messenger. About nine o'clock, however, he walked down before the prisons and spoke a word of cheer to their inmates. They were wretched, but hope was awakened in them by his presence and fearlessness.

There was evident consternation among the dons. That American signalling the Don Quixote every morning as she swept into the harbor, and the idea of a fleet outside, its commander ashore, communicating with it by a fast-sailing brig, and that commander defying the governor, breaking through the guards, conversing with the prisoners, and those martial songs by night, were ominous circumstances in the eyes of those contemptible tyrants!

About noon it was reported that the prisoners would have a trial! A little advance this! The government had begun to yield to its fears, what it would not to its sense of justice.

The next morning, the 23d, the entire standing army, consisting of sixteen filthy half-breeds, and a corps of about sixty volunteers, mustered at the beat of the drum before the prisons. Twenty-one of the prisoners were brought out between the lines, marched to the governor's house, and seated on the grass in front of it. They were emaciated and pallid, but resolute. The American pushed his way through the crowd of officers and citizens, seated himself within twelve feet of the prisoners, and manifested to them by the sincerest compassion and most resolute acts, that if they died he died with them. He had agreed with them to appear before the prison at the middle hour of night, on the twenty-fourth, and go with them to freedom or a brave death, if they were not fairly tried and on evidence condemned, or released before the following midnight. This promise they felt would be kept.

The trial, as it was called, soon commenced. Each man was summoned singly from his seat to a lower room in the governor's house, and called upon to produce his passport. Most of them replied, that they were arrested in their fields or workshops, and were not permitted to go to their residences for papers or anything else.

To this the Alcalde who sat in judgment said, "I have no evidence before me of your lawful right to remain in California."

The next question was, "What do you know of a revolutionary movement under Graham?"

The reply was, "I know nothing of any such movement or intention."

"What meant that advertisement for a horse-race, put forth by Graham?"

"It meant what such advertisements have meant for the last five years: a wish on the part of Graham to run his American horse in California."

"Nothing more? Nothing more?"

This was the form of trial in each case. The only favor they craved was, that they might have an interpreter who understood both languages. This was denied them. A miserable tool of the government, who spoke the English so badly that he could never make himself understood, succeeded, by his manner of translating their answers, in making them confess themselves guilty of high treason, and other misdemeanors worthy of the bullet.

After all had passed this ordeal, a Botany Bay Convict, by the name of Garner, was called in evidence on behalf of the government. His testimony removed all lingering doubts. He established the unqualified guilt of all. Graham, in particular, who had been preferred over him as commander of the foreign riflemen in Alvarado's revolution, and whom he had previously attempted to kill, he declared to have formed a scheme of ambition, which, had it not been discovered, would have dug the grave of every Spaniard in California!! This man's testimony was written out and signed by his murderous hand. It may be in due time a blister on his perjured soul.

The reported confessions of each prisoner were reduced to writing in the Spanish language. They contained, as I afterward learned in Mexico, things never said, accounts of acts never performed, and bequests of property to their persecutors, their jailers, and to those, who, on several occasions, thrust sabres at their hearts when nearly helpless in the dungeons of Monterey, which I need not say were never made. Few of them could read Spanish, and none were permitted to peruse these documents. They were compelled to sign them, as poor Morris was, by threats of instant death if they refused. Thus ended the trial of one hundred and sixty-odd Americans and Britons, before a court of Californian Arabs! What its judgment would be was the painful question in every mind! A few of them had been sent to their places of residence without arms, or any intimation whether it would be the sublime pleasure of the villains that they should live or die: the greater part were remanded to the prisons. And again, while they sat, stood, and laid on the mud floors of their cells, and clanked their fetters and handcuffs, they sang "Hail Columbia," and "Rule Britannia," as another night of wo passed away! That spectre fleet and its commander were the only hope between them and death. On this they leaned!

On the morning of the twenty-third the drums beat at early dawn, and the whole military force paraded before the dungeons. An imposing display was that. The clanking of rusty swords and scabbards, the jingling of loose gun-locks, and the right-about-face-forward-march operations of these bandy-legged, pale-livered, disconsolate sons of Mars, praying to the saints that they might not be annihilated by such terrible events, told a story of valor, which future ages ought to hear with appalled ears! The times which try men's souls have always been remarkable in some way; and this day was chiefly conspicuous for beef and beans. The quantity of these articles which they devoured at breakfast, was incredible; and the grease and dirt which they consumed, the glare and quick twinkling of the eyes for more, and the panting obesity of their persons when the meal was ended, indicated great perseverance, if not indomitable bravery.

As in other countries talent is measured by impudence, moral worth by long faces and stereotyped solemnity of countenance, and rank by the elevation of the nose and the successful villainy of ancestors, so in California, with the same unquestionable good sense, do the cavalieros measure their manliness of character, their bravery in arms, their civil and social elevation, by the capacity of their stomachs and their eloquence in boasting. Never were men happier or more thoroughly self-content than the troops of Monterey at their beef and beans. The events of THE REVOLUTION were discussed with full mouths and laboring throats. Los Espanioles del Alta California, to wit, every Indian with a drop of Spanish blood under his filthy skin, were *muy bravos*, extremely brave, and their conduct in the late troubles was second to nothing recorded since the siege of Mexico under Cortes!

It is said by some one who pretends to know, that the world generally estimates us by the value we set upon ourselves. Whether this opinion be founded in truth or not, I am unable to determine. But certain it is, the Genius of Glory in these days seems to be in her dotage. Homer, Socrates, Luther and Washington, wear her laurels with so much grace, that the old jade appears to think it a mere amusement to make immortal men. Accordingly she throws the poet's wreath upon moon-struck rhymsters, the philosopher's crown upon heads with long hair and dirty beards, that of the Reformer upon apes and brass-mounted women, and even tries to make men out of male Californians. Sad mistakes are all these; and particularly the last.

About ten o'clock the troops were reviewed by Don Jose Castro. A little after eleven, all the prisoners except forty-six were pardoned. These the government would not liberate. They had acted a conspicuous part in Alvarados' revolution, and were feared as likely to demand for themselves and their companions the fulfilment of the promises which he had made them. The American had suggested that they should be sent to the Consuls of their respective governments at Tepic. A ship which had been chartered for that purpose (the Roger Williams, of Boston), was floating in the harbor. The doors of the prisons were opened; the emaciated tenants came out, chained two and two, hand and foot, some of them with no clothing except a pair of ragged pantaloons. The Spaniards had robbed them not only of their cattle, horses, mules, and freedom, but also of their wardrobe. They were marched towards the shore, clanking their chains. Poor Graham and Morris were so heavily loaded with irons that it required four stout Indians to carry them.

The American mingled among them, and dissuaded them from a contemplated insurrection on ship-board. Three Californian women followed the prisoners. They were wives, and had children. They clung to their husbands and wept aloud. Castro ordered them to be driven away with blows. They were beaten with swords, but would not go. They led their children, and helped bear the chains that were galling the bleeding limbs of those whom they loved.

They said, "the soldiers have taken all our horses, cattle and property, and now they take you away from us for ever! May God take our lives! Oh, Mary, mother of God, pray for us!"

As they were going down to the boat, poor old Graham

seemed entirely broken-hearted. The American said to him, "Be brave, Graham, be brave! Let no Tennessean ever think of yielding in this way. Raise your head and keep it erect. Once landed at San Blas, you are safe. I will see you when you land."

"Ah," said Graham," I never can be a man again after having these feet bound with irons by a Californian; never again! I could bear to be a prisoner to a brave and decent people, but to be caught and cooped up, chained and exported like a tub of lard, by these here scabs of mankind, is mighty bad! No, I never shall be a man again, Mr. ——. Here, take my hand. We should have been riddled with bullets if you had not been here, could the rascals have drawn a bead close enough to hit us! I never shall be a man again! Irons on the legs of a man who fought for them, who made the cowards what they are! With my fifty rifles about me, I could drive the devils from the whole coast or lay them away to rot. But I won't think on't. I never can be a man again!"

They put him and some others into a boat and pushed off for the ship. "Farewell, Mr. ——, farewell: but stop, hold on!—have you got money enough to get home with? I will let you have some in San Blas. But I never shall be Graham again!"

The boats continued to ply between the ship and the shore until all were carried on board. The multitude then retired to the town. Deep feelings struggled in every breast at the termination of this affair. Alvarado was mad that he had not shot Graham, to whom he owed $2,235 and other obligations; those cavalieros who had been rejected by ladies to make way for foreign suitors, were enraged beyond measure that most of them had been left in the country. The ladies generally rejoiced that no blood had been shed; the wives of those who had been sent on board the prison-ship, sat on shore beneath the tree where the cross was erected by Padre Junipero, and wept upon the necks of their children, until the ship was out of sight. The American suggested that the town might be taken, and the perpetrators of such outrages be disposed of at rope's end; but the proposition was discountenanced by the residents. The church was opened, and a *Te Deum* sung for the deliverance of the country! After this, each class true to their leading emotions, gathered in knots about town, and talked of these strange things till supper separated them for the night. During the evening some of the officers of government called at Mr. Larkin's, and informed the American that the governor had sent the prisoners to the American and British Consuls at Tepic, via San Blas, and that the vessel would put into Santa Barbara for provisions and other prisoners.

The twenty-fourth morning of April was clear; the sun came up the eastern hills on a landscape of sweet things. No one born and dwelling in the rugged, changing seasons of the North can know, without experiencing, the delights of a climate like that of California. From spring to spring again all is friendly; from morning till morning comes again all is pleasant to breathe and to see; from hour to hour the body feels in the air a balmy blessing; from moment to moment the blood leaps vigorously through the frame.

Near eleven o'clock the troops were in motion, and Mr. Larkin and myself went down to the public green, to see what might transpire.

We found the green covered with the people kneeling and crossing themselves, and the priest in full robes performing high-mass near the door of the governor's dwelling. His Excellentissimo was kneeling with his officers before the altar as devoutly as if he had been obedient to the commandments from his youth till that time. It was shocking to hear him respond to the prayers for repentance, while any observer might see the malignity with which he had sought the lives of his friends, struggling among the muscles of his face and burning in his eyes!

The services being ended, the governor retired into his house. Thanks had been given to God for saving the country from danger which never existed, and for protecting the villains that pretended its existence as an excuse for shedding blood.

No other event occurred that day worthy of being noticed, except the wives of those poor fellows who were floating down the coast in the prison-ship went weeping through the streets, beseeching all they met to go down to Santa Barbara and bring back their husbands.

I spent my time among the foreigners, who had been let out of prison, in gathering information relative to the country, which will be given in another part of the volume.

The evening was passed at Mr. Larkin's. We were happy, not because we felt no danger around us, for there was much of it. But we were glad that no more groans came up from the damp dungeons! That none of our countrymen were calling for air, and water, and food, from those infernal dens! Alas, for those who were on their way to Mexico We thought of them sadly; they might be dying; but we called hope to our aid, and believed that better hours would soon dawn on their misery. More than one hundred of our countrymen were released from impending death! Bolts grated no more! chains clanked no more on the silent night! And we felt in our own persons something of that returning security to life which sends through the soul of the most reckless and inexpressible sense of pleasure.

The next morning the green before the governor's house was graced with a portly effigy of Senor Judas Iscariot! One ankle out of joint, and other parts disarranged, for the especial gratification of his inferiors in moral qualities. The senor was assumed to be dead. His optics glared rather sorrowfully upon the multitude around him, as if loth to look the last time on congenial hearts! He held in his hand a scroll, containing a last will and testament, in which his several virtues and possesions were bequeathed to various persons residing in the country.

In the afternoon the American and some other gentlemen

were invited by an English resident to a *festa* on the shores of the bay. And being in a mood to seize upon anything to divert thought from the unpleasant reminiscences of the past week, we gladly accepted the invitation, without knowing indeed what a Californian *festa* might be. Dr. Bale was one of the guests, and kindly conducted us to the place selected for the ceremonies. It was among the trees, a short distance southwest of the anchorage; a wild, rude spot. The old trees, which had thrown their branches over the savage before a white man had touched the shores, were rotting on the ground, and formed the fuel of our fire! The ancient rocks stood around, covered with the moss of ages! The winds sang in the trees! The ringing cadences of the towering pine, the deep bass of the strong spreading oak, the mellow alto of the flowering shrubs, the low, soft voice of the grasses, nature's great Æolian lyre, breathed sweet music! The old wilderness was there, unshorn, and holy, responding to the songs of birds in the morn of the opening year.

When we arrrived, half a dozen brunettes were spreading cloths upon the grass, and displaying upon them boiled ham, dried beef, tongue, bread, pies, cigars, and various kinds of wines, from the vineyards of the country; so that a *festa* proved to be an invitation for us to eat and drink among a group of joyous children and smiling lasses. Yes smiling, hearty Californian lasses. Who is not glad to see me repeat words that speak of the smiles of women? I do not mean those heart-rending efforts at grinning, which one so often meets in mechanical society; but those pulsations of genuine joy and truth, which come up impulsively from woman's real nature, shedding on the dwelling-places of the race the sweetest elements of the social state. It is that sunshine of our moral being which beams on our cradles, on the paths of our childhood, on the stormy skies of misfortune in the years of manhood, which warms the chilled heart of age into renewed life, and shines on till sight and sense are lost in the dark gateway to the after state!

We ate and drank freely. Who could do otherwise? The mellow laugh of childhood, the holy kindness of maternal care, the pride of the paternal heart, the love of woman, the sky and fragrant breezes of a Californian lawn, the open sea, the giant woodlands, the piping insects, the carolling of a thousand birds, the voices of a boundless hospitality, invited us to do so. The finest dish of all the goodly array of fat things, the brunette lips excepted, was the roasted mussels. The Indians in attendance gathered a number of bushels, piled them upon a large log fire, and in a few minutes presented them to us, thoroughly cooked and delicious to the taste. Indeed I hope for no better fish. They are tender as an oyster, with as fine flavor; and the abundance of them is really remarkable! The coast is lined with them.

Our *festa* ended near sunset. It had been as agreeable as our hosts' best attentions could render it. The ladies also had vied with each other to make the occasion happy. But their gladness was forced. A deep gloom like that which the thunder-cloud throws over the flowering meadow-land, saddened their smiles, arrested the laugh half-uttered, bent the figure, and shaded the warm glow of joy in the eye, with the cold watchfulness of alarm! Such was the influence of that prison ship, the last speck of which had been watched, as it sunk, hull, spars, and streamer, over the bending sea, freighted with chains and the misery of fellow-countrymen, that the heart could not be persuaded into happiness!

CHAPTER VI.

A Ride—Vale of San Carmelo—Indians employed—The Surf—Bay of San Carmelo—Mission Edifices—Belfrey Bells—Deserted and Sad—An Indian Lawyer and his Wife--A Speech—Return to Monterey—Embarkation--Weighing Anchor—An American Tar—Tom's New Axe—General Training Day—Becomes a Salt—Tom's opinion of the Land and its Inhabitants—A fine breeze—Punto Concepcion—Islands—A calm—A night on deck—Landing at Santa Barbara—The Prison Ship—El Mission de Santa Barbara—Its Fountains, Tanks, Church, Pictures and Cemetery—The Prisoners—Taking leave of them.

In the afternoon of the twenty-fifth, three or four Americans and an English physician rode out on horseback to the mission of San Carmelo, one league and a half southwesterly from Monterey. The road leading to it lay over an undulating country, covered with the growing wild grasses. Its general aspect much resembled that of the broken lands of Illinois The hills, however, were higher, the gravel of the roads coarser. The trees were a species of soft, low oak, pine and birch. A kind of clover and some other species of grasses crowned every knoll and height. And the odor of that vegetation! Incense from the boundless altar of nature! The teeming fields of spring on the rich hill sides, sending up into the broad sky the sweet perfume of opening leaf and flower. The glancing flight of the butterfly, the nimble leaps of the hare, the hurried snort of the startled deer, the half-clad Indian lounging in the genial sun-light, mottled the view along the way.

The valley of the mission is a charming one. It comes down from the north-eastern highlands, accompanied by a clear bright stream, to the sea. It is ten miles in length, two miles wide near the ocean, and narrower as it rises among the lofty ridges. Rio Carmelo winds very much; and in its bends are many stately groves, between which lie the forsaken fields of the mission, overgrown with wild grass and brush. Not entirely forsaken, for here and there is found an Indian hut, with its tiled roof, mud walls and floor, tenanted, but falling to decay. The inmates are the spiritual children of the old Padres, who taught them rude agriculture, architecture, and the Being and worship of God. Since the departure of those good men, the fields have been neglected, and the Indians have sunk into vice and degradation. A sad thing is it to see the furrow of civilisation turned back; the thistle usurping the place of the wheat; rank weeds choking the vineyard, and the rose trodden in the dust! But so it is in the valley of San Carmelo. The Indians in different sections were planting small plats of beans and maize. A mule and an ox yoked together were used for draught.

We rode to the water-side to look at the surf. It was a glorious sight that heaving up of the Great Deep on the land! The shore was bold and lined with huge buried reefs. On these the swells, walls of bending water ten feet in height, dashed, broke, roared and died—a sheet of quarrelling foam—over the beach for miles around the bay. And as each wave retired, that beach of shells reduced to dust by the battering sea, sent up its countless hues, from pearly white to the richest violet, dancing and trembling over the green lawn on which we stood. This bay of San Carmelo is a large open bight, so filled with sunken rocks and sand bars, and so exposed to the winds from the south-west, as to be useless for a harbor. But it is a wild and grand thing to look out upon in storm or calm. On the south, rude rocks, old trees and desert hillocks bound it. On the north the lofty pines crowd down to its billows. On the north-west opens the valley of the missions. Over all its blue waters rave the surges, if the winds be up; or if still, in come the great swells, alive with porpoise and seal, and bellow and die on the shore of San Carmelo.

The mission buildings are situated on the north side of the valley near the sea. They stand on elevated ground, which overlooks the bay and seven or eight miles of the vale. They were inhabited by a family of half-breeds, who kept the keys of the church. The edifices are built around a square area of half an acre. On the west, south, and east sides of it, are the Indian houses with their ruined walls, scalloped tile roofs, clay floors and open unglazed windows. On the north side are the church, the cells and dining hall of the Padres. The latter is about forty feet by twenty, lighted by open spaces in the outer wall, grated with handsomely turned wooden bars, and guarded by plank shutters, swinging inside. At the west end of this room is a small opening through which the food was passed from the kitchen. On the north side and east end are four doors opening into the cells of the friars. Everything appeared forsaken and undesirable. And yet I could not forbear a degree of veneration for those ancient closets of devotion; those resting-places of the wayfarer from the desert; those temples of hospitality and prayer, erected by that band of excellent and daring men, who founded the Californian missions, and engraved on the heart of that remote wilderness, the features of civilisation and the name of God.

There was an outside stairway to the tower of the church. We ascended it and beheld the broken hills, the vales and the great heaving sea, with its monsters diving and blowing; and heard it sounding loudly far and near. We saw the ruined mission of San Carmelo, and the forsaken Indians strolling over its grounds! On the timbers over head, hung six bells of different sizes—three of them cracked and toneless. Formerly one of these rang to meals, to work, and rest; and the others to the various services of the Catholic faith. Dr. Bale informed us, such was the regularity of these establishments that the laboring animals stopped in the road or furrow, whenever the bells called the Indian to his duties But prayers are no longer heard in San Carmelo; the tower no longer commands obedience to God; the buildings are crumbling to dust; the rank grass is crowding its courts; the low moss is creeping over its gaping walls; and the ox and mule are running wild on its hills.

The walls of the church are of stone masonry; the roof of brick tiles. The whole structure is somewhat lofty, and looks down upon the surrounding scenery, like an old baronial castle, from which the chase, the tournament, and the reign of beauty have departed. An oaken arm-chair, brown and marred with age, stood on the piazza, proclaiming to our lady of Guadaloupe and a group of saints rudely sketched upon the walls, that Carmelo was deserted by living men.

My respect for the profession of "glorious uncertainties," will not permit me to leave this valley without introducing to the kind regards of the reader a brother lawyer. He lived on the banks of the Carmelo in a little mud hut, surrounded by some beautiful fields under good cultivation. His stock consisted of a number of tame cows, a few goats, uncounted flocks of domestic fowls, and a dozen dogs. When about a quarter of a mile distant, the dogs opened their artillery in a running fire upon us; the cocks flew upon the fences and crowed terribly; the pullets cackled; and altogether, the commotion surprised our horses into a general snort, and ourselves into a laugh, prolonged and loud as our lungs could sustain, at such a welcome to the residence of the only professional lawyer in the Californias!

We rode up briskly in the midst of this cackling, crowing and barking, and dismounted before the door of a tolerably comfortable hut, in the standing presence of the brown, flat-nosed, broad-cheeked, ragged Indian Esquire. His head was bare, his leathern pants full of holes and glazed with grease, his blanket hung in tatters. His wife hobbled out as blind as a fire-dog, and decrepid with years and hard labor. One or two other Indians stood about among the hens and ducks, grinning and squinting at us in much wonder and humility! Such was the group on the hen-dog-Indian side of the scene. Ourselves occupied the other.

We stood at our horses' necks, one hand on the rein, and awaited something, we knew not what. The Esquire rolled his little black eyes in delight to see us; put one hand on the hip, and stood on one leg, and then changed into an opposite position; shaking and giggling with joy meanwhile, and apparently not knowing where to begin to entertain either himself or us. At length, Dr. Bale came to his relief, by referring to the fact that he owned more land before the mission was founded, than he now seemed to enjoy. At this he took fire, and went into a dissertation on the titles of the Padres and Indians; the substance of which, I learned from the Doctor, was, that the Padres had taken possession of the valley about forty years before, had taught the Indians to work and pray, had given a portion of his lands to other Indians, and when civil troubles came, had killed most of the cattle and sold the hides and tallow to ships, for hard dollars, and with bags of these dollars left the country and the Indians who had earned them. "There," said he, pointing to his blind wife, "is all they have left me of my wife; she worked hard and is blind; and these little fields are all they have left me of my broad lands."

His violent gesticulation and tone of voice led me to the belief that he was tinctured with mania. The poor fellow and his wife excited our commiseration deeply, and I cannot remember them, even now, without reviving the pity I felt for the "Indian lawyer" and his poor blind wife, tottering about her lowly hut.

From these premises we turned rein for Monterey. Our Californian steeds laid hoof to the rough road in a manner worthy their Arabian sires. Speed, speed! Backward the gravel flew from their willing feet, as we mounted the heights. Gully and rock were leaped with a joyful neigh! We reached the highland when the sun was a hand's breadth above the ocean. His burning farewell lay on the verdant hill-tops. Onward! speed onward! The Bay is before us; its crested billows are gilded, like fretted gold, with rays from the uppe. rim of the sinking sun!

On the twenty-eighth of April the Don Quixote had completed her business with P. I. Farnham & Co.'s ship Alciope, and was ready for sea. Captain Paty had laid in a generous supply of fresh beef, vegetables, and other comforts for his passengers; the foreign residents had presented the American with many little tokens of regard, in the form of fruits, wines, &c., to make the voyage comfortable.

Eleven o'clock, A. M., we took leave of our countrymen, and others of the Saxon blood, on the rock where the prisoners' chains had lately clanked, and shoved off for the ship.

One of the unpleasant circumstances attending journeys in wild and dangerous countries, is, the parting from persons of kindred feelings with whom we have wept or rejoiced. Many who had suffered in Monterey were still there. They had escaped an apparently certain doom, and I had felt keenly every shade which progressive events cast on their fate, or lifted from their hopes of being saved from the death of felons. They were saved! They were glad! But the fear of returning tyranny still hung over them. The same malignity held the reins of power; and the dungeon and bullet were under the control of the same demons. It was hard parting with those brave and abused men. The throats of villains could be made to bleed! The walls of justice and mercy could be reared around the social state in California. The acting government could have raised no force to prevent it. Britons and Americans could have done it; and the halter been made to claim its own. But that prison-ship and my hearth called me.

" On board!" " On board!" Our boat lies under the lee of the good barque Don Quixote; the ropes of the gangway are seized; and we stand on deck. " Man the windlass;' " heave the anchor, cheerily, boys," is ordered and done.

This is always a cheering time on ship-board. "Heave ahoy;" and the old salt's eye brightens, his step quickens, and his voice rings gladly, as link after link of the ponderous cable tumbles aboard, till the flukes of the anchor lie high on the bows, and the ship is given to her helm and the breeze.

The wind, the sea, and good planks between him and the bottom, and the stars and stripes at the mizen, are the substantial comforts of an American tar. Supplied with these and a clear sweep from the headlands, he will leave the shore without a feeling that it will ever be his wish to return. Indeed, the real sailor, he who has wound every yarn of his happy hours around the windlass, despises the land. We had in the Don Quixote an example of this kind. He was a tall, slabsided Yankee, from the State of Maine; with a hand like a grappling-iron, hung to a mass of shoulder and chest that would have been formidable among buffalo. His deck name was Tom; to which the adjective *long*, was sometimes prefixed, as he explained it, "in order to add a fathom to its scund."

When sixteen years of age, he had heard that Maine was noted far abroad for its long mortals and heavy fists; and dreamed that he was not so deficient in these qualities as to be excluded from the distinction which might arise from them. He therefore determined to avail himself of the first favorable occasion for reaping the harvest of that notoriety to which he seemed to be born. Nor did he wait an unpleasant length of time for such an opportunity. His father returned home one evening with a new axe, purchased for Tom's especial use, in the lumber forest. It was the night previous to "the General Training-day," at Portland; and he proposed, as the morrow would be a leisure day, that Tom should test the metal of his axe, in cutting away a dry hemlock tree which had fallen across the public road. A mere suggestion from the father was the law of his household. Tom, therefore, ate his breakfast, next morning, with becoming submissiveness, and about seven o'clock struck his new axe into the dry hemlock

Long Tom Sassafras.—P. 105.

It rose, fell, and clinked in the hard knots; and occasionally sinking into the wood a depth sufficient to hold without his aid, left him at liberty to chew his tobacco, and think of his condition.

The neighboring lads came riding past. They jeered him for his want of spirit, once, again, a third time, and onward, until Tom began to think that his situation was not quite so agreeable as it would be, if he, also, with a pistareen in his pocket, were on his way to the gingerbread carts of the parade ground. To be kept at work on General Training-day, was at war with all precedent; that was a holy day for young people throughout all the land of johnny-cakes. A little reflection, therefore, convinced him that his father's requirement was somewhat unkind; a little more thought and considerable love of gingerbread, demonstrated that chopping wood on that day was not to be done by Long Tom Sassafras; and depositing his axe in the corn-house, he went to the General Training, received a flogging from his father in the presence of an auctioneer of Yankee Notions, shipped on board a lumber sloop bound for Boston, and from that time became a Salt.

Tom considered the land well nigh a nuisance. It had a few points of value It was useful as a hiding-place from a storm; useful as a hospital for "a fresh" to cure the scurvy; as a convenient substitute for a "log" to show when the voyage is ended; as a lumber yard for the wherewithal to build keels; and as a place in which small fish may rendezvous. But the sea was a greater part of the Globe; the home of freemen; where they have a plenty of sound air to breathe, and nothing but the will of Heaven to curtail their movements. "On the land it is otherwise. One's tarpaulin is knocked off at every second step on their brick-decked gangways; every lubber in straps and tights who sees fit to pass before you can up helm, runs into you, carries away your bowsprit, and d.....ns your eyes because you could not luff into the walls of a building to give him lee-way. And then the land is all mud and reefs; everything upon it is dirty; the Ladies, God knows I love the Ladies and pity them, can't keep themselves tidy. I've seen many a brace of them that required a fortnight's holy-stoning to get down to their natural color. They are obliged to paint themselves to cover up the dirt and keep from looking weather-beaten. I never knew a sensible sailor that wasn't glad to leave the land for the glorious old sea. Their ideas, those land lubbers, about what is comfortable and beautiful, are not worth a ball of spunyarn. They talk to you about the dangers of the sea, just as if there was no lee coast to run one's head and toes against on the land; about the shady groves on a May-day, just as if there were no May-day shade under the brave old canvass of Neptune; and about the purling brooks and the music of birds, just as if there were neither water at sea, nor any albatross to sail and scream in the sun, nor happy petrels to sing in the storm. And about being buried in the sea! This they think is a dreadful thing! They thrust their eyes half out of their heads when you tell them it is better to be eaten clean up by a decent shark, than to be stuffed away a few feet under ground among toads and worms and other varmints! And if you tell them that when a fellow dies at sea, they sew him up in a strong bit of canvas, and hang a weight to his feet, read prayers over him and drop him solemnly into the ocean, and he goes down into the clear clear water, two or three miles perhaps, and there sleeps high above the bottom, high above dirt and worms, the lubbers think he is out of the latitude of the resurrection and Heaven and all. I am for the sea. I would not mind shipping on the quarter-deck a voyage or two, to see how it would seem to whistle the boys into the top-gallant stays in a dead north-easter. But I should want to be before the mast. That's the home for me, boys."

"Haul taut the weather main brace there"!

"Aye, aye, sir;" and away skipped our Maine boy to his duty.

We had a fine breeze from the time we weighed, till twelve o'clock on the twenty-ninth, when the wind died gradually away to a calm. During the night we lay off Punto Concepcion ; a rough ragged point of land forty miles north-west of Santa Barbara. On the thirtieth, a light breeze bore us early in the morning past San Miguel. This is an island, about fifteen miles from the coast. It is ten miles in circumference, with a rocky, barren and dry surface, marked here and there with a few fruitful spots and streams of water. At nine o'clock we were off Santa Rosa ; an island about the same distance from the land, twenty miles in circumference, piled with lofty barren hills, interspersed with a few forests and fertile districts. Next came Santa Cruz ; an oblong island forty miles in circumference, with some woodlands and fruitful vales. Farther off shore and southward, are the islands of Santa Barbara, San Nicholas and San Clemente. They lie in a line running south-east and north-west, and form the outer wall of the roadstead, called the Canal de Santa Barbara. These islands have much high land, composed of dark shining rocks, apparently of volcanic origin. They are partially covered with trees, but a greater portion of their surface is barren sands and rocks. They are densely populated with goats.

Near night a calm came on, and our sails, after flapping awhile, hung lifeless upon the spars. This was a very annoying circumstance. All on board felt extremely anxious to be in Santa Barbara that night lest the prison-ship should leave before we arrived. About twelve o'clock, however, a slight breeze sprang up, which bore us along two knots the hour. The air was so bland on deck that I chose a berth among some loose sails in the long boat, in preference to the heated cabin. It was a pure night. No vapors obscured the sky. No harsh winds disturbed the waters. Every living thing seemed reposing and smiling in its dreams of joy. The birds on the land and water should be excepted. They were twittering softly one to another, coursing through the air and marshalling and gabbling among the waves, as if keeping vigil over the slumbers of Nature!

The coast from Monterey to the Canal de Santa Barbara is broken into elevated hills, fringed with forests of pine and oak, and covered with the wild grasses From these flow many valuable little streams, which gurgle and plash down deep and verdant ravines to the sea. It is a beautiful wilderness; a country for the wild horse, the mighty grisly bear, the undomesticated cattle of a thousand hills; a blithe domain for the human race, when true and valiant men shall govern it.

The first sound that fell upon my ear on the first day of May, was the rippling of the water at the ship's side. She was moving slowly down the Canal de Santa Barbara. At nine o'clock we cast anchor before the town, lowered the boat and shot away to the beach. The prison-ship was lying at anchor in the roadstead! Our countrymen were incarcerated at the mission! We might be of some service to them; and that expectation gave us all infinite pleasure, in being again in their neighborhood.

Santa Barbara is situated on an inclined plane, which rises gradually from the sea side to a range of picturesque highlands, three and a half miles from the sea. The town itself is three quarters of a mile from the landing. The houses are chiefly built in the Spanish mode, adobie walls, and roofs of tile. These tiles are made of clay, fashioned into half cylinders, and burned like brick. In using them, the first layer is placed hollow side up; the second inversely, so as to lock over the first. Their ends overlap each other as common shingles do. This roofing serves very well in dry weather. But when the driving southwesters of the winter season come on, it affords a poor shelter. Very few of the houses have glass windows. Open spaces in the walls, protected with bars of wood, and plank shutters, serve instead. Mr. A. B. Thompson, a wealthy and hospitable American merchant, has erected a residence in the centre of the town, which bears very striking testimony to his being a civilized man.

There is an old Catholic mission, one mile and three quarters above the town, called El Mission de Santa Barbara. The church itself is a stone edifice, with two towers on the end towards the town, and a high gable between them. The friars complimented Father Time, by painting on the latter something in the shape of a clock dial. In the towers are hung a number of rich toned bells, brought from old Spain nearly a hundred years ago. The roof is covered with burnt clay tiles, laid in cement. The residence of the Padres, also built of stone, forms a wing with the church towards the sea. The prisons form another, towards the highlands. Hard by are clusters of Indian huts, constructed of adobies and tile, standing in rows, with streets between.

The old Padres seem to have united with their missionary zeal a strong sense of comfort and taste. They laid off a beautiful garden, a few rods from the church, surrounded it with a high substantial fence of stone laid in Roman cement, and planted it with limes, almonds, apricots, peaches, apples, pears, quinces, &c., which are now annually yielding their several fruits in abundance. Before the church they erected a series of concentric urn fountains, ten feet in height, from the top of which the pure liquid bursts, and falls from one to another till it reaches a large pool at the base; from this it is led off a short distance to the statue of a grisly bear, from whose mouth it is ejected into a reservoir of solid masonry, six feet wide and seventy long. From the pool at the base of the urn fountains water is taken for drinking and household use. The long reservoir is the theatre of the battling, plashing, laughing and scolding of the washing-day Around these fountains are solid, cemented stone pavements, and ducts to carry off the surplus water. Nothing of the kind can be in better taste, more substantial, or useful.

Above the church and its cloisters, they brought the water

around the brow of a green hill, in an open stone aqueduct, a rapid, noisy rivulet, to a square reservoir of beautiful masonry. Below, and adjoining this, are the ruins of the Padres' grist-mill. Nothing is left of its interior structure, but the large oaken ridgepole. Near the aqueduct which carries the water into the reservoir of the mills, stands a small stone edifice ten feet in length by six in width. This is the bath. Over the door, outside, is the representation of a lion's head, from which pours a beautiful jet of water. This little structure is in a good state of preservation. A cross surmounts it, as, indeed, it does everything used by the Catholic missionaries of these wilderness regions. Below the ruins of the grist-mill is another tank one hundred and twenty-feet square, by twenty deep, constructed like the one above. In this was collected water for supplying the fountains, irrigating the grounds below, and for the propulsion of different kinds of machinery. Below the mission was the tan-yard, to which the water was carried in an aqueduct, built on the top of a stone wall, from four to six feet high. Here was manufactured the leather used in making harnesses, saddles, bridles, and Indian clothing. They cultivated large tracts of land with maize, wheat, oats, peas, potatoes, beans, and grapes. Their old vineyards still cover the hill-sides. When the mission was at the height of its prosperity, there were several hundred Indians laboring in its fields, and many thousands of cattle and horses grazing in its pastures. But its splendor has departed, and with it its usefulness. The Indians who were made comfortable on these premises, are now squalid and miserable. The fields are a waste! Nothing but the church retains its ancient appearance. We will enter and describe its interior. It is one hundred and sixty feet long by sixty in width. Its walls are eight feet in thickness. The height of the nave is forty feet. On the wall, to the right, hangs a picture representing a king and a monk up to their middle in the flames of purgatory Their posture is that of prayer and penitence; but their faces do not indicate any decided consciousness of the blistering foothold on which they stand. On the contrary, they wear rather the quiet aspect of persons who love their ease, and have an indolent kind of pleasure in the scenes around them. On the other side, near the door of the confessional, is a picture of Hell. The Devil and his staff are represented in active service. The flames of his furnace are curling around his victims, with a broad red glare, that would have driven Titian to madness. The old Monarch himself appears hotly engaged in wrapping serpents of fire around a beautiful female figure, and his subalterns, with flaming tridents, are casting torments on others, whose sins are worthy of less honorable notice. Immediately before the altar is a trap-door, opening into the vaults, where are buried the missionary Padres. Over the altar are many rich images of the saints. Among them is that of San Francisco, the patron of the missions of Upper California. Three silver candlesticks, six feet high, and a silver crucifix of the same height, with a golden image of the Saviour suspended on it, stand within the chancel. To the left of the altar is the sacristy, or priest's dressing-room. It is eighteen feet square, splendidly carpeted, and furnished with a wardrobe, chairs, mirrors, tables, ottoman, &c.

In an adjoining room of the same size are kept the paraphernalia of worship. Among these are a receptacle of the host, of massive gold in pyramidal form, and weighing at least ten pounds avoirdupois, and a convex lens set in a block of gold, weighing a number of pounds, through which, on certain occasions, the light is thrown so as to give the appearance of an eye of consuming fire.

A door in the eastern wall of the church leads from the foot of the chancel to the cemetery. It is a small piece of ground enclosed by a high wall, and consecrated to the burial of those Indians who die in the faith of the Catholic Church. It is curiously arranged. Walls of solid masonry, six feet apart, are sunk six feet in depth, and to a level with the surface. Between these the dead are buried in such manner that their feet touch one wall and their heads the other. These grounds have been long since filled. In order, however, that no Christian Indian may be buried in a less holy place, the bones, after the flesh has decayed, are exhumed and deposited in a little building on one corner of the premises. I entered this. Three or four cart-loads of skulls, ribs, spines, leg-bones, arm-bones &c., lay in one corner. Beside them stood two hand-hearses with a small cross attached to each. About the walls hung the mould of death!

On the first of May the American made application for permission to see the prisoners, and was refused. He had heard that they were in want of food, and proposed to supply them; but was forbidden by Jose Castro, the officer in charge. The prison-ship had arrived at Santa Barbara on the twenty-fifth of April, and landed forty-one of the prisoners. Four others were retained on board to work. These forty-one men, during the whole passage from Monterey, had been chained to long bars of iron passing transversely across the hold of the ship. They were not permitted to go on deck, nor even to stand on their feet. A bucket was occasionally passed about for particular purposes, but so seldom as to be of little use. They were furnished with a mere morsel of food, and that of the worst quality. Of water, they had scarcely enough to prevent death from thirst; and so small and close was the place in which they were chained that it was not uncommon for the more debilitated to faint and lie some time in a lifeless state. When they landed, many of them had become so weak that they could not get out of the boat without aid. Their companions in chains assisted them, although threatened with instant death if they did so. After being set ashore, they were marched in the midst of drawn swords and fixed bayonets, dragging their chains around bleeding limbs, one mile and three-quarters, to the mission of Santa Barbara!

Here they were put into a single room of the mission prisons, without floor or means of ventilation. The bottom of the cell was soft mud! In this damp dungeon, without food or water, these poor fellows remained two days and nights! They had not even straw on which to sleep!

At the end of this time it coming to the ears of the Friar in charge of the mission, that one of them was dying of hunger and thirst, he repaired to the prison and inquired of Pinto, the corporal of the guard, if such were the fact! The miniature monster answered, that he did not know. The Friar replied, "are you an officer and a Catholic, and do not know the state of your prisoners! You, sir, are an officer of to-day, and should not be one to-morrow." The good man entered the cell; found one of the Englishmen speechless; administered baptism, and removed him to the house of a kind family, where I found him on my arrival; still speechless and incapable of motion. The Friar extended his kindness to the other prisoners. He ordered Castro to furnish them food and water. But the villain, evading so far as he was able, gave them barely enough of each to tantalize them, until the arrival of the American in the Don Quixote; when that fleet, laying off the coast, commanded by such a man, charmed his benevolence and mercy into activity. From the first of May, therefore, they had food and water, and were permitted to take the air and bathe daily.

On the fourth, the American was permitted to see the prisoners. They had been scrubbing themselves at the great tank; and were allowed, at his suggestion, to take their dinner in the open air. They had evidently suffered exceedingly since they left Monterey; for their countenances had lost the little color which the dungeons of that place had left them. Their hands looked skeleton-wise; their eyes were deeply sunken in their sockets; they tottered when they walked! Poor men! For no other fault than their Anglo-Saxon blood, they fared like felons! They had a long voyage, and slavery in the mines of Mexico before them, and were sad

They asked the American if he would lead them in an attack upon the guard. But he pointed out the hopelessness of such an attempt in their enfeebled condition, and comforted them with the reiterated assurance that he would meet them at San Blas.

While this conversation was going on their dinner arrived. The first course consisted of batter cakes, called tortillas, with a small quantity of boiled beef hock. A sad pittance, and of the meanest quality. But one of them told the American with much pleasantry, that it was an attempt to surprise him with the richness of their fare! The next course was a soup. I stood by the kettle while they dipped and ate it. As they approached the bottom of the vessel they hauled up two old cloths of the most filthy description, besides other things which it would ill become me to name! They ate no more! Starvation itself lost its appetite at such a spectacle! The American remonstrated with the officer in charge for allowing such baseness. The fellow promised. But why speak of a Spaniard's promise? It can be likened to nothing so well as his justice. Both are as unreliable to one in his power, as the thunder-cloud at night is, for light to him who treads on precipices!

As this was the last interview which we expected to have with the prisoners before they would leave California, it was suggested that they should write to their friends at home. To this they gladly assented. We therefore furnished them with implements for that purpose. But the jealous tyrants in charge saw fit to prohibit this last consolation of the doomed! While, however, the villains were engaged in consultation about it, I took their names and places of residence, and promised if they should be executed, or sent to the Mexican mines, to give their friends the sorrowful intelligence of their fate.

We now took leave of them. As we shook them by the hand their tears flowed freely. One said, write to my sister in Maine; another, write to my mother in Boston; another, write to my uncle in London, and he will inform my parents; another said write to my wife in *******. Her heart is already broken by my abandonment. Another tried to speak of his home; but grief choked his utterance. Graham was himself again. That hardy and high-toned energy of character which nature had given him, seemed to rise over misfortune, as his corporeal powers decreased. He was greatly enfeebled by his sufferings, and thought he might die on the passage to San Blas. "But," said he, "I reckon these villains will see me die like a man. And if I do die, I wish you to go to Tennessee and Kentucky, and tell the boys of our sufferings. My bones on the stake, their rifles will make spots on their vile carcases. Two hundred Tennessee riflemen could take the country; and it's a mighty pity it should be held by a set of vagabonds who don't regard the honor of God or the rights of men. I have been here now seven years; have always been a peaceable man, except when I took part with the Californians against the tyranny of Government officers sent up from Mexico. And now I am lassooed like a bear for slaughter or bondage, by these very men whose lives and property myself and friends saved. Well, Graham may live to prime a rifle again! If he does, it will be in California! Farewell to you. I hope we shall meet in Mexico." The old man brushed a tear from his weather-beaten generous face, and we left him.

The American repeated his visit to the sick Englishman. He had neither ate, drank, nor spoken. His limbs were entirely cold and motionless; fast sinking. The ladies in attendance were very compassionate, and bestowed on him every kindness he was capable of receiving. Yet how inhuman the power which, calling itself a Government, authorises such murders! The halter which swings at the bidding of a civil tribunal, the axe which flashes along the grooves of the guillotine, have their horrors; and the head picked up by the mob and shown while life yet speaks from the eyes, and the dying love of Freedom still clothes the countenance, shocks human forbearance! But to be killed by inches, to be sent to the arms of death by the long agonies of thirst and famine, for no crime save that of being an American or Briton, is a sacrifice at which malice itself in its soberer moments shudders and turns pale. So was this man dying. He breathed heavily. One of Castro's officers came in, and remarking that he was undoubtedly a feeble man, kissed his hand gallantly to the ladies and retired.

The evening was spent with Mrs. J. A. Jones, the Californian spouse of the former American Consul at the Hawaian Islands, and her sisters. A stroll, a *tête-à-tête*, and the sweet guitar! The air was balmy; the smiles were deeply sympathizing; the laugh savored richly of the dearest impulses of the soul; the music was the warm breath of the great living principle of the best affections. All beyond was barbarism and wilderness! The vast pampas, the unexplored streams, the unpruned forests, the growling hosts of beasts that war with life and gnaw each other's bones; the roaring seas; the wild men, women and children, unlocated, homeless,—the untamed fields of earth and the deserts of the human heart lay outside; within was our little company. Will the reader tarry here awhile and listen to tales of olden times? They tell of heroic deeds, of martyrdoms, and glorious conquests. They will bring back the events of buried years; will show the deeds of those who acted here and died; and as the scene moves on, this charming land, with all its countless beauties and its grey and noiseless wastes, will appear.

Guitar Player.—P. 116.

CHAPTER VII.

An Incomparable Wilderness—A Strange Period—Phrenzy—An Indian Fire—Gentlemen by the Grace of God *versus* Gentlemen by the Grace of Pelf—A Sight of a Great Sea—The first Voyage around the Earth—A Surrender—Victims—Fleet—Voyage—Another Voyage—Murder—Massacre—Another Voyage—Shipwreck—Beaten to death in the surf—The Dead and their Requiem—Gathered at their Ancient Altars—A Return—Another Voyage—An Arrival from a Ten Years' tramp among the Savages—An Expedition by Sea and Land—Death of the Discoverer of California.

Any part of the earth with its forests, its native grasses, herbs, flowers, streams and animals, unmolested by the transforming powers of that race which derives a livelihood from agriculture, commerce, and their attendant handicrafts, is a spectacle of great interest. The seasons as they come and go—the spring with its rich blossoms and leaves—the summer with its fulness of vigor—the autumn with its dropping fruits—and the winter, that Sabbath of the year, when nature rests from her toil—all bring to the old wilderness unnumbered charms. But who can portray them? They are so closely grouped, so richly tinted, so mellow, so sacred and grand, that a long life is required to perceive them. And I often think, if we should study the ancient woods and towering rocks, and the countless beauties among them, through all our days as we do in childhood, we should be drawn nearer to virtue and to God!

California is an incomparable wilderness. It differs from that which overhung the Pilgrims of New England. That was a forest broken only by the streams and the beautiful lakes in which the Indian angled for his food. This is a wilderness of groves and lawns, broken by deep and rich ravines, separated from each other by broad, and wild wastes. Along the ocean is a world of vegetable beauty; on the sides of the mountains are the mightiest trees of the earth; on the heights are the eternal snows, lighted by volcanic fires! But this is not the place to describe the features of this remarkable country. I have said there is a tale of olden times connected with it and its people, which must first be given. A strange period in the history of man is that, in which the Californias became known to Europeans. The latter years of the fifteenth, and the first of the sixteenth century, embrace it. It is a barbarous era of human energy—not the energy of well-directed reason—but of that recuperative force of human nature which for centuries bends under ignorance and inaction, and then, like some central spark, ignites the mass, and flows forth over every opposing obstacle.

The attempt to take Palestine from the Infidels has called out the combating and religious faculties in conjunction. Veneration for the Church and its rites is the ruling idea; the cross is transferred from the cathedral to the field of battle, and with solemn hymns to God the people of Europe march to their graves on the desecrated plains of Jerusalem. This religious battling has an end; but its influence on the minds of the people has been immense. They have wrapped their faith around their lances; turned from commerce, the subjugation of the soil, and general industry, to war upon opinions—to an unsettled state of fanatical vagabondism, which turns the world loose upon itself in a religious phrenzy that is forced to seek an outlet among the waves of the western seas.

Half the solid land of the globe with its boundless forests, its Amazon and Mississippi Rivers, its mountain ranges, its unnumbered forms of animal life, its savage infidels—all its vastness, beauty and gold, catches the restless fancy of the age, and Columbus is among its sea-weed—sees the light of the Indian's evening fire, and invites the enthusiasm of the Old World to the New. It comes. It is love of wealth, power, and faith!

Pizarro.—P. 119.

Cortes.—P. 119.

Venice, Genoa and Florence are bringing overland, from the East Indies, so much wealth, that kings are tributary to them. The palaces of the merchant princes outvie those of the cut-throats Royal by the Grace of God. And the leading cord of events now is, to find a shorter route to the silks of Hindostan. For in this lies the possibility that these Grace of God gentlemen may rid themselves of their unpleasant dependence upon the coffers, navies and armies, of these free States. Portugal, Spain, France, England, enter the lists of this great Tournament of El Dorado. The prize sought to be wrested from the hand of Dame Fortune is, a water passage through the American Continent, by which the ships of the discovering nation may reach the East Indies. Columbus, Balboa and Cortez on the part of Spain, seek it along the shores of the Gulf of Mexico; but the Continent spreads itself an everywhere present barrier to their hopes. This Vasco Nunnez de Balboa in 1513 is in the Gulf of Uraba; and an Indian chief called Panquiaca conducts him over the Cordilleras range of the Isthmus Darien, to Michaelmas Gulf on the Pacific. The Great Pacific Ocean is first seen by this man. His name is written among the heroes of those benighted years. It is dyed in the blood of many thousand slaughtered Indians. He leads Pizarro to the foul murder of the Incas! He opens the arteries of Guatimala! In 1519, Fernando Magellano, in the service of Portugal, discovers the Strait which bears his name, sails across the South Pacific, and touches at the Ladrone and Philippine islands. Among the latter group himself and many of his companions perish. Juan Sebastian del Cano succeeds to the command, traverses the Indian Ocean, doubles the Cape of Good Hope, and moors safely on his native shore. Two passages to the East Indies have now been discovered, and the earth for the first time circumnavigated in 1522. The Pacific has been seen at Darien, and ploughed in the Antarctic latitude. But its northern parts are yet unexplored. Hernando Cortez, the student of Salamanca, the magistrate of San Diego de Cuba, the murderer of Montezuma and Guatimozin, the slender, five feet seven inch conqueror of Mexico, undertakes this.

On the thirteenth of August, 1521, Mexico surrenders to Cortez, and the King of Mechoacan, whose dominions extend to the shores of the Pacific, also submits to this magistrate of San Diego. Men are sent to explore three different points for a ship-yard on the coast of the Great South Sea; forty Spaniards, carpenters, sawyers, and blacksmiths, are sent to the chosen port; iron, anchors, cables, sails, rigging, pitch, oakum, bitumen, and other naval stores, sufficient to build two brigantines, are borne by Indian slaves and a few mules, from Vera Cruz to Zacatula; a distance of six hundred miles!

But misfortune is beginning to tread on the heel of Cortez' enterprise. These materials, soon after their arrival at Zaca tula, are consumed by fire. He has used all his private funds in the purchase; but as his credit is still good, a thousand Indian backs, stout and subservient, are again gored and broken by similar burthens. And the mountain path-ways from Vera Cruz are a second time thronged with victims, dying under the bales of materials for building the magistrate's brigantines. Cortez sees them rise from keel to top-mast, constructed with very sharp bows, and masts leaning forward, carrying triangular sails; and although ill-shaped, they run near the wind. In 1524, this fleet sails under command of one Christopher de Olid, on a voyage among the unseen waters of the North! This expedition, however, results in nothing but wind and storm, and the return of the ships in a miserable condition.

Great minds in different ages have reposed belief in strange things. Cæsar trusted in the entrails of birds; the British Parliament enacted laws against witchcraft; and this Cortez, in 1524, believes in a nation of immense women, called Amazons, inhabiting a very large island whose shores are strewn with pearls and gold! A sufficient variety of taste has human credulity, to give it a keen appetite and capacious throat. Cortez determines to discover the habitation of these large ladies. But in 1528 his fame falls into the hands of Spaniards who treat it with the same respect as they already have that of Columbus; that is, begin to dig its grave.

To avoid the vexations which the Viceroy of Mexico, and a few other envious men, are throwing around him to cripple his efforts, he sails to Spain and presents himself to his King. He is received at court with marked kindness, is made Marquis del Valle de Guaxaca, Captain General of New Spain and the provinces and coasts of the South Sea, discoverer and peopler of those coasts and of the island of pearls, gold and Amazons, with a grant of the twelfth part, for himself and heirs, of all the territory that he shall discover and conquer. These powers, privileges and honors fire anew the volcanic spirit of this five feet seven inch slender student of Salamanca. In 1530, therefore, after having agreed with his sovereign to prosecute his discoveries in the South Seas at his own expense, he returns to Mexico; and finding the Audiencia, the Council of Government, still inimical to him, determines at once to undertake the manifold duties of his office.

Accordingly in May, 1532, he appoints Diego Hortado Mendoza, a relative of his, commander of two ships which he has built at Acapulco, and sends him on a cruise into the Pacific. The crew of one of these vessels mutinies and brings her back to Xalisco. The other, under the personal command of Mendoza, is never heard of after she leaves port. Misfortune never weakens Cortez' resolution. On advice of his kinsman's loss and the ill fate of his expedition, he proceeds to Tehuantepec, and superintends the building of two other ships. These sail in 1534 for the fabled island of Amazons, under command of Hernando Grijalva and a cousin of Cortez, Diego Becera Mendoza. Grijalva proceeds three hundred leagues to a desert island which he calls San Tomas, and returns. Ximenes, the pilot of the other, kills the commander, and having assumed the command, sails up the Gulf-coast of California as far as the bay of Santa Cruz. Here himself and twenty of his crew are destroyed by the Indians. After this event the sailors take the vessel down the coast of Mexico to a port called Chiametla.

Ximenes' people, in the true spirit of the race to which they belong, represent the country in which their pilot has been killed, as fruitful and thickly peopled, and the sea around it, stored with great quantities of pearl beds. So that the misfortunes of former voyages only serve to arouse the unconquerable spirit of this magistrate of San Diego de Cuba, to further effort in search of the rich islands and countries in the North Pacific. He accordingly gives public notice, that Hernando Cortez, the conqueror of Mexico, Marquis del Valle, His Majesty's discoverer, &c. &c., designs to take command of a fleet for this purpose. Spaniards from all parts of the country enter his camp at Tehuantepec; three new ships are launched, well supplied with stores for a long cruise, and sent northward to Chiametla; thither Cortez goes, with a large body of priests, officers and soldiers, and several families, designing to settle in the territories he may discover; the ship of Ximenes, lying at Chiametla, empty and plundered, is fitted up as the fourth vessel of this little squadron; and Cortez and a part of his followers sail into the unknown north; enter the bay where Ximines was killed; and call it Santa Cruz, Bahia de la Paz.

Having landed his people and stores at this place, he sends his ships back to Chiametla for a part of the stores and people which have been left. But tempests fall upon them, and contrary winds so thwart them, that only one ever returns to La Paz. Their stores and provisions consequently wane fast; the country around is desolate and barren; death gnashes his teeth upon them, and starvation walks a ghastly image through their pallid ranks; but Cortez sees a difficulty only to conquer it. He immediately puts to sea in his only remaining ship; crosses the gulf; coasts along its eastern shore for the space of fifty leagues, amid infinite dangers from rocks, currents and tempests; finds his lost ships stranded on the coast of

Wreck of Cortes's People on the coast of Cal.fornia.—P 123.

Senora, and the bodies of his companions rotting and beating among the breakers! A sad end to those men was that! A dolorous termination to Cortez' hopes of discovery! and dreadful to the people of La Paz, on a heated and desolate shore, starving and thirsting, the living eating the dead and drinking their blood! On his return he finds the few wretched ones who yet live, mad with hunger! They shout with wild maniac joy, and rush into the surf! They try to swim to the ship for food and are cast back upon the shore by the surges! Many perish in the angry waters! Cortez lands and gives them food in sparing quantities. But the tides of life have been ebbing too long! Their dying energies are overtaxed! They die by twenties and are buried among the brambles with the holy water sprinkled on them for a coffin and winding sheet! The rude cross of wood stands over each one's grave, the symbol of faith and life to come! And now the deep desert, red and toneless, hears their requiem, in the clanking cable of Cortez's ship, as the wailing crew heave the anchor, and depart from the eastern shore of Lower California!

Meantime report at Mexico says that the murderer of Guatimozin and Montezuma has perished in the western seas. Cortez is the name of a corse bloated and sunken in their depths. The caciques of the fallen dynasty shout for gladness among the mountains of Mexico. Their enslaver no longer breathes. The great relentless heart of Cortez is rotting. His fiery eye has ceased to burn. His unconquerable soul no longer hovers over their native vales, and the sound of his terrible voice is for ever hushed. This belief rouses their lost courage. They gather around their ancient altars. The holy Sun is besought to blight their oppressors with his fervent fires, and send life, love, and true hearts among his fallen children. They worship in their ancient temples, and vow that they will be free.

The Marchioness Donna Juanna de Zunniga, daughter of the Count de Aguilar and cousin to the Duke de Bejan, has loved the student of Salamanca, and become his second wife

And the love of this woman still burns ardently, and alone, for her absent husband. The Audiencia at Mexico are Spaniards, and as such can lay aside their jealousy of Cortez when his prowess is required to save their necks. A virtue this which never fails to grow where Castilian blood fertilizes the human frame. The Caciques now line the mountain sides with their followers; the war-cry bounds across the vale of the city. "Cortez is dead, and we can be free!" is sung on all the heights from the Gulf to the Pacific. That Audiencia now loves Cortez. They condole with his wife on her probable loss, and allow her to send a ship with letters from herself urging his return. The Caciques press towards their holy city, and its sacred lakes. The avenging passions of enslaved millions growl through the land, and the clash of savage arms, their dancings and songs, mingle in one direful din on the ear of the Viceroy. He sends entreaties that Cortez will return and save the country. These messages from the Viceroy and his wife reach him on the coast of Senora; he sails back to La Paz; leaves Francisco de Ulloa in charge of a part of his people; returns to Acapulco; goes to Quahunahuac to meet his anxious wife; and thence proceeds to Mexico. The poor Indians learn that the murderer of their Emperor lives! They lay down their arms, and every hope of freedom.

Ulloa has followed his master, and awaits his orders at Acapulco. In May, 1537, he is again ordered to sea with three ships, the Santa Agueda, La Trinidad, and Santo Torres. He touches at Santiago de Buena Esperanza; at Guayabal; crosses over to California, and follows the coast to the head of the Gulf. Along this coast he sees many volcanoes, bare mountains, and barren valleys. Whales abound in the sea; and on the land he finds large, heavy, and very crooked sheep's horns; also naked Indians taking fish with hooks made of wood, bone, and tortoise-shell, who wear bright shells about the neck, and use the maws of sea-wolves for drinking vessels! After a year's cruising in the Gulf, or Ma de Cortez, Ulloa returns to Acapulco.

About this time Alvar Nunnez Cabeza de Vaca and his three companions, Castello, Dorontes, and a negro called Estevanico, arrive at Mexico. They are the only survivors of three hundred Spaniards who landed in Florida with Pamfilo de Narvaez, ten years before, with the intention of conquering that country. They have been defeated and driven from Florida, and having wandered on foot through Louisiana, Texas, and other parts inhabited by savages, they appear among their countrymen naked, and so changed in their personal appearance, that their language is almost the only evidence of their origin. This Alvar Nunnez Cabeza de Vaca relates such surprising tales of his adventures, and the gold, pearls, &c., seen in the north, as to kindle anew the avarice of the Spaniards. The excitement, however, does not reach its height until the return of a monk who has travelled over those countries with the design of Christianizing the natives. This man has seen rich countries covered with grains, fruits, countless herds of black cattle, and mountains shining with the precious metals.

The Viceroy and Cortez are enemies. They both conceive the design of penetrating these countries. But the former induces the creditors of the latter to vex him with legal proceedings while he himself dispatches an expedition by sea and another by land, to discover and conquer these wonder-born regions. The land force is led by Francisco Vasquez Coronado. He marches at the head of one thousand chosen men; and after many hardships reaches his destination, in 52° N. Lat., three hundred leagues north of Culiacan, Cinaloa, and Valle de Senora. He finds a province here composed of seven towns in which are about four hundred men and a proportionate number of women and children. The largest has two hundred houses of earth and rough wood. Some are four and five stories high. The entrance to each floor is from the outside by means of stairs, which, for security, are removed at night.

The country not being strewn with gold and gems, however, as the soldiers anticipated, they propose to return. But Coronado sends a body of them three hundred leagues farther north, in search of two cities, called Quivira and Axa. They find only a rich country abounding in fruit, cattle and wild beasts. Meeting with nothing, therefore, in all these regions to gratify their cupidity during a search of three years, they return to Mexico and report to that effect. This expedition has traversed the interior of Upper California. The armament, meantime, has sailed to the place of rendezvous on the Pacific coast of Oregon, and awaited in idleness the arrival of the land expedition. But as Grijalva was spending his time in searching for a land of gold, and the fabled cities of Quivira and Axa, instead of seeking his countrymen at the appointed place, the commander of the fleet found it convenient to return to Mexico. He is soon after disgraced and dies of chagrin. Thus terminate the Viceroy's expeditions!

The friends of Cortez bruit this failure of his enemy to defraud their chief of his rights. But the star of that great man is sinking; and they cannot stay its fall. Thwarted and overreached by his enemies, and finding the mind of his sovereign poisoned by their machinations, he resolves to present himself again at Court and demand his rights. Accordingly, in 1540, he embarks with his two sons for Spain; attends the King in his unfortunate expedition to Algiers; and after spending seven years in vain efforts to regain the favor of his monarch, expires of grief and disappointment at Castillya de la Cuesta, while on his way to meet his daughter at Cadiz. Thus dies the conqueror of Mexico and discoverer of California!

CHAPTER VIII.

Three hundred years ago—The Capitana, Almiranta, Frigate and Barco Longo—A rare Bird—Mazatlan—A Fog and a Reef—San Barnabe—Laying down Arms—Rich Shores—Game—Nature's Salt Works—Departure—A Northwester—A Separation—Signal Fires—A Desert—Fish—A Saline Lake—Tracts and a Meeting—An Island—A Precious Mountain—Amber—Cerros—Circumnavigating—San Hypolito—Up the Coast—A Gale—Out of sight—Comes to Anchor—Bahia San Francisco of the South—Native Cattle—Indian Courtesy—A Meeting—Another Bay—A Battle—Weighs—San Diego—Savages—Graves—Santa Catarina—Its Inhabitants and Customs—Its Productions—A Temple—A line of Islands—His Majesty and Hospitality—A Blow—Four Canoes—Rio San Carmelo—Monterey in 1602—Death—The Almiranta dispatched to Mexico—A Horrid Disease—The Country—Its People and Animals—Bahia San Francisco of the North—Cape Mendocino—Death! Death!—Return to Mazatlan—Death—To Acapulco—Lamentations!!

In 1542 the Viceroy of Mexico sends Juan Rodriguez Cabrillo from the Port of Navidad with two ships, on a voyage of discovery up the coast of California. He touches at Santa Cruz, la Magdalena, Cape del Enganno in lat. 32°, La Cruz in 33°, de la Galera in 36½°, the Bay of San Francisco in about 37° 40′, and sees a large Cape, in lat. 40°, which he calls Mendocino, in honor of the Viceroy. In March, 1543, he reaches 44° without making any additional discoveries of importance. At this time, the cold being very intense, he turns his ship homeward and enters the harbor of Navidad on the 14th of April, 1545. No other expeditions are undertaken to California, until 1596; when Count Monterey, the reigning Viceroy, receives an order from Philip II. for making discoveries and settlements in California. In obedience to this order, Sebastian Viscayno is appointed Captain-general of the Expedition, and Capt. Toribio Gomez admiral. Both are persons of great worth, enterprise and skill. Two ships, the Capitana and Almiranta, are purchased, and a frigate built expressly for this service. There is besides a *barco longo* for surveying creeks and bays, and such other services as cannot be performed with deeper keels. Three barefooted Carmelites, Padre Andrez de la Assumpcion, Padre Antonio de la Ascencion, and Padre Tomas de Aquino, accompany the expedition in the capacity of spiritual advisers; and Capt. Alonzo Estevan Peguero and Ensign Gaspar de Alarcon, as counsellors in relation to the proceedings of the expedition. Capt. Geronimo Martin is likewise attached to it as draughtsman of the coasts, islands, and harbors which shall be discovered. This body of officers are men of enterprise and skill; and supported by the best seamen in Spanish America, great results are anticipated from the voyage!

On the 5th of May, 1602, the fleet sails from Acapulco. Strong head winds and currents buffet them for many days; but on the 19th of May, they reach Puerta La Navidad, and put in to obtain ballast and repair the Capitana. All which being dispatched with the utmost speed, they proceed on their voyage and reach Cape Corrientes on the 26th of May. Having surveyed this coast, and the adjacent country, they sail northward to the Islands of Mazatlan. These they reach on the 22d of June. They are two in number, lying near each other, and making a fine roadstead between them and the main shore. In this the Capitana and Almiranta come to anchor. The frigate having been separated from them soon after leaving Navidad, they fear she is lost; but they are glad to find her lying in a river which empties into this roadstead. The officers and priests visit one of the islands. Great numbers of sea birds, about the size of a goose, having a bill nearly half a yard in length, legs resembling those of the stork, and a large crop in which they carry small fish to their young, cover the beach; deer and wild goats abound inland. These islands lie at the entrance of the Gulf of California.

Having passed a part of the day among them, they steer across the mouth of the Gulf, and on the 9th of July make Cape San Lucas. As they stand in, a heavy fog falls upon them, and completely conceals the shore. For a day and a half they lie thus enveloped, out of sight of each other, and in great danger. At length it clears up a little, and the Almiranta discovers that she is within twenty-five fathoms of a reef of rocks, on which she barely escapes being dashed in pieces. Having borne away from so fearful a doom, they enter a bay where they rejoice to find the frigate already anchored. This is the day of San Barnabe, and accordingly the harbor is named in honor of that saint.

Their attention is soon attracted to the natives, who, armed with bows, arrows, and spears, line the shore, shouting fiercely, and throwing sand in the air. General Viscayno lands with twelve soldiers, the priests and officers. But the natives are so intimidated by the lighted matches and arquebuses that they are near losing all communication with them, when Padre Antonio de la Ascencion, advancing alone, making signs of peace and friendship, induces them to stop, embraces them all kindly, and gives assurance that no harm is intended them. They now lay down their arms, and intimate that the soldiers must do the same before they will advance. The Padre conveys this wish to his friends, and calls a little negro boy to bring a basket of biscuit to distribute among them. At sight of the negro they are greatly pleased, and tell him, by signs, that there is a village of people like himself not far thence, with whom they are on friendly terms. Having received beads and other presents, they retire to their rancherias, or settlements, much pleased, though apparently not entirely free from apprehension. After this, the general and others walk about to examine the shore. Not far distant they observe a pond of clear water, on the borders of which lie great quantities of sardine and pilchard, which have been thrown up by the breakers. The next day they visit another spot, where they find the shore for some distance strewn with pearl oysters of the most brilliant and various hues.

The little fleet lies in this bay several days to repair, and take in wood and water. The boats, meantime, are kept constantly abroad taking fish. Soles, lobsters, pearl oysters, &c., are procured. The quail, wood-pigeon, rabbits, hares, deer, lions, tigers, are seen on the hills; various kinds of trees, as the pitahaya, fig, lentisk, and a great variety of plum shrubs, which, instead of gum, emit a very fragrant odor, grow in the valleys. In the vicinity of the anchorage is a low tract of ground subject to be inundated by the sea, during the prevalence of the southwesterly winds. Its shape is such that when the waves retire a large quantity of water is left, which evaporates and leaves a deposit of fine white salt. The Indians of this region go entirely naked. They are, however, extremely fond of ornamenting their hair, and of painting their bodies in black and white stripes.

Having finished the repairs about the time the moon changes, and having by the distribution of goods produced a favorable state of feeling among the soldiers, the Captain-General, about the first of July, orders the squadron to put to sea. But they run only three leagues, when a northwesterly wind springs up, which soon increases to such a gale that they are compelled to put back into the bay of San Barnabe. Three times they stand out, and as often are compelled to return. At last they determine to leave the *barco longo*, which the Capitana has towed, much to the detriment of her progress, and on the 5th of July, for the fourth time, attempt to gain the open sea. The Almiranta and Capitana with great difficulty make some headway against the tempest. But the frigate is obliged to part company, and run in under the land. When the gale abates, the commander is desirous of uniting with the frigate, and for this purpose lays in for the shore. On the 8th they make land under the brow of some lofty hills, where they are becalmed. This range of highlands they call Sierra del Enfado, or Mount

Tedious. On the 16th a breeze fills their sails, and the ships stand away for the harbor de la Magdalena. Here they are enveloped in a fog so dense that a man cannot be seen at six paces. The Capitana runs into the harbor, but the Almiranta is compelled to turn her prow seaward. When the fog clears up, therefore, they have lost sight of each other. The people of the Capitana mount the hills which skirt the harbor, and build signal fires on the heights. These are seen by the people of the Almiranta; but mistaking them for the fires of the Indians, continue to stand off. The Captain-General now becomes very anxious for the missing ship and frigate; and, as soon as the gale abates, sails in quest of them. He first explores the bay of San Jago; but not finding them there, proceeds to Magdalena, and, to the joy of all, anchors near the frigate.

They weigh anchor again on Sunday morning the 28th of July, and that they may not be parted again, the Capitana takes the frigate in tow. A gale which comes on from the northwest after they leave the harbor, prevents them from standing as far from the shore as they desire. But they bear away along the coast, and soon after heave in sight of a bay which seems to be formed by the mouth of a river. This the frigate is sent to survey. But ascertaining the mouth to be crossed by a line of impassable breakers, they continue their voyage. On the eighth of August they discover another bay. Being now very much in want of wood, water, and fresh food, some soldiers are sent on shore to search for them. The country, however, is perfectly barren and destitute of all. An island is in sight which promises the required aid. It proves to be small, with a soil of gravel and sand, and thronged with gulls. The creeks are frequented with immense numbers of sea wolves, and a great variety of fish. The boat is sent out with fishing tackle, &c., and in an hour two men take a supply for both vessels.

Transfiguration day is passed here; and Padre Antonio celebrates mass. After service, the sergeant and some soldiers being out in search of water and wood, find a lake filled with very good salt. Near it are some pits containing brackish water. Around these they discover innumerable foot prints, and other signs which, to their inexpressible joy, clearly indicate that the crew of the Almiranta have been here before them! They therefore take a small supply of this miserable water, and sail for the island of Cerros in search of their companions. On their way they pass a very high barren mountain upon the main coast, showing every variety of color, on a bright shining surface. It is affirmed, by a sailor from Peru, to be a bed of silver and gold! They are very desirous to ascertain if this opinion be true; but the wind will not permit them to land.

They soon after enter a good harbor, which they name San Bartholome. Here the General sends Ensign Alarcon and some soldiers ashore for water. The only thing they find worthy of notice is a kind of resin, or gum, which being rather offensive to the smell, they do not think worth taking to the ship. They believe it to be amber, and report enough of it to load a large ship. As no water is to be found on this barren shore, they continue their search for the lost vessel.

On the last day of August they come to anchor at the island of Cerros. While they are furling their sails, Padre Tomas de Aquino discovers the Almiranta approaching them. The most extravagant joy is manifested on board both ships at this meeting. Capt. Viscayno learns that she has been lying in a fine harbor since the nineteenth; that she has just weighed for the purpose of circumnavigating the island in search of the Capitana, and that supplies of wood, water, salt, &c., may be had at her last mooring ground. Accordingly, the little fleet runs into the Almiranta's old harbor. Here the General orders his men to pitch a tent for the Padres, and take in supplies. But the water is found so remote, that the General sends Ensign Juan Francisco and Sergeant Miguel de

Legar with twelve soldiers, over the island, to see if there be not some spring or stream more accessible.

After a long search they report the discovery of a rivulet about two leagues distant. Everything is now ordered on board and the fleet proceeds at once to the mouth of the stream. While they are taking in water, the General orders the frigate to make the circuit of the island. On their return, the cosmographer reports it to be about thirty leagues in circumference, to have high mountains covered with cedar and pine, and to be inhabited by savages, who answered all their signs of peace with the most threatening gestures. On the main coast a large bay was observed, which seemed to run far inland. All the ships of the fleet being supplied with water, they set sail on the ninth of September. Their course is northerly, towards the main shore. They make it on the eleventh, and discover a fine bay, which they call San Hypolito. Anchors are dropped and preparations made for surveys. For this purpose the General orders some soldiers ashore under Capt. Peguero and Ensign Alarcon. The country is found very beautiful. A broad and well-beaten road leads inland from the coast to a large hut covered with palm-leaves, capable of containing fifty persons. While returning to the ship they take a great quantity of the best fish, on which all hands feast sumptuously. Thus fed, and joyful that they have found so desirable a country, they raise anchors and stand up the coast.

As they sail along they see many large fires, which they deem an indication that Indian villages are numerous. But they have proceeded a few leagues only, when a violent gale springs up from the northwest, which compels them to run in under some lofty hills bordering the sea. To the southeast of this anchorage is seen a line of white cliffs on which there appear to be a great number of Indians. The General, therefore, orders the frigate inshore with the cosmographer to take a chart of the coast and ascertain the condition of the natives. On coming in close under the heights she is becalmed at such a distance from the shore that they cannot land. The sea, meanwhile, running very high outside, obliges the ships to lie to for twenty-four hours, during which time the frigate drifts out of sight and the Almiranta is near foundering. In the morning they endeavor to continue their voyage. But the wind increases till evening, when a thick fog envelopes earth, sea, and ships. The Almiranta being in much jeopardy from the injuries received the previous night, the General determines to look for some harbor where they may be secure against the heavy storm presaged by the fog. He finds none; but much to their surprise, the following day opens clear, and with a gentle breeze, which carries them off the Mesas, near which the frigate left them. The promises of fair weather, however, prove very deceitful; for before night a gale, more violent than any they have experienced, and accompanied by a thick fog, overtakes them. The ships lie to all night under reefed mainsails; but before morning they lose sight of each other.

The General now makes every effort to fall in with the Almiranta; and keeping close in shore for this purpose, very unexpectedly meets the frigate. But as he gets no tidings of the ship, his fears for her safety are not lessened. He therefore puts into a fine harbor which they have discovered northwest of Cape Enganno, and there awaits her. He believes that, if still in a sailing condition, she must, by pursuing her instructions in regard to her course, necessarily pass near the mouth of this bay. They call this harbor Bahia de San Francisco. In a rancheria near the anchorage they find a species of onions. Goats' horns, also, are strewn over the ground. The surrounding country is level, fertile, and very beautiful. The plains are fed by large herds of cattle and deer. The crew of the frigate point out an island a little north of the anchorage which they call San Geronimo; and the Captain-General orders some of the seamen ashore to examine it. It proves to be heavily wooded, and frequented by immense flocks of birds. Its shoals abound in the finest cod and other fish Of these they take a supply for all the ships. Beyond the island they discover a large bay into which a considerable creek empties itself with a strong current.. The frigate goes in to survey it. They observe great numbers of naked Indians fishing in the creek, who approach the Spaniards with the liveliest marks of joy, offer them the best of their fish, and show them several wells of pure fresh water. When these things are reported to Captain Viscayno, he orders a tent to be pitched for the celebration of mass, and preparations made to lie here till the Almiranta comes up, or all hope of her is lost.

They take in wood and water. Every morning the Indians bring them a supply of fish for the day, and pay such deference to the Spaniards, that they never visit the rancherias in the neighborhood, without first soliciting the permission of the General and the Padres. The Spaniards return their courtesy with trifling presents, which enlist their wonder and admiration so deeply, that immense numbers of Indian men, and women with two infants each, flock from the neighboring rancherias; pronounce Spanish words after the soldiers; eat with them; and in other ways show a disposition to cultivate the most friendly and intimate acquaintance. The females are clad in skins, and show much propriety of conduct. These Indians carry on a considerable trade with their inland neighbors by furnishing them with fish, and receiving in return net purses, curiously wrought, and a root called *mexcalli* or *maguey*, boiled and prepared as a conserve. Of both these articles they give great quantities to the Spaniards in return for the beads and other trifles. They inform their visitors that up in the country there are a great many people who wear clothes and beads, and have fire-arms. They are supposed to refer to Onate's land expedition from Mexico.

Having now abandoned all hope of the Almiranta, it being twenty-eight days since she parted from them, the General, on the twenty-fourth of October, stands out to sea. Just as he leaves the bay, to his great astonishment and joy, the long absent ship is seen approaching.

Being now all united again, the General gives orders to continue the voyage, and run into the first harbor discovered. They soon see a large bay, which the tender is ordered to explore. It is well sheltered from the northwest winds; but as its shores are lined with great numbers of warlike Indians instead of landing they proceed up the coast. A north wester, however, soon obliges them to put back, and come to anchor. This being the anniversary of St. Simon and St Jude, they give the name of both saints to the bay. The next morning Captain Peguero and Ensign Alarcon are sent ashore with some soldiers to look for wood and fresh water. Finding none of the latter, they dig some wells in a moist spot overgrown with sedge and flags. While doing this, the Indians seem very brisk and bold; but do not molest the Spaniards till some presents are offered them. Construing this act into a sign of fear on the part of their visitors, they at once become impudent, attempt to steal, and even go so far as to try to take one of the boats from the boys who are left in charge of it. To deter them from further violence, one of the soldiers, as they are going off to the ship, fires his piece in the air. But the Indians finding no one hurt, grow more insolent than ever; and the next day when a small party goes on shore to obtain water, they become so very troublesome that two soldiers who have their matches lighted, order them to stand back. But this only increases their audacity. One of them throws his bow over the head of a soldier. The pilot draws his sabre, and severs it. They now draw up in form, and place their arrows on their bow-strings. The soldiers, who have lighted matches, are ordered to fire upon them! In a moment six Indians lie bleeding upon the sand! Their companions snatch them up and bear them away!

The news of this occurrence spreads like the wind among the neighboring rancherias, and in a short time two hundred Indians painted fiercely, wearing plumes upon their heads, and armed with bows and arrows, rush down to attack the

Spaniards. The Ensign, on seeing them, orders his men to make ready The Indians, however, do not relish the appearance of the arquebuses, and remain at a distance, talking and gesticulating in the most earnest manner. At length they send one of their number with a little dog, in token of their desire to make peace. The man, while making the treaty, eyes the arquebuses very keenly, and signifies that four of his people are already deceased, and others dying of their wounds; and in token of their sincere wish not to hear from these gods of fire again, he makes a number of presents to the soldiers who bear them, and retires.

The squadron leaves the bay on Wednesday the first of November. Continuing along the coast, they come to the mouth of a very large bay, sheltered on all sides, except the sea-ward one, by lofty mountains. It is protected at the entrance by two islands, which they call Todos Santos. The frigate and the Almiranta run in to make surveys. But the Capitana standing off, and night approaching, they dread another separation so much that they put out and rejoin the General. The next morning preparations are made to enter it again, for a more deliberate examination. But a favorable breeze springing up, they conclude to leave it for their return, and continue the voyage.

On the fifth of November they fall in with four islands, which they call Coronadas. On the tenth they enter the famous harbor of San Diego. The day after their arrival, Ensign Alarcon, Captain Peguero and eight soldiers are sent out to explore. They first direct their steps to a heavy forest which lies on the northwest side of the bay. This is ascertained to be about three leagues in width and half a one in breadth. The trees are chiefly oaks, with an undergrowth of fragrant shrubs. Obtaining a fine view of the bay from the heights, they ascertain it to be spacious, land-locked, and every way desirable; and returning to the ships, report such to be its character. This result being deemed satisfactory by the General, he orders a tent pitched on shore for the celebration of mass, and preparation to be made for repairing the ships. One part of the crews therefore is assigned to clean and tallow the hulls, another to fill the water casks, and another to procure wood and keep guard.

One day when each department is employed at its appointed task, a sentinel posted in the forest sees a large body of Indians coming along the shore, naked, painted with red and white colors, and armed with bows and arrows. In order if possible, to avoid bloodshed, the General desires Padre Antonio to go and offer them peace. He is accompanied by Ensign Juan Francisco and six soldiers. Signs of peace being made with a bit of white linen, the Indians immediately deliver their arms. The Padre embraces them all affectionately; and thus the best understanding is at once established. But observing so large a number of persons on board the ships, they retire in much apprehension; and after consulting some time together, send two of their women alone to the tent. They approach with a timid air; but being kindly received and presented with beads, biscuit, &c., they return and make such a report to their people as soon brings the whole troop down to the water side. They are generally naked; their bodies striped with white and black paint; and their heads loaded with feathers. Their light paint seems to the voyagers, to be compounded of silver and other materials; and on being asked what it is, they give the Spaniards a piece of metallic ore, saying, "it is made from this." They add that far up in the country there are many people, wearing beads and clothes like theirs, who make of this metal such ornaments as the General has on his purple velvet doublet.

All desirable preparations being made, they sail from this beautiful bay of San Diego. While they have tarried in it, many of the crew who had been sick of the scurvy, have recovered, and many others have died. It is a sorrowful occasion for those who still live, to part from the graves of their companions. They are interred on the borders of the magnificent forest northwest of the bay; and the well known trees which spread their branches over them, are discernible as they leave the land! They scarcely clear the headlands of the harbor when a terrible northwester comes down upon them and changes their grief to fear. They see another voyage begun which may terminate their own lives. But they keep their course and soon make another large bay. It is surrounded by a level, beautiful country, the inhabitants of which make fires on the heights along the coast, and by every sign in their power, invite the fleet to anchor. On approaching the land, however, they find no shelter from the northwest wind and stand out again to sea. A few leagues brings them to the large island of Santa Catarina.

On the twenty-eighth they anchor in the bay. The inhabitants of Santa Catarina make the most noisy and earnest invitations for them to land. The General therefore orders Admiral Gomez, Capt. Peguero, and Ensign Alarcon, with twenty-four soldiers, to land on the island, and learn what the natives so earnestly desire. As soon as they reach the shore, they are surrounded by Indian men and women, who treat them with much kindness and propriety, and intimate that they have seen other Spaniards. When asked for water they give it to the whites in a sort of bottle, made of rushes.

They explore the island. It appears to be overgrown with savin and a species of briar. A tent is pitched for religious service, and Padre Tomas being ill, Padres Antonio and Andrez celebrate mass in presence of all the people. These Indians spend much of their time in taking the many varieties of fish which abound in the bay. They have boats made of plank, capable of containing twenty persons. In these they carry long slender poles, to which harpoons of fish-bone are attached by long ropes. They strike with the harpoon and pay out rope till the fish is unable to run longer, and then if it be small, take it into the boat, or if large tow it ashore. They prize the sea-wolf most highly, as well on account of its flesh, which they eat, as its skin, of which they make most of their clothing.

The women of this tribe are beautiful, modest, and extremely well conducted. The children have fine complexions and are very amiable. They live in large huts, dispersed in rancherias, and have many convenient utensils made of rushes Their island abounds in a small root resembling the common potato, which is much prized as an article of food. On this island is a very large level enclosure, with an altar in the centre surrounded by a circular wall or partition of various colored feathers. Within this circle is a figure painted with a great variety of hues, and resembling the image by which the Indians of Mexico typify the devil. In its hands are the figures of the Sun and Moon. As the soldiers approach this place they discover two very large crows within the enclosure, which rise on their coming up and alight on some rocks in the vicinity. Before the guide can remonstrate, their pieces are levelled and both birds fall. This act calls forth the bitterest lamentations from the Indian, who evidently regards them as sacred to his deity. Santa Catarina has several fine harbors. It abounds in partridges, quails, rabbits, hare and deer. The people are very numerous, and exhibit much ingenuity in pilfering from their visitors.

On the twenty-first of December the squadron leaves Santa Catarina to explore other islands which extend in a line nearly one hundred leagues up the coast. They are found to be inhabited by shrewd, active people, who trade much among themselves and with their neighbors on the continent. Between a portion of them and the main land is a channel called the Canal de Santa Barbara. After exploring them, the fleet puts back to the continent, near the southern mouth of this channel. Before they reach the shore, however, four men come up to the Capitana, and row three times round her with the most astonishing swiftness, all the while chanting a kind of wild measure, similar to what the Indians of Mexico call *almatote*. By this the Spaniards understand that they have the Indian king or *cacique* on board. And so it proves; for when the ceremony is over, his majesty steps on board the

Capitana, and after walking three times around the quarter-deck, addresses himself in a long speech to the General and his officers. This being concluded, he adopts the more intelligible method of signs, to inform the Spaniards that the natives of Santa Catarina have sent his majesty advices of their visit, and have also spoken of their bravery, generosity, and the many presents made by them. All these things have kindled in his majesty a desire to cultivate the acquaintance of such illustrious persons; and he backs his protestations of regard by the proposition to furnish them with everything they desire to eat and drink, and with the moderate supply of ten women each! To prove his ability in this last offer, himself and son will remain as hostages while one of the soldiers shall go on shore and ascertain the fact. As it is near night, however, the General very ungallantly declines his offer in behalf of himself and crew; and his majesty at length departing, it is thought best to improve the fair wind then coming on, to prosecute the voyage. Setting all sail, therefore, they progress rapidly till they nearly complete the survey of the channel. The breeze leaves them opposite a cluster of islands, six in number, and about two leagues distant from each other. The channel is ascertained to be about twenty-four leagues in length. The main coast is beautifully diversified with woodland and lawn, among which are several Indian villages.

The following night the wind changes to northwest, and blows a tremendous gale for about sixty hours. The waters in the channel are lifted into mountains. The ships are driven almost uncontrolled among the islands. The greatest fear prevails that all will be lost. On the third day, however, the tempest abates. The Capitana and Almiranta are safe, and with the fair weather stand in for the continent. But the frigate is missing. The coast is skirted with lofty mountains which shelter some fine bays. From one of these, four canoes run out at the same moment, filled with savages bringing a large quantity of excellent sardines. These Indians are tall, fine-looking people. They cover themselves with goat-skins before entering the ships; and as if sensible that language not understood would be of no use, they utter not a word, but express their thoughts by signs. Appearing very good-natured, and not disposed to pilfer, the Spaniards present to them some clothing and trinkets, with which they seem delighted. The next day, others coming on board urge the General to bring his ships to their country, in order that they may furnish him with plenty of fish and acorns.

The frigate now rejoins the ships. She has been driven among the islands, and experienced much hospitality from the natives. They now all get under way and stand nearer the shore in search of a harbor. The whole coast has been enveloped in a thick fog since the gale. A fair wind, however, springing up, they run along the edge of the mist till the fourteenth of January, when the weather clearing, they find themselves under a ridge of high mountains, white at the top, and clothed with wood at the base. This range they call Sierra de Santa Lucia. Four leagues beyond it a river tumbles through a ledge of rocks into the sea. Its banks are covered with black and white poplar, willow, birch, and pine. This stream they call Rio San Carmelo.

Two leagues farther on is a splendid harbor, between which and the mouth of the Carmelo, is a heavy pine wood, forming a cape. This is Punto de Pinos. In this harbor the squadron comes to anchor. The crews are very much reduced by sickness. The master and mate of the Almiranta are both unable to leave their births; the Captain-General and his mate are scarcely able to appear on deck; a great many of the soldiers and boys are very sick; and sixteen have died since leaving Bahia de San Francisco. Under these circumstances it is resolved that the Almiranta shall be sent back under the command of Admiral Gomez, with the two pilots Pasqual and Balthazar, and all the sick; th t she shall take a sufficient number of sound men to man her; and that the rest shall go on board of the Capitana and frigate. The General will send advices and a chart of all his discoveries, with a request that a reinforcement and supplies may be sent on early in the spring, to enable him to complete the survey of the coast and Gulf.

In accordance with this arrangement the sick are put on board with great care; Padre Thomes de Aquino is assigned to accompany them, and on the twenty-ninth of January the Almiranta sets sail for Acapulco. The disease which preys so distressingly and fatally on the ships' crews is one of a very singular character. It is supposed to arise from the action of the cold winds of this region upon the relaxed constitutions of persons who come into it from warmer climates. The patient is seized with violent pains throughout the system, which are soon followed by such extreme sensibility as forbids the slightest touch. This latter symptom is often so excruciating as to draw tears and groans from the stoutest men. Soon after this the surface becomes spotted with an eruption of a purple color, fine and sharp, feeling as if shot were inserted under the skin. These are followed by wales or lines of the same color, similar to those raised by the infliction of severe blows. They are about the width of two fingers; appear first on the upper posterior portion of the thigh; but soon spread themselves to the flexure of the knee. Wherever they appear the parts become rigid, and remain in the position in which they were first seized. The whole system now swells prodigiously, and the patient cannot be moved in any manner without suffering extreme torture. The disease finally extends itself to all parts of the body, affecting particularly the shoulders, head and loins, and causing the most distressing pains in the kidneys. No relief can be obtained by change of position; for the slightest motion is agony. In time the entire body is covered with ulcers so exceedingly sensitive that the pressure of the lightest bed covering is intolerable. At length the gums and jaws swell so that the mouth cannot be closed, and in many cases the teeth drop out! The violence of the disease and the debility arising from it are such, that the patients frequently die while talking with their friends. Such is the dreadful pestilence that has swept the Captain-General's ranks, and now fills the Almiranta with groans, shrieks, prayers and curses!

While she is making her way back to Acapulco, the Capitana and frigate remain in the harbor of Monterey to take in wood and water, and explore the adjacent country. They find this finely diversified with lawns and groves of pine, firs, willow and poplars, with an abundant undergrowth of roses and fragrant shrubs. The open lands are also dotted with clear, pure lakes. The country is inhabited by a great variety of wild beasts. A large bear, a species of horned cattle similar in size and shape to the buffalo, and another which, from the description, might be ancestor of the *Americana Horribilis*, are among the most remarkable. The voyagers give to this latter beast the size of the wolf, the form and horns of the stag, the skin and neck of the pelican, a tail half a yard in width and twice as long, and a cloven foot! If it were a native, one might be led to speculate on the propinquity of sulphur! The country also abounds in deer, rabbits, hare, wild-cats, bustards, geese, ducks, pigeons, partridges, thrushes, sparrows, goldfinches, cranes, vultures, and another bird about the size of a turkey. On the seaboard are great numbers of gulls, cormorants, and other sea-fowl. The sea abounds in oysters, lobsters, crabs, sea-wolves, porpoises and whales. On the shores are many rancharias, the residents of which are an affable, generous people, living under some form of government. They use the native arms and subsist chiefly on fish and game. They seem fond of the Spaniards, and express the most sincere sorrow at their intention to leave them But this is unavoidable. Both vessels run out of the harbor with a fair wind, on the fifth day of January, 1603, and stand away northward.

Soon after passing the harbor of San Francisco, in Lat. 37° 45′, they lose sight of each other, and the Capitana puts back into it, to await the arrival of the frigate, and also to survey the harbor and surrounding country. Another reason which the Captain-General has for wishing to stop here is to ascertain if there be any remains of the San Augustine, which had been driven ashore in 1595 with other vessels sent by the Government from the Philippine Islands, to survey the coast of California. The pilot of this squadron, Francisco Valanos, is acquainted with the country. He reports that they left a large cargo of wax and several chests of silk on the shore of this harbor. The General, therefore, runs the Capitana in, and anchors her behind a point of land called Punta de los Reyes. Becoming more anxious, however, for the fate of the frigate, he weighs the next day and runs out in search of her. A gentle northwester takes him up the coast within sight of Cape Mendocino, when a violent southwester, accompanied by sleet and a heavy sea, combined with the sickly state of the crew, induces him to seek a southerly harbor, in which to await the coming of spring and the reinforcement from Mexico.

They are now in a deplorable state. Six seamen only are able to be on deck. The officers are all sick. The Padres are scarcely able to administer the last rites to the dying; and the few well ones are in dreadful consternation lest a storm come on, and the ship go down, for want of men to manage her. This determination of General Viscayno, therefore, raises the spirits of the healthy, and cheers the sick to their best efforts. When the wind changes so that the fog is dispersed, the pilots take an observation and find themselves in Lat. 42°, opposite a cape which runs eastwardly, and unites with a range of snowy mountains. This they call Cabo Blanco de Sebastian. The lost frigate runs very near the Capitana during the storm spoken of, but not being able to live in such a sea, she comes to anchor under a huge rock near Cape Mendocino. The pilot, Florez, when the storm abates, finds himself in Lat. 43° north, near Cape Blanco, and the mouth of a large river, whose banks are covered with ash, willow, and other trees, well known to the Spaniards. This river they are very desirous to explore, supposing it will conduct them to the great city reported by some Dutch mariners, to exist in this region; or that it is the Strait of Anian, connecting the Atlantic with the Pacific! The worthy pilot, however, has no chance of immortalizing himself by running through Smith's river to the city of Manhattan. The current is against his course and his fame; and he turns back with the determination of sailing to Acapulco without unnecessary delay.

Meantime the Capitana is making all possible speed for La Paz, the harbor selected for her winter quarters. Occasionally, in her progress, she is visited by the trading canoes of the Indians. But nothing of moment befals her save that her crew grow more and more sickly, till she reaches a large island lying east of Santa Catarina, when only three persons beside the Captain-General are able to keep the deck. There is no conversation, no mirth on board! Orders are conveyed in the quiet tone of conversation! The good Padre Andrez moves quietly about among the sick, the sole physician, nurse, priest and confessor of that gloomy hospital! Now he bears medicine to the sick, and smoothes their pillow; now he administers the extreme unction, and anoints with holy oil the dying; now he seals the lips and closes the eyes of the dead! Prayers and groans alone are heard; except when the burial service is hurriedly chanted, and the sudden plunge announces that some one is gone from among them for ever!

These terrible afflictions induce the General to abandon his intention of wintering at La Paz, and to run directly for the islands of Mazatlan, where he can procure better treatment for his dying crew. On the third of February he reaches the island of San Hilario and passes on to Cerros. Here he stops and obtains a supply of wood and water. On his departure, he leaves letters and signals for the frigate, in case she should touch there, and turns his prow for Cape San Lucas. He reaches it on the fourteenth of February, and standing directly across the mouth of the Gulf, enters a harbor near the island of Mazatlan on the seventeenth of the same month. An account of his condition being sent to the Viceroy, he determines to go in person to San Sebastian, a village about eight leagues from the harbor, for more immediate aid. He starts on the nineteenth with five of his soldiers. But being utterly ignorant of the country, they take the wrong path, and wander two days in the wood without food or water. At length they fall into a broad beaten road, and while resting themselves by the wayside, a drove of mules, laden with provisions, comes along. These are going from Castile to Culiacan. The General learns from the muleteers that an old friend of his has become the Alcalde of the latter place, and immediately accepts their offer to convey himself and soldiers thither.

At this town they are furnished with every comfort for themselves and those on board the ship. The poor seamen and Padres! They are now reduced to the most lamentable condition! Helpless, covered with ulcers, and unable to speak or eat! Among other things that are sent them, is a kind of fruit which is considered a specific for this disease. It bears among the natives the cognomen, *Xocohuiltzes.* It resembles an apple. The leaves of the plant are exactly like those of the pineapple. The fruit grows in clusters. The rind or shell is yellow, and contains a pulp full of seeds. Its flavor is slightly tart. Its medical properties are such that it cleanses the mouth reduces the gums, fastens the teeth, heals the ulcers, purifies the blood, &c. Its virtues were accidentally discovered by an officer who was attending the burial of a victim to this frightful disease, from his own ship. He was himself somewhat infected, and passing under a tree, plucked and ate some of the fruit. In a few minutes he voided from the mouth a large quantity of purulent matter, mingled with blood. The soreness was at the same time much relieved, and the gums contracted upon the teeth so that they no longer rattled in his mouth. The poor seamen and soldiers have suffered most deplorably from this malady. By the use of this fruit they begin to recover. Nor have the Padres been less afflicted. Such is the condition of their hands and mouths, that the crucifixes which they have held and often caressed, while the disease has been devouring their frames, are covered with a filthy gore! Their couches, as well as those of the crew, are masses of putrid matter! But now all are creeping on deck; the ship and its appurtenances are cleansed; their rotting frames begin to heal! On the 21st of March they are so far restored that the Capitana puts to sea, and after a pleasant sail of eight days, moors in the bay of Acapulco. When her anchor runs, and the pallid forms of the few survivors are seen at the bulwarks, the horrid spectacle chills every tongue! The people gather on the shore in silence. But soon mothers call the names of those who, many months before, have been buried in the sea! Fathers seek their sons whose graves the wolves have opened in the forest of San Diego! Mothers, in the excess of maternal sorrow, demand of the Captain-General their offspring, who have fallen, muscle and bone, morsel by morsel, before the terrific pestilence! A few recognize among the living, the disfigured countenances of their friends, and rushing on board embrace them with loud lamentations! The Almiranta rides hard by The frigate arrives in as deplorable a state as the Capitana. Her crew is reduced to a number scarcely sufficient to remember the sufferings and the names of those who have died. Thus terminates the voyage of Viscayno. He has explored the whole Pacific coast of Upper and Lower California.

CHAPTER IX.

A.D. 1615—A.D. 1633-4—Don Pedro Portel de Cassanate—A.D. 1647—A.D. 1666-7—A.D. 1683—Indians—A Battle—All busy—Orders from Mexico—Ships dispatched—A Garrison and Church—An Expedition into the Interior—Despatches arrive—A Determination—Padre KINO—Padre JUAN MARIA SALVA TIERRA—The Jesuits—Powers granted—SALVA TIERRA goes to California—The Resurrection—Insolence—An Attack—A Repulse—A General Onset—A Route—Peace—Arrival of Padre Piccolo—An Exploration—Condition of the Conquest SALVA TIERRA goes to Senora for Food—An Expedition to the Gila and Colorado of the West by Padres KINO and SALVA TIERRA—Return to Senora—Padre SALVA TIERRA leaves for California—Another Expedition to the Gila and Colorado by Padres KINO and Gonzales—Indians and Rivers—Death—Last Days of Padre KINO—A lost Grave.

No other expedition of any moment is undertaken to California until 1615, when Captain Juan Iturbi obtains a license for making a voyage at his own expense. One of his two ships is captured by a Dutch pirate. With the other he reaches the coast of Cinaloa, and procures supplies from a Jesuit Missionary, Padre Ribas, preparatory to crossing the Gulf. But before leaving port he is ordered out to convoy the Philippine ship to Acapulco. This done, he returns to Mexico, and by exhibiting the pearls he has taken fires anew the wonder and cupidity of the whole country. The Californian pearl fisheries are soon thronged. A few find what they desire, but an infinitely greater number are disappointed. The results, however, lead to the granting of a license to Francisco de Ortega to make a voyage up the Gulf. He sails in March, 1632. Accompanying him is Padre Diego de la Nava, the newly appointed Vicar-general of California.

On the second of May they land at San Barnabe bay; and having made a special survey of the coast from this point to

La Paz and purchased some pearls of the Indians, they touch at Cinaloa, and in June go thence to report their proceedings to the Viceroy. In 1633 and '34, Capt. Ortega makes two other voyages for the purpose of forming a settlement in California; but finds the country so barren that he is obliged to abandon his design. He now proposes to have a garrison established at some proper point for colonization, and a sum of money granted from the royal treasury to maintain settlers for a definite period. But while he is agitating these measures, he has the mortification to learn that his pilot, Carboneli, has not only obtained a license for making a voyage, but asserts the practicability of settling the country farther north, without depending on the government for supplies. This pilot sails in 1636; but to his chagrin nowhere finds such a country as he has promised; and, after obtaining a few pearls, returns to confess his failure.

After this, an expedition is undertaken at His Majesty's expense. The governor of Cinaloa receives orders to pass over to California and survey the islands, bays, coast and face of the country, preparatory to making a chart for the use of navigators. He does so. Padre Jacinto Cortez, a missionary of Cinaloa, accompanies him in order to ascertain if it be practicable to Christianize the Indians. They complete the survey in July, 1642, and soon after send their charts, pearls, and other things procured, to the Viceroy.

A change is now taking place at Mexico. The Viceroy, Don Diego Lopez Pacheco, Marquis de Villena and Duke of Esclona, returns to Spain under suspicion, and is succeeded by Don Juan de Palafox. The Marquis successfully vindicates himself against the malicious charges of his enemies, and procures an expedition to California to be ordered under Admiral Don Pedro Portel de Cassanate. This man is empowered to build and equip fleets, and make settlements in California, and do such other acts as he may deem best calculated to bring the natives of that country into the church. The spiritual welfare of this expedition is committed to Padres Jacinto Cortez and Andrez Baes, Missionaries of Cinaloa.

Having arrived at Cinaloa, Cassanate receives instructions to go out and meet the Philippine ship which it is feared will fall into the hands of English or Dutch pirates. He brings her safely in; and while he is making preparations to sail again to California, two of his ships are burned. Discouraging as this circumstance is, he resolves not to be defeated by it. Two others are built at Cinaloa in 1647–8, in which he sails to the place of destination. But he finds the country, as far as he explores it, barren and dry. Before he completes his survey, however, he receives orders to go a second time and conduct a Philippine ship into Acapulco. This done, he proceeds to lay the results of his expedition before the Viceroy.

This excellent man is soon after promoted to the Government of Chili; and California is neglected till 1665, when Philip IV. again orders its reduction. The execution of this effort is entrusted to Don Bernado Bernal de Pinadero. But the Spanish treasury is now exhausted; the nation and its colonies are impoverished. Two small vessels only, therefore, are built in the Valle de Venderas. In 1666 they sail to the coast, rob the poor natives of some pearls, and make their way back to report that expedition also, a failure. The Queen mother, acting as Regent, orders Pinadero to make another attempt. In this he is accompanied by the celebrated Padre Kino. This likewise results in nothing valuable. In the following year Francisco Luzenilla obtains a license for a voyage at his own expense. This proves, like all others, fruitless of results worthy of note. In 1667, the importance of making a settlement in California for a rendezvous of ships trading to the Philippine Islands, is again brought before the Council of the Indies; and it is finally determined to instruct the Viceroy and the Archbishop of Mexico to send out Admiral Pinadero again, if he will give security for the performance of that duty according to the decrees of Council; and if he decline, to make the offer to any person who will undertake it, at his own expense ; and if none so offer, it is ordered to be accomplished at the expense of the crown. Admiral Pinadero having refused, Admiral Otondo accepts the proposition. The spiritual Government is conferred on the Jesuits. Padre Kino as superior, and Padres Copart and Goni accompany the expedition.

They put to sea from Chacala on the eighteenth of May 1683, and in fourteen days reach La Paz. They think it singular, on landing, not to see any Indians; but as soon as they begin to erect a garrison, considerable numbers appear, armed and hideously painted, who intimate by signs that the Spaniards must leave their country. After some effort, however, on the part of the Padres, and uniform kindness from the officers, soldiers and seamen, their intercourse becomes apparently unconstrained and friendly. Soon, however, circumstances occur which arouse suspicion. The reported murder of a mulatto boy, added to some indignities towards the garrison, indicate the need of great watchfulness on the part of the voyagers. Danger lurks near them. The Guayacuros among whom they sojourn, offer to unite with their enemies, the Coras, for the extirpation of the Spaniards. The Coras appear to entertain the proposition, but report it to the Admiral on their earliest opportunity. The soldiers are thrown into such a panic by the discovery of this plot, that the Admiral and Padres are obliged to exert all their authority and persuasion to induce them to meet the event with fortitude. The day of the intended massacre arrives. The Indians appear, to the number of thirteen or fourteen hundred. A *paderero,* or cannon, is fired among them, by which ten or twelve are killed and several wounded. The remainder retire in confusion to their rancherias. The garrison is safe; no one even wounded. But this victory does not discourage their fear of the Indians. The dry crags, the treeless sands and thirsty torrent-chasms are, to the anxious minds of the timid men, peopled with forms of death; and every howl of the lean wolf upon the heights, grates like a coffin screw on their ears. Otondo is, therefore, obliged to weigh anchor for Hiaqui on the Senora shore. Here he sells all his pearls, and pledges his plate for stores. Like a brave man bent on his end, he seeks again the Californian shore, and on the sixth of October anchors at San Bruno Bay, in Lat. 26° 30′.

On the same day, Otondo, the three Padres, and some soldiers, explore for fresh water, and find it in a narrow vale one mile and a half from shore. Near this they establish a garrison, build a rude church, and some huts. And now Otondo sends two ships to Mexico with an account of his proceedings, and a request for more money; takes possession of the country in the name of the king; goes fifty leagues westward in the month of December among mountains and desert vales; ascends an elevation, where he finds several leagues of table land, with a temperate climate and a fresh-water lake of small size; advances beyond, on a toilsome journey over steeps and depths, in search of a peak from which to see the Pacific Ocean; fails to do so, and returns to San Bruno. The Indians whom they meet are much delighted with the paternal kindness of the Padres. Otondo employs himself a year in like explorations at different points along the coast. The Padres are busy meantime in learning the language of the Indians and instructing them in the Catholic religion. They translate the Catechism, teach it to the children, and these in turn teach it to their parents. The voice of heathenism utters prayers to Jehovah on the Californian mountains!

The Padres find no word in their language to represent the resurrection of the dead. That idea has not existed in their minds, and consequently has no expression in their language. Resort is had to a very ingenious method of finding one which will present it. Some flies are immersed in water until animation seems extinct. They are then placed among ashes in the heat of the sun till restored to life. The Indians who witness the operation cry out, Ibimuhueite! Ibimuhueite! This word or expression is afterward used to represent the resurrection of the Saviour, and conveys to the Indian a clear conception of that holy event. The Padres instruct during the year four hundred adults and many children, but baptize none except those who are at the door of death. Some of these sick indeed, recover, and prove useful teachers. Most of them, however, die, holding fast their new faith. In these several ways do the priests and Otondo consume the year. At its close, dispatches arrive from the Viceroy requiring an account of proceedings, and forbidding any farther attempts to be made for the conquest and settlement of California which should involve the Government in expense.

On the reception of these dispatches a council of the Padres and military officers is held, the determination of which is, that a small ship shall be sent with dispatches to Mexico, that the Padres shall continue to teach the Indians, and Otondo to explore the country and pearl beds. In September, 1685, however, a peremptory order comes prohibiting farther efforts at settling the country, and ordering, if possible, to keep possession of what is already conquered. But it has now become apparent that San Bruno must be abandoned. No rain has fallen for nearly two years; dearth, thirst, and hunger, stand near them; and to escape is the settled desire of all, except the priests. These men of iron souls would stay to teach the savage. But Otondo weighs anchor, and with priests, soldiers, seamen, and three native converts, squares his yards for the harbor of Matanchel, on the Mexican shore.

This is the last expedition of the civil power of Spain to conquer and settle California. PADRE KINO has begun to conquer it with the Cross; and we shall follow him in his triumphs and trials while he achieves it. The professor of Ingoldstadt, PADRE KINO, the devotee of San Xavier, traverses Mexico preaching to his brother Jesuits the glories of martyrdom, and the rich reward of those who save from wo the doomed and lost In order to forward his zeal, he is appointed to the charge of the Missions on the Senora coast, whence it will be easy to send supplies across the Gulf to the more barren regions of the peninsula. PADRE JUAN MARIA SALVA TIERRA is designated to lead the way on the California side. He solicits contributions; obtains Padre Juan Ugarte, a professor in the college at Mexico, as a fellow-laborer; fifteen thousand dollars to be pledged the Society of Jesuits for the enterprise; ten thousand more to be given it as a fund for one mission; prevails upon the Commissary of the Inquisition at Queretaro, Don Juan Cavalero Y. Ozio, to subscribe funds for two other missions, and obligate himself to pay whatever bills shall be drawn on him by PADRE SALVA TIERRA.

The license for the Jesuits to enter California is granted on the fifth of February, 1627. The special warrants empowering PADRES KINO and SALVA TIERRA to enter California are subject to these conditions: that they waste nothing belonging to the king, nor draw upon the government treasury without express orders from his majesty; that they take possession of the country, and hold it in the name of the King of Spain.

The powers granted them in these warrants are, to enlist soldiers at their own expense; appoint a commander, whose immunities shall be accounted the same as in time of war; to commission magistrates for the administration of justice in California; and discharge all these from their service at will. With full powers both civil and ecclesiastical, therefore, and the treasury both of the Inquisition and of many private individuals to draw upon, PADRE SALVA TIERRA goes from Mexico to Guadalaxara; thence to Hiaqui, in Senora; and thence on the tenth of October, 1697, with five soldiers, Estevan Rodriguez Lorenzo, Bartolemé de Robles Figueroa, Juan Caravana, Nicolas Marques, and Juan, with their commander, Don Luis de Torres Tortolero, embarks for the scene of his future trials. A great moral hero, with his little band, kneeling in prayer on the deck of a galliot, bound for the conquest of California! The sails are loosened to the winds; they leave the harbor;

but they have proceeded hardly a league, when a squall comes on, which strands them on the beach. All now appear to be lost. But they save themselves in the long-boat; and when the tide rises, the galliot floats again, and proceeds on her voyage. A holy voyage is begun; its consequences are full of hope to man!

On the thirteenth they touch at San Bruno, in California, and at San Dionysio, ten leagues south of San Bruno. At the latter place, fifty Indians receive them with joy. A fine watering-place, discovered in a deep and fruitful glen, indicates the place for an encampment. The provisions, baggage, and animals, therefore, are landed, and the barracks of the little garrison built; a line of circumvallation is thrown up, in the centre of which a temporary chapel is raised; before it a crucifix, adorned with a garland of flowers, is erected; and "the image of our Lady of Loretto, as patroness of the conquest, is brought in procession from the galliot, and placed with proper solemnity." On the twenty-fifth of October, formal possession is taken of the country in the name of the King of Spain.

Thus commences the religious conquest of California by PADRE SALVA TIERRA; a voluntary exile from the highest circles of European life; a great man, with a strong and kind heart; abandoning kindred, ease, and intellectual society, for the well-being of the stupid and filthy natives of the Californian deserts.

The Padre now sends the galliot to Hiaqui for Padre Piccolo, some soldiers and provisions. Meantime he applies himself with unceasing assiduity to learning the Indian language and teaching religion. He pursues the same course as he would with stupid children; induces them to learn the prayers and catechisms, by rewarding attention and industry with something to eat. By thus addressing their strongest propensity as a stimulant for the acquisition of knowledge, he hopes to awaken and instruct their higher faculties of thought and sense of right. In the latter he, for a time, fails.

For the savages, dissatisfied with the amount of food which the Padre gives them, fall upon the animals of the post, destroy them, and steal corn from the sacks. Nor are they satisfied with this. They meditate a general attack on the garrison, in order to destroy or drive the people from the country. The good Padre knows their designs, but continues his kindness. Their insolence increases. On the thirteenth of November, the tribes meet to strike a decisive blow. Four savages come to the camp about noon, while the garrison are eating. The sentinel tries to prevent their entering the trenches, and one of the boldest of them deprives him of the staff used as a halberd. The soldier cries out, and Tortolero running up, wrests it from the Indian with such force and boldness, that the invaders are frightened and retire. At this moment the Indian Alonzo de Tepahui, who keeps the swine and sheep in a valley overgrown with rushes and flags, is assaulted by another party. But aid being immediately rendered, himself and animals are saved. And now falls a shower of arrows and stones from five hundred Indians, advancing to attack the camp.

Ten men and one Californian Indian compose the garrison. And how shall they be so detailed as to meet this numerous force? Tortolero, the acting commander, stations himself and Bartolemé de Robles on the entrenchment facing the lower part of the valley, the post of greatest danger; on the opposite side are Juan de Peru and the Indian Alonzo de Tepahui; on the side looking towards the river, stands the bold and active Indian Marcos Guazavas; on the remaining side is Estevan Rodrigues; the Maltese Juan Caravana has the care of the paderero, or cannon, placed at the gate of the camp; and near to him is Nicolas Marques, the Sicilian, as assistant gunner; SALVA TIERRA and Sebastien, his Indian, occupy the centre, in order to give aid where there should be the most need. The forces have barely time to make this disposition of themselves, when the savages begin to advance on all sides, with dreadful shouting and outcries. They are repulsed with as little destruction of life as possible. PADRE SALVA TIERRA desires that course to be pursued. The Indians return to the attack repeatedly for two hours, throwing stones, arrows, and wooden javelins into the trenches, when suddenly the whole body retreats and the action ceases. Half an hour elapses, and they return reinforced, and press upon the trenches with rage so fierce and deadly, that the hope of successful resistance without the paderero grows faint. The Padre, therefore, consents to have it fired. The match is applied. But instead of destroying the Indians, it bursts in pieces and flies about the camp, knocking Juan Caravana senseless to the ground. The Indians against whom it has been levelled, perceive this misfortune, and send notice of it to others with the remark, that since the paderero does not kill, they need not fear the smaller pieces. Of this they are the more persuaded, because the Padre has ordered the soldiers to shoot over them. And the kind old priest, now that the Captain thinks it necessary to fire into the Indian ranks, rushes between the guns and the savages, beseeching them not to press on sure destruction! Three arrows shot at him are the reward of his kindness. Happily, the Padre is not injured. But he withdraws and leaves them to their fate. And now they fall before the muskets of the soldiers! The wounded and dying groan on every side! A route succeeds! They fly in confusion to their villages!

Soon after, messengers of peace arrive. The first is a Chief. He weeps; he talks in broken grief; he acknowledges himself the cause of these disturbances; he first formed the plot, inspirited and drew in the other tribes; he and they have sought vengeance; but are now sincerely repentant. Next comes a band of women leading children. They seat themselves at the gate of the camp, and weeping bitterly, and promising good conduct for themselves and their husbands, offer the children as hostages. The good Padre is greatly rejoiced to see these signs of sorrow; explains to them the wickedness of their acts; and promises them peace, friendship, and other good things, if their husbands prove true to their league. And receiving one of the children in order to remove all suspicion from their minds, sends them to their friends and homes with shouts and other demonstrations of great joy. And now night comes on in this vast waste of burned mountains! The little chapel is opened for worship. Special "thanks are returned to God, His most holy mother, and Saint Stanislaus for his manifold favors."

On examining the camp next morning, it is found "that most of the arrows stick in the pedestal of the cross; whilst the cross itself, and tent which serves for a chapel to 'our lady of Loretto,' are untouched." None of the garrison are killed; two only are wounded. These are the brave Tortolero and Figueroa; and they adore the holy cross as the standard of their faith; "they sing *Ave Maria* to our lady as their Captain, and unanimously determine to remain in the country." This garrison is called Loretto. To it, for many years to come, will centre the events of the country. Even now it is a bright and lone starry point: the only lamp of truth that burns, from Cape San Lucas to the north pole, is at Loretto. The only civilized men that live on all that extent of coast, breathe this first night after the battle, with their hands clenched on their guns, in the tents of the garrison at Loretto in Lower California!

On the twenty-third of November a long-boat arrives from Señora with Padre Francisco Maria Piccolo—a missionary among the Tarahumares, who has left his former field of toil, for this new one in California. Padre Salva Tierra has, by his arrival, a companion at his prayers, and in his labor among these savages. The soldiers now erect some works of defence within the camp; the trench is enlarged and fortified with a palisade and thorny branches of trees; a chapel is built of mortar and stone, with thatched roof, for the image of "our Lady of Loretto;" three other structures are raised, one for the Padres, one for the Captain, and one for a magazine; and near to these are raised the barracks. The Padres employ themselves with the Indians. A small tribe is allowed to take up quarters near the camp.

The native priests, perceiving by this movement of their people, that their authority is diminishing, raise a party to oppose the Padres. They steal a long-boat and break it in pieces; attack a party in pursuit of them, and are driven from the ground; repent, and are again received into favor by the forgiving Padres. Don Pedro Gil de la Sierpe sends PADRE SALVA TIERRA a bark called San Firmin, and a long-boat called San Xavier. With these they bring wood, fruits, and horses and cattle, from the opposite coast of Senora. The Padres understand the Indian languages; they also have horses to bear them in their travels; and they undertake, in the beginning of the year 1699, to explore different parts of the country. Padres SALVA TIERRA and Piccolo visit a place called Londo, eight leagues northward from Loretto. Here is found a populous village and some tillable land. But the inhabitants flee as the Padres approach. They call it San Juan de Londo. Next they attempt to penetrate Vigge Biaundo, lying south of Loretto. On the tenth of May, the soldiers, after much suffering among the rugged precipices, refusing to go farther, Padre Piccolo determines to go alone, and climbs the precipices till he comes to a village, where he is received by the savages with the most cordial demonstrations of love. He instructs them four days; names the place San Xavier, and departs. Some portions of this mountain valley can be irrigated and tilled for grains and fruit trees. The neighboring heights are craggy and barren; about their bases are some fine pasture lands.

From San Xavier, Padre Piccolo goes westward to the sea, and explores its coast in vain for a harbor and habitable lands. During this journey he discovers, four leagues southwest from San Xavier, a large village of tractable Indians. They reside on the head waters of a fine stream running westward into the Pacific;—a beautifu. spot among a dreary desolation, which he consecrates to San Rosalia. At San Xavier, during his absence, the Indians and soldiers have built with sun-dried bricks some small houses and a chapel. The Indians from San Rosalia are there; and PADRE SALVA TIERRA consecrates the Chapel to San Xavier, with great devotion and joy. This done, Padre Piccolo is left in charge at San Xavier, and PADRE SALVA TIERRA returns to Loretto.

The shipping of the mission at this time consists of two vessels, the San Firmin and San Josef, and the long-boat San Xavier. The number of settlers already in California of Spaniards, half-breeds, and Mexican Indians, is six hundred persons; and as the means of supplying them with food from the country produce, has not increased in proportion, it becomes necessary to redouble their diligence to obtain them elsewhere From Mexico they can export nothing, for the Captain of the Garrison at Loretto, having been prevented from using the converts in the pearl fishery, and thus ruining their health, and the Padre's hope of rearing them for Heaven, has, by his misrepresentations of these benevolent men, rendered ineffectual Padre Ugarte's efforts in that quarter. Unfortunately also at this juncture, the two ships of the California missions are cast away! Nothing is left them now but the long-boat! Distress is creeping upon them! The fearful, maddening expectation of starving to death begins to be talked of in Loretto, when PADRE SALVA TIERRA takes the leaky long-boat and goes to the great presiding genius of the missions, PADRE KINO, in Senora, for relief. These Padres are devoted friends. They meet and embrace each other warmly, and relate, in the shades of a beautiful evening, all the hardships which have befallen them; and the success that has attended their labors among the savages. PADRE SALVA TIERRA has reduced the Indians for the space of fifty leagues about Loretto; founded four towns, in which are six hundred Indian Christians; two thousand adult Catechumens, besides many children; all of whom are now starving!

PADRE KINO entered Senora in 1687. He was appointed to

the lonely missions in the neighborhood of the Indians in the upper country, called Pimeria Alta, a district extending three hundred miles to the northward of Senora, and embracing the vallies of the Gila and the Colorado. He went alone among these wild Indians; learned their language; formed them into communities; prevailed upon them to cultivate grains and raise cattle; and, by the aid of subordinate agents, has reformed their civil polity; and indoctrinated them in the mysteries and hopes of the Catholic faith. And such is the reverent love of these savages for the excellent Padre that they greet him everywhere as little children do a kind parent, who comes to bless and love them. This influence he uses only for their good. He procures from his Sovereign an edict against their being seized by the Spaniards and immersed in the mines to labor till dead! He acquaints the Vice-Royal Government at Mexico that the military powers often accuse them of rebellion, and make war upon them for the base purpose of taking them captives to dive for pearls and dig in the mountains for the precious metals, and procures a cessation of such barbarity. This is a great work of mercy. For previously, in all those regions, it has been customary for the civil and military authorities to make the Indians labor on the lands or in the mines five years after their conversion. They pay for Christianity in their hearts by the servitude of their bodies. And seldom do the poor Indians live to be free again, after this chain of avarice is put upon them. Very many are the clusters of little wooden crosses, near these mines, which stand over the graves of those who have been worked to death in their deep and dismal depths! PADRE KINO gives them liberty; builds them houses and chapels; teaches them agriculture and many other useful arts. Their animals now range on a thousand hills; their ploughs turn the soil of a thousand fields; and their belfries send their peals for prayer and praise up a thousand vales!

Such is the result of the labors of PADRE KINO in Pimeria, and such the happy condition of the numerous tribes of Indians on the waters of the Gila and Colorado in the year 1700. These Padres have wrought well in the vineyards of the Faith. And they are now met to converse about the fate of these labors. They have learned that malice has destroyed their interest in Mexico and Spain. They know that the lives of the garrison at Loretto depend on their sole energy and means. And well would it be for the distressed everywhere if the relief which they need were dependent on such hearts and heads as those of the Padres Kino and Salva Tierra. The Indian farms are laid under contribution, and the keel of genuine mercy is fast cutting its way to Loretto to feed the dying! Words, wishes, speeches, associations, societies, general and special committee rooms, and newspapers devoted to "the cause," are the outlets and substance of benevolence in the seventeenth century—an untiring chase after the shade of a great idea. In the seventeenth, these hated priests of an odious order, whose name has come to be the common term of the most refined knavery, and even introduced into our lexicons as the appellation for the basest villany, perform acts of the highest virtue, endure hardships of the severest character, and make sacrifices of the noblest nature, for a class of beings who will never have intelligence enough to appreciate them.

After succors are sent to California, these Padres agree to explore the northwest country, in order to ascertain whether California be an island, or whether it be merely a peninsula. This question is deemed of great moment to the missions in California; for if supplies can be sent by land from Padre Kino's mission to Loretto, the expense of shipping to carry them across the Gulf will be avoided, and the certainty of their arrival much increased. Accordingly, it is agreed that Padres Kino and Salva Tierra shall take different routes towards the Colorado. They determine to visit, on the way, Padre Kino's converts at the several missions in that region, and meet at Mission de Dolores. Accordingly Padre Salva Tierra goes by San Ignacio,

San Diepo de Uquitoa, and San Diepo de Pitquin, to river Caborca, and follows its course to Tibutama, Axi, Concepcion de Caborca; while PADRE KINO takes the route by Cocospera, San Simon and Jude; strikes the river Caborca and follows its banks through Tierra Tibutama, and other villages, to the place of rendezvous. Thence the Padres, accompanied by ten soldiers, go northward to San Eduardo de Baissia, San Luis de Bacapa, and thence twelve leagues to San Marcello. This latter place lies northeast from the mouth of the river Colorado, fifty leagues north of the latitude of the Gila, the same distance from the river Caborca and the same distance eastward from San Xavier del Bac. The soil of this valley is fit for tillage and pasturage, and abounding in water for all uses. It is surrounded by deserts and lofty mountains. Here they are informed by the Indians of two ways to approach the mouth of the Colorado; the one to the right over the mountains and valley of Santa Clara, the other and the shorter along the coast over a broad tract of sands. The Padres desire to examine the coast, and for this reason, unfortunately, choose the latter route They travel thirty leagues on the south side of the mountains in search of the Gulf; pass a large section of the mountains, composed of pumice stone; and on the nineteenth of March, arrive at the sandy waste. On the twentieth, PADRE KINO and Captain Mateo Mange, ascend a lofty peak in Lat. 30° N., and not only see the Gulf but the opposite shore and mountains of California. On the twenty-first they reach the beach. Want of fresh water, and the difficulty of wading in the loose and burning sand, compels them to return to Marcello, and take a higher track, in Lat. 32° 30′, where they ascend a hill of moderate height, from which are clearly seen the mountains of California, the termination of the Gulf, the mouth of the Colorado, the junction of California with the continent! The PADRE KINO joyfully returns to San Marcello to build a church and give directions for a new mission, while SALVA TIERRA goes to Caborca Delores and the other missions of Senora, collecting charities for California, and with heightened expectations of saving the lives of his friends at Loretto, ships himself and them in the old long-boat San Xavier at the mouth of the river Hiaqui, and arrives at Loretto the latter end of April, 1701. Joy fills the camp on the arrival of the good Padre; and earnest thanksgivings are offered in the chapel by his spiritual children on account of his return.

Here we leave California for a brief space to follow good old PADRE KINO through the labors of his last days. In November of 1701 he takes another excursion to San Marcello by a new route, and thence onward, to the Gila. He fords this river at San Dionysio near its junction with the Colorado; and having viewed the neighboring country, repasses the Gila and descends the Colorado twenty leagues, among the villages of the Yumas and Quinquimas. Here vast numbers of Indians come to see the Padre and hear him speak of the white man's God. The Colorado at this place is two hundred yards wide. The Indians swim it. If they desire to take anything across, it is placed in a water-tight basket, made of rushes and herbs called Corysta, and floated along before them. PADRE KINO crosses the river on a raft made of tree-tops, and finds on the other shore, great numbers of Quinquimas, Coanopas, Bagiopas and Octguanes Indians, to whom he explains, by means of interpreters, the nature of the true God and the after state. He travels on foot three leagues to the residence of the chief of the Quinquimas. The country over which he passes is level, and covered with a soil fit for tillage and grazing. He calls the place Presentacion de Nuestra Senora. In this neighborhood he sees ten thousand Indians. PADRE KINO is very desirous of travelling to Monterey and Cape Mendocino. But it being impossible for his animals to ford the river, he reluctantly gives up the hope of progressing farther, and returns to his missions in Pimeria.

In February, 1702, PADRE KINO journeys in company with Martin Gonzales. On the twenty-eighth they arrive at San Dionysio, at the junction of the Gila and Colorado. On the way and at this place the Indians throng the path of this good man, kneeling like children to a loved grandsire for a blessing. In March they advance as far as the village of the Quinquimas, and name it San Rudesindo. These Indians show much love towards the Padres, and even towards the beasts that bear them. The good Padre Gonzales is affected to tears by these demonstrations; and strips off a part of his own wardrobe to clothe an aged man who follows him. They now travel down the Colorado to its entrance into the Gulf. Here many Indians come from the western shore and entreat the Padres to pass over into their country. They learn from them that the Pacific is ten days' journey from this place. The night of the tenth is spent at the point where the river and the Gulf meet. The tide rises very high and swashes near their couches; horned night-owls hoot on the crags; Padre Gonzales groans with extreme illness! These Padres have designed to cross the river at this place, and travel over the mountains to the Pacific Ocean. But PADRE KINO sees the necessity of returning with his sick brother. He succeeds in getting him to the mission of Tibutama, where he dies. Death in the wilderness, to one who goes into its depths to sow the seeds of salvation, is sweet. The desires of the mind touch the earth lightly. Their objects are things of thought and trust. The hand of hope is laid on the skies! The eye follows it to the temple of immortal faith; is absorbed and fixed there, to the exclusion of everything material. The pains incident to the separation of the living principle from the body, are like brambles which one passes to fields of flowers and fruits, singing birds, pebbly streams, and odorous shades. And the grave itself becomes in truth the pass-way only to the full enjoyment of the proper objects of the moral sense, without limit or satiety. So this missionary dies, and is buried among the graves of Indian Christians at Tibutama.

The years 1703, 1704, and 1705, PADRE KINO spends in building up the missions of Pimeria, and in resisting the persecution raised against him because he will not permit the owners of the mines and plantations to enslave his converts. Having no one to assist him in so wide a province, he is almost constantly travelling from one mission to another, exhorting, encouraging, disciplining, and protecting his spiritual children. These duties task severely the tottering strength of the good old man. But he labors without intermission or discouragement, as he ripens for his reward. Nor does his ardent interest in the Californian missions abate. Every few months he forwards to Loretto his largesses of provisions and animals. But as the expense of supporting shipping for that purpose becomes more and more apparent and perplexing, he determines once more to attempt an exploration of a land route, by which supplies can be sent from the mission on the Gila down the coast to Loretto. Accordingly, in 1706, he turns his footsteps again towards the Colorado, in company with the chief military officers of Senora, and the Franciscan monk, Manuel de Ojuela. This last expedition of Padre Kino results in confirming his previous discoveries. But being unable to penetrate to Loretto, he returns to his missions, and defends them with the same dauntless courage against the avárice and cruelty of the miners, and the civil and military powers, till 1710, when he passes from the scenes of his benevolence and trials to his grave.

There are few good men in the world. Consequently, when one of this class dies, there is a jewel lost from the crown of earthly virtue. ALL feel the loss of its light, and grope nearer to the ground in their way onward to their destiny. Padre Kino has given his best energies to the Pimerian and Californian missions. The poor Indians on both sides of the Gulf have been accustomed to eat his bread and receive his blessing. The bells now toll through all Pimeria and Senora, at Loretto and San Xavier. The Indians kneel in their rude chapels, and pray for his soul, and invoke for him the good fellowship of departed saints Padre Kino is buried among the heights of Pimeria, the scene of his trials and hopes. His grave is lost among the driving sands of those desolate regions; but his good deeds will live for ever

CHAPTER X.

Meeting of PADRES SALVA TIERRA and Ugarte— A Plot—Burning of San Xavier—Ugarte at San Xavier—Famine—A Runaway—A Murder—A Campaign—Rejoicings—A Tempest—An Arrival of Food and Soldiers—Measures for the Advancement of the Conquest—Exploration of the Interior—Sacking of San Xavier—Massacres—A Court Martial—An Execution—Peace—Expedition to the North—Distress—A Council, and its Results—Endurance—Roaming and Starving—An Attack—SALVA TIERRA leaves California—His Return—Extension of the Conquest—Ligui, and a great Example—A Chastisement—A murderous Attempt—Mulege—Cada Kaaman—The Triumph of the Good—Poison—Death.

DURING the absence of PADRE SALVA TIERRA in Pimeria, Padre Ugarte has arrived at Loretto with a few supplies. The meeting of these two men in that distant land is warm and hearty. They have labored long in the same cause—have hoped ardently for the same result—the growth of the tree of life on the shores of California. The one has used his utmost energies at Mexico and Guadalaxara to procure the means to support the other, while breaking up the ground and casting in the seed. And when all his efforts are closing in disappointment, and the dark night of malice is casting gloom over them, and his expectations are giving place to despair, he flies to his fellow-laborer in the wilderness, to die with him, if need be, in a last struggle to bring the Californian Indians within the fold of the Catholic faith. After thanks are rendered to God for the favor of meeting again, the Padres earnestly resolve to sustain the sinking missions. It is agreed, therefore, that Padre Piccolo shall go to Mexico and make farther trial to obtain funds for that purpose. He accordingly puts to sea, but is driven back by a tempest; and again he leaves the harbor, but is again compelled to return.

These unfavorable trials induce him to postpone his voyage to a more favorable season. He returns, therefore, to his mission at San Xavier, and Padre Ugarte remains at Loretto with Padre Salva Tierra, to learn the Indian language, and assist wherever his services may be needed.

Another class of events now transpire which change somewhat the aspect of affairs among them, and give hope of better things. The military commandant, who has, by his misrepresentations, rendered abortive the efforts of Padre Ugarte, at Mexico, finds that the authorities will not relieve him from subordination to the Padres, and resigns. Captain Don Antonio Garcia de Mendoza is therefore succeeded by one Isadore de Figueroa. This man, however, proves unworthy of his trust in a difficulty with the savages of San Xavier. The Indians of that mission plan the murder of Padre Piccolo. And led on by the conjurors, or priests of their old religion, they come down upon the few converts who remain faithful, with such violence as to get possession of the premises; and enraged at the Padre's escape to Loretto, burn the mission buildings and furniture. A number of the converts have been killed in this outbreak; the fields of San Xavier, the only grounds within the limits of the missions on which grain can be grown, are laid waste; the success of the savages in this instance will embolden them to attack Loretto. All these, as reasons, determine the Padres to send Captain Figueroa with his soldiers to chastise them and recover the mission. Accordingly he marches his troops to San Xavier. The Indians flee before him. The soldiers desire to pursue them. But the commander forbids it; and otherwise shows such a want of courage and manliness, that the soldiers depose him, and elect in his stead, Don Estevan Rodriguez Lorenzo, who leads them in pursuit among the breaks of the mountains; but without success.

At the end of this year, 1700, Padre Ugarte having learned the Indian language, and the Indians of San Xavier having become satisfied and peaceable, it is resolved to rebuild the mission and put it under his charge. Accordingly he leaves Loretto for that purpose. But on arriving there, the Indians, through fear of the soldiers that accompany him, run into the mountains. The Padre, nowise discouraged by this circumstance, takes up his quarters on the site of the burned mission, and awaits their return. Meanwhile the soldiers, not having Indians to serve them, prove troublesome. They abuse the Padre and one another in such manner that he determines to trust himself with the Indians, rather than any longer suffer their insolent behavior; and accordingly sends them back to Loretto. After the departure of the soldiers, Padre Ugarte remains alone all day about the ashes of the mission and the graves of those who were killed at the time it was destroyed! He does not know how soon they will fall upon him likewise, and take his life. Night comes on and passes away; and he is yet alone. At daylight a little Indian lad comes shyly, about the Padre's couch; is treated kindly by him; examines the fields, and hastily returns to his tribe: and shortly afterward the good Padre is surrounded by hundreds of Indians rejoicing at his arrival, and protesting that soldiers are disagreeable members of their community. The Padre and the Indians now unite their energies to rebuild the mission. The first labor of Ugarte is, to secure their regular attendance on the catechising, the prayers and mass; and by kind and affable treatment, to alienate them from their sorcerers; the second is, to accustom them to till the land and take care of the cattle. To accomplish these objects he induces them early in the morning to attend mass; after which he feeds those who will engage in erecting the church or clearing the land for cultivation, or making trenches for irrigation, or digging holes for planting trees, or preparing the ground for sowing seed. In the progress of these labors the good Padre works more than any of them. He is overseer, bricklayer and farmer. He is first in bringing stones, first in treading clay for mortar, in mixing sand, cutting, carrying, bringing timber, removing earth and fixing materials; sometimes spading up the ground, sometimes splitting rock with a crowbar, sometimes turning water into the trenches, and at others leading the beasts and cattle, which he has procured for his mission, to pasture and to water. By his own example he teaches them to throw off their natural sloth, to feed themselves and live like rational beings. But this great example does not suffice to wean them from a love of the woods, and a listless and starving inaction. A thousand times they try his patience, by coming late to mass and to work, and by running away and jeering him, and sometimes threatening and forming combinations to take his life. All this the old man bears with unwearied patience, kindness, and holy fortitude. In the evening the Padre leads them again to their devotions. At this time the rosary is prayed over, and the catechism explained; and this service is followed by the distribution of some provisions.

At first these Indians jest and jeer at the service, and mock at what he says. This the Padre bears patiently, till he finds forbearance increases the evil, and then makes a very dangerous attempt to suppress it. An Indian in high repute among his fellows for physical strength, stands near him during service, and mocks at all that he does. The other Indians, regarding bodily strength as the only quality of greatness, are vastly pleased that their champion seems the superior of the Padre. Ugarte perceives by their bearing, that he is losing their confidence. He therefore seizes the savage, in the midst of his profanity, by the hair of his head, and swings him to and fro, with determined violence, till he begs for quarter. This so frightens the tribe that they afterwards behave with strict decorum when engaged in religious duties. The work of building the mission edifices, however, goes on slowly. The Padre, careful not to weary his Indians with labor, at frequent intervals instructs their stupid minds in the best methods of performing their tasks, and most especially, in the knowledge of their Maker. In succeeding years he enjoys the pleasure of seeing his neophytes well instructed in the doctrines of the Catholic Church, inured to patient labor, and residing in comfortable houses. He has turned the mountain streams along the crags, and changed the barren dust of the mountains into cultivated fields, burdened with harvests of wheat, maize, and other grains. He even makes generous wines, sufficient to supply the missions in California, and an overplus to exchange in Mexico for other goods. He likewise breeds horses and sheep, cattle and mules. Indeed, such is the success of Padre Ugarte's fortitude and industry, that in 1707 he becomes the Purveyor-General of the missions, and relieves them by the produce of his converts' labor, from some of the fears of starvation on that desolate coast.

Thus has this excellent man, in the course of seven years, opened, by his individual influence on the Californian Indians, a large plantation, the products of which, in favorable seasons, feed thousands of savages and seven hundred whites. His efforts now take another direction. His sheep, brought originally from the opposite coast, have increased to such an extent, as to yield large quantities of wool. This the Padre determines shall be made to clothe his naked Indians. He, therefore, with his own hands, makes spinning-wheels, looms, and other weaving apparatus, and teaches his Indians to use them. In order to perfect them in these manufactures, he obtains a master weaver, one Antonio Moran, from Tepic, under a salary of five hundred dollars per annum, to instruct them in weaving, and various other handicrafts. By these new manufactures, the missions are saved vast expenses for sail-cloth and baize. The Indians are clad; the grains and vegetables, although not a full supply, are ordinarily sufficient to prevent famine. The cattle and the other animals being added to these, suffice to meet the necessities of the Californian missions. A deed of true benevolence performed, where human praise can never speak of it, is a jewel in the crown of our nature, which can never be dimmed. How it beams on the robes of the good man as he steps into his grave! How it glistens in the tear of silent gratitude that is shed over the tomb of the dead, as ages crumble it into dust! How rich a halo does it throw back on all after time, a remnant light of Bethlehem's holy star, to lead the living to the same happy use of their capacities! These Indians' remote descendants will forget this good man. But his deeds will live in their virtues.

We will now look into the movements of Padres Salva Tierra and Piccolo. Near the end of the year 1701, the provisions which Padre Kino has sent to Loretto, are exhausted, and Padre Piccolo's departure to Mexico for a supply is hastened. He sails on the second of December, leaving the Padres, the garrison and Indians in absolute want. For sixty days they subsist on roots, wild fruits, and a few fish which they find washed up on the shore. On the twenty-ninth of January, 1702, however, their distress is changed to gladness by the arrival of a boat from Padre Piccolo, laden with meat, maize, and other provisions. This supply, in the bountiful hands of Padre Salva Tierra, lasts but a short time; and want returns upon them with all its horrors. At length the last filthy piece of meat is consumed, and they betake themselves, Indians and Padres and garrison, to the shores for fish, and to the mountains for Pitahayas and other fruits and roots. Amidst these sufferings occurs a difficulty with the Indians. A soldier by the name of Poblano has married one of the Indian converts. In the month of June her mother visits her and invites her home to the joyful ingathering of the Pitahayas. They go away in the night unperceived, and run to the mountains. The next morning the soldier pursues them a limited distance, but returns unsuccessful. A day or two afterwards, he goes with a Californian Indian near a village, where they hear a great deal of shouting and merriment. An old Indian, whom they meet, advises them to return, because their lives will be endangered by proceeding. The soldier insults the old man and shoots him. The noise of the discharged musket rouses the village, and the soldier dies, pierced with arrows. His Indian companion is wounded, but brings to Loretto information of this misfortune.

The Padres of San Xavier return to Loretto, and prepare to march in pursuit of the murderers. The Indians, learning this movement, gather all their forces and destroy the corn fields of San Xavier, and a few goats, on whose milk the Padres are subsisting, during this calamitous famine. The soldiers arrive in time to prevent the destruction of the buildings. At length the parties begin to skirmish, and four of the Indians are killed. But their numbers and violence increase daily. The troops suffer incredible hardship among the precipices, and breaks of the mountains. Distress and consternation are beginning to seize them. Death is looked for as inevitable. But they rejoice again; they breathe freely again; a bark comes over the tranquil and heated sea, with provisions and a recruit of soldiers; and runners are sent from Loretto to San Xavier, to give all a speedy share of the joyful news; they eat and drink again in the Californian missions! The Indians are intimidated by the arrival of fresh troops, and submit; and the grateful Padres give thanks to God in a solemn Te Deum for this unexpected deliverance.

Great anxiety is felt in California for the fate of Padre Piccolo. No tidings of him have been received since he left the port of Loretto. He has, however, arrived safely at Cinaloa, about the first of February, 1702, and sent them supplies; has hastened thence to Guadalaxara and Mexico; by indefatigable exertions has obtained six thousand dollars from the Government for the payment of soldiers; and having collected charities from a few individuals, has purchased goods for the relief of the most urgent necessities of the missions; has obtained a guarantee of Don Josef de La Puente Marquis de Villa Puente, for the support of three new missions; and from Nicolas de Arteaga, an offer to support another; and from the Government, six hundred dollars per annum thereafter; has secured the appointment of two Padres, Juan Manuel de Bassaldua and Geronimo Minutili, as missionaries to California; and has purchased a vessel at Acapulco, called Nuestra Senora del Rosario; has embarked at Matanchel with his goods, provisions, his brethren, and some artisans, for Loretto. Fine breezes bear them into the Gulf; then a tempest swoops down upon them and compels them to throw overboard that part of the cargo which is stowed on deck; but helping gales bear them to their destined port, on the twenty-eighth of October, 1702.

And now again the cross is raised before the people; the lofty anthem of thanksgiving swells up the parched mountain, and every knee bows to God and Senora de Loretto. Most of the garrison had been discharged for want of money to pay their wages; few have remained to protect the Padres. Joyfully now do they all gather about Padre Piccolo, with warm effusions of thanks for his expedition, and engage anew to bear arms, and beseech the mercies of God for the missions of California. This reinforcement of troops, artisans, and Padres, and the supplies of provisions and money, and the guarantees for the support of four new missions, and the promised annuity from the Government, encourage PADRE SALVA TIERRA to form higher designs for the enlargement of his operations. To effect them in the best manner, he confers with all the Padres on the best measures; and the conclusion is, that Padre Ugarte shall go to Senora and procure cattle for breeding, and horses and mules for draught and riding; that Padre Minutili shall remain at Loretto with PADRE SALVA TIERRA; and that Padre Bassaldua shall accompany Padre Piccolo to San Xavier, where he may learn the Indian language, and otherwise prepare himself for future labor. In obedience to these determinations, Padre Ugarte sails in the beginning of November; but after being absent a few days, is driven back by contrary winds. In December he sails again, and happily arrives at Guaymas, Pimeria, in February 1703. He reappears at Loretto with a fine quantity of black cattle, sheep, horses, mules, and provisions.

In March of this year, PADRE SALVA TIERRA re-commences

exploring the country. He takes with him the Captain and some soldiers, and proceeds to San Xavier, where he is joined by Padres Piccolo and Bassaldua. Thence they travel with great difficulty over the thirsty mountains to the Pacific, and search the coast far northward for a harbor, fresh water, and tillable land. None is found which will shelter ships from the prevailing winds. Some land, with a good soil, is discovered; but the absence of water for irrigation renders it useless. By going south, however, they fall upon the little river San Xavier. Here they find a few Indians who, after running away, are persuaded to show themselves friends. On their return these Padres pass two rancherias, the inhabitants of which they induce to move nearer to Loretto. This journey proves fruitless. They have discovered no suitable place for the establishment of a new mission. In May, they make another, in search of a river emptying into the sea one hundred and twenty miles north of Loretto. Having arrived near Concepcion Bay, they fall in with a large rancheria of Indians, who seize their bows and arrows and come out to destroy them. The Californian Indians, however, who are acting as guides to the Padres, explain the benevolent object of their visit; and all are received as friends, and treated with the kindest hospitality. These Indians inform the Padres of a large tract of crags and abysses lying between them and the river that they seek, which it is impossible to pass, and they return to Loretto.

A dismal misfortune now falls on California. Some Indians arrive at Loretto full of fright and sorrow, from whom the Padres learn that the wretch who formed the last conspiracy, the murderer of the soldier Poblano, and incendiary of the mission of San Xavier, has fomented discontent, assembled the rancherias, and massacred all the adult converts at San Xavier, except the few who have escaped to Loretto. This sad news determines the Padres and the Captain to punish those factious individuals, in such a manner as to prevent such outrages in future. Accordingly the Captain and soldiers fall on the conspirators at night, kill a few, among whom is one of the most active in the massacre; but the leader escapes. The Captain, however, declares he shall die. But the roughness of the country prevents pursuit. Another means of arresting him is adopted. The Indians are told that they shall never have peace until they surrender this chief of villains, and in a few days he is brought into the mission of San Xavier. A court-martial is now called, and the culprit arraigned, tried, and condemned to death! The Padres interfere to save him. But the Captain will not yield. The prisoner confesses that he intended to destroy all the converts and the Padres; that he has burnt the chapel and the images; that he has had a chief hand in the murder of Poblano; that he has been inducing the Indian women to marry the soldiers, in order to have more killed in the same manner; and the Captain will not release him from the punishment which he deserves for such terrible acts and intentions. All the Padres, therefore, gather at San Xavier to attend the last hours of the miserable man. They teach him to look at the fearful scenes which will break on him when the spirit's eyes open on eternity; exhort him to kiss the cross of redemption and lift his love to him who bled upon it for sins like his. He is taken to the plain in chains, blinded, made to kneel down and is shot! This is the first execution for a capital crime in California. Its influence is salutary. The Indians become peaceable, and regular in their duties.

The Padres make use of restored peace in exploring the country to find sites for new missions. The river Mulege, at the north, is visited by Padres Piccolo and Bassaldua in the bark San Xavier. They find arable land on its banks, a league in width, which appears suitable for a mission station. They therefore proceed to Senora to obtain riding animals wherewith to explore the southern shore for a land route to Loretto. Having returned, they descend the coast a few leagues, where a range of dry volcanic heights arrests their progress, and compels them to abandon their design, and re-embark for Loretto in the San Xavier. On their way, they put into Concepcion Bay which lies south of the opposing Mountains; send the bark to Guaymas for supplies; go by land along a path partially cleared by the preceding expedition; arrive at a valley which they call San Juan de Londo, where they meet PADRE SALVA TIERRA; and thence proceed in great haste to Loretto. Misfortune calls for their sympathy.

An ordinance has been issued by the Viceroy at Mexico, prohibiting any one from engaging in fishing for, or trading in, pearls, on the Californian coast, without a license from the Government, countersigned by the military commandant at Loretto. The object of this regulation is to prevent avaricious individuals from drawing the Indians away from the missions; an evil which the Padres have long endeavored to extirpate. But notwithstanding this regulation, two vessels have come upon the coast without license, and are fishing off Loretto, when a tempest breaks them from their moorings and strands them in the bay. The crew of one of them, seventy in number, are saved, and fourteen of the other succeed in gaining the shore. These eighty odd men the Padres clothe and feed a whole month,—the time required to get their ships off and repair them,—when the one with seventy souls sails for Mexico. This unexpected draught upon the small stores of the missions bears so heavily upon them, that the arrival of Padre Piccolo from Senora, with the bark partially laden with provisions, barely saves them from starvation. Near the close of the year the twelve survivors of the other crew are taken to the continent by Padre Minutili, who has been appointed to the missions at Tibutama. But their presence for so long a time at the garrison has greatly increased the sufferings of all the stations. It is now 1704, the seventh year of the religious conquest of California. It seems to be the last of the missions. The Padres have labored incessantly. Many of the natives have been baptized, and are becoming accustomed to labor. The lands are somewhat productive, and the manufacture of cloth is considerably advanced. Their attendance on the ordinances of religion gratifies the Padres, and civilisation seems to be taking root among these savages. But as the converts increase, the number of persons to be fed and clad are multiplied. And as the necessities of these grow, the hopes of a proper supply become more precarious. The vessel in which grains are to be brought from the opposite coast requires overhauling before she can put to sea. Without her the money for the payment of the garrison cannot be obtained from Mexico. But as the Padres have no means of repairing her, Padre Bassaldua, for life or death, sails in her towards Mexico, and Padre Piccolo, with equal self-devotion, embarks for Senora in the leaky and shattered bark San Xavier.

The mission of San Josef, on the continent, has been annexed to the Californian missions, in order that the Padres may use its resources for a uniform supply of provisions and animals. The brave Padre Piccolo is passing now between this station and Loretto, with all possible speed and activity. But the little provisions he is able to collect, ill suffice the wants in California. And as this little is often spoiled in the leaky boat before its arrival, starvation is again expected at Loretto. Meantime Padre Bassaldua arrives on the coast of Mexico with his creaking, leaky vessel; proceeds to Guadalaxara and Mexico; urges the execution of the Royal Orders for the support of the mission ; is unsuccessful; collects enough to repair his vessel; procures a small supply of necessaries from benevolent individuals; sails in company with Padre Pedro Ugarte, who has been appointed to fill the place of Padre Piccolo, and in the latter part of June rounds into the bay of Loretto, to add to the number of the desponding and starving! The Padres send the vessel and the bark to the continent for provisions. But the shattered condition of these craft, and the northwest gales, twice oblige them to put back empty. And when at last they succeed in making the voyage, little relief comes of it. There is a want of every necessary of life among the Padres and soldiers. The latter complain that their certificates of services sent to Mexico have not been honored; and the former see that some decided step must be taken either for the salvation or abandonment of the missions. PADRE SALVA TIERRA calls together the Padres and the Captain, and another officer of the garrison, to deliberate, and informs them that they can expect no speedy relief from their friends at Mexico; that he cannot more clearly depict the melancholy condition of their affairs than their common sufferings do; that he is summoned to Mexico to confer concerning the execution of the Royal Orders for the relief of the missions; but that he will not leave California until the missions are either relieved or destroyed. He desires, however, that others will fully deliberate, and freely determine whether they shall all remain there, and suffer for the glory of God, or go to Mexico, and await a more favorable juncture for renewing the conquest. He himself is ready to eat the wild fruits, and in other respects fare as the converts do, rather than abandon them. Padre Ugarte opposes leaving the country. Padres Piccolo, Pedro Ugarte and Bassaldua agree with him: and the Captain declares that he is astonished to hear a proposition of the kind; that he will solemnly protest against the Padres, if they should abandon the conquest. Nevertheless, notice is given to the people, that whoever will, may embark in the vessel going to Mexico, and that bills shall be given them for the arrears of their wages. But instead of embracing the offer, they all refuse to leave the Padres. The fear of an insurrection among the soldiers on account of the non-payment of wages and want of food being removed, the Padres dispatch the vessel and the bark to Guaymas for supplies. While they are waiting for these, Padre Ugarte sets an example of patience and fortitude. He goes into the mountains and woodlands, gathers the wild fruits and digs edible roots, reminds his spiritual children of the death in Canaan, and God's goodness to Jacob—while the soldiers and officers vie with the good man in all his works of love.

The Padres do not abandon their determination to found the other missions, for which funds have been promised. With this design in view, and also to bring new matters of interest to the minds of the distressed people, Padres SALVA TIERRA and Pedro Ugarte visit the district of Ligui, lying on the coast south of Loretto. A single soldier and two Indians accompany them. As they approach the village, many Indians rush from an ambush and begin to fire their arrows at them with great fury. The soldier, Francisco Xavier Valenzuela, draws his scimitar and brandishes it briskly in the sun with one hand, while with the other he fires his musketoon in the air. These movements so frighten the savages that they throw their weapons and themselves on the ground, and allow the whites to approach them. The two Indians interpret for PADRE SALVA TIERRA. He assures them that he comes only to do them good; that he has brought Padre Ugarte to live with them as a father, who will lead them to a happy futurity. On hearing this, they affectionately embrace PADRE SALVA TIERRA, and bid their wives and children to come from their hiding-places. The Indians are sad that the Padres do not remain longer with them, and can only be comforted by a strong promise that Padre Ugarte will soon return. They baptize forty-eight of the children, and depart for Loretto.

In the month of August, of this year, the vessel and bark return from Guaymas with provisions. Close upon this happy event, follows another, which causes much grief to the Padres and the Indians. PADRE SALVA TIERRA is appointed visitor to the missions of Cinaloa and Senora. The prospect of losing the society and fatherly love of this great and good man, causes deep sorrow among all ranks. He is also called to Mexico by order of the Viceroy, to attend an assembly to be soon convened by command of his Sovereign, in which the propriety and possibility of executing certain royal orders concerning the conquest and settlement of California are to be discussed. Before he departs, he consecrates the new church at Loretto, and appoints to the command of the garrison, Juan Baptiste Escalante, a distinguished warrior, against the Apaches on the Gila, and Nicolas Marques, as Lieutenant, to fill respectively the places of the worthy Captain Estevan Lorenzo and Ensign Isidro, who, to the sorrow of the Padres, have resigned their posts on account of some bitter feelings towards them among the soldiers

These matters being settled to the satisfaction of all parties, he appoints Padre Juan Ugarte to the supreme government of the garrison and missions, and on the first of October sails for the continent. He goes to Guadalaxara, confers with the Audiencia of that department, passes on to Mexico, and finds himself appointed Provincial of New Spain, and missionary of California. The good Padre, overwhelmed with this unexpected distinction, urges, with sincerity and zeal, his unfitness for the office, and his desire to labor and die a simple missionary among his Californian Indians. But the Padres assure him that the rules of his order will not permit him to decline; and persuade him, that under so good a man as Provincial, the church will cheerfully further his pious desires for the conversion of the Indians of California. The PADRE JUAN MARIA DE SALVA TIERRA, therefore, in hope of bettering the condition of his converts in that forlorn wilderness, enters upon the duties of Provinical Bishop of New Spain.

PADRE SALVA TIERRA in his official character communicates with the Viceroy, and lays before him his views of the proper measures of his Government for the furtherance of the missionary enterprise in the territories under his charge. He states, generally, the advances of the Spanish power in those vast realms by means of the Jesuits, and that in order to hold these conquests, the power by which they have been obtained must still be exercised. The honor and benefit of the Crown and of the Catholic Church demand this of his Excellency's Government. He is favorably heard, and all classes of people second his views. But the delay and selfishness which have ever characterized the Spanish power in America and elsewhere press on the track of the good Padre, and he is forced to leave Mexico on a visit to the churches of his Diocese, without any decided assurances that his views will be acted on. The poverty of the Crown, while half the world is digging gold and silver for its coffers, is an additional cause of this inaction.

We next find PADRE SALVA TIERRA, in 1705, appealing to the Jesuit College and the Audiencia of Guadalaxara, to succor the missions. Soon after this he lands at El Mission del Nuestra Senora de Loretto, amid the general joy of the Padres, soldiers and Indians. To the latter, particularly, he has been a father; and they dance and shout around him in an ecstacy of gladness to see again his grey head and benevolent face.

The PADRE finds his brethren in great wretchedness, but full of unwavering determination to carry forward the work which he has so valorously begun. Padre Piccolo, who has been appointed visitor of the missions of Senora, in order that he may have authority and opportunity to draw provisions more regularly for those of California, has been forwarding at intervals whatever he could gather from those poor establishments. But this has been sufficient only to prevent starvation or the abandonment of the country. However, the missions still exist, and the venerable PADRE SALVA TIERRA is happy. Their discomforts have been much increased during his absence by the growing tyranny of Capt. Escalante, who has become impatient of his subjection to the Padres, and abusive to the Indians and soldiers. An account of this state of things having been forwarded during the PADRE's tarry there, he has brought with him Don Estevan Rodriguez Lorenzo to supersede Escalante—an arrangement which results in much satisfaction to the missions.

The Provincial remains two months in California; but he does not excuse himself from his usual arduous labors. His new dignity furnishes no pretext for idleness. He bends all his energies to the well-being of the natives; takes measures for the establishment of two new missions; the one at Ligui and the other at the river Mulege. The small number of his associates, however, is an obstacle to the accomplishment of his wishes. There are but three Padres with him. One of these is required at San Xavier, and one at Londo. This distribution will leave but one to take care of the magazines, disburse the stores, nurse the sick, and perform the spiritual functions at Loretto—a task which no single man can perform. Accordingly, Jayme Bravo, the lay companion of PADRE SALVA TIERRA, is induced to take upon himself the temporal affairs of the garrison and mission, and thus leave the Padres free to pursue their religious labors. This arrangement being made, the Provincial departs for Mexico about the last of November, 1704, and the Padres Pedro Ugarte and Juan Manuel de Bassaldua commence the exploration of the new stations. The former goes twelve leagues south, to Ligui, and the latter forty leagues north, to the river Mulege; while Padre Juan Ugarte takes care of the missions at Loretto San Xavier and Londo.

The Ligui Indians are found to be peaceable, but so extremely indolent that the Padre can get no help from them in the construction of the mission buildings. His ingenuity and patience, however, are equal to his necessities. He feeds the boys of the tribe with sweetmeats, makes them small presents, and by his paternal address, soon attaches them so strongly to his person, that they follow him wherever he goes. He resorts to many artifices to habituate them to labor; lays wagers with them on their comparative dexterity in pulling up bushes, removing the earth from the sites of the buildings, and challenges them to dance with him on the clay of which the bricks are to be made. The boys sing and poach the mud with their feet, and so does the Padre. And in this way he clears his ground and erects the buildings of his mission. He also teaches these boys the Spanish language, and they teach their own to him. He explains to them the catechism and prayers, and they do the same to their parents. Thus, with untiring

A California Indian.

patience, firmness and labor, does he bring the mission of San Juan Baptista into form, and its Indians under his control And not these only; but going many miles into the woods and the breaches of the mountains, he gathers in the wandering, feeds and clothes them, and teaches them to till the ground and live like men. At last he succeeds in humanizing the greater portion of these rude people. They call him Padre, follow him to the labor of the field, and gather about the altar in his humble church to worship. All are industrious, well-fed, well-clad, and happy.

As the Padre, however, is felicitating himself on these results of his labors, an accident occurs which well nigh ruins all. He is called to baptize a sick woman, with whom he finds an old sorcerer employed according to their ancient customs. The Padre bids him depart, administers extreme unction to the woman, remains with her till death, buries her according to the forms of the church, and after reprimanding severely the converts who have lent their sanction to the juggler, dismisses them with much indignation. This severity of the Padre rouses the sullen fierceness of the Indians to such extent that, instigated by the disgraced sorcerer, they form the design of murdering him. They use the utmost secrecy, and make death the penalty of divulging their purpose. The Padre always has a boy sleeping in his apartment; and when at length the night of the massacre comes, this boy desires that he may be allowed to spend it with his friends, the Indians. The Padre objects! The boy urges! The Padre inquires the reason; and the boy, after much hesitation, tells him, "Because, father, this night they are going to kill you!"

On hearing this, he sends for some of the chief ones, and with a resolute and dauntless air tells them, "I know you have formed the design to kill me this night. But remember! With this musket I will, when you come, slaughter you all." Having said this, he quickly leaves them full of consternation at what they have heard.

Oppressed with fear, they retire to their associates in the

design; consult much, and at last conclude to seek safety from the Padre's musket in flight. In the morning their lodges are deserted; not an Indian is in sight of the Mission San Juan Baptista Ligui. On the following day the Padre goes out to seek his lost flock. They are found hidden away among the cliffs, and flee at his approach. After considerable parleying, however, they are convinced that the Padre seeks their good alone, and return to the mission thoroughly persuaded that he loves them, but can never be made to fear them.

This excellent man continues at his mission, enduring every privation, till 1709, when the severe fatigues of years weigh him down and compel him to seek health in Mexico. Thither he goes in the character of negotiator and procurator of the missions. No sooner, however, does he recover his health in a tolerable degree, than he returns and resumes his labors. But illness again compels him to leave this inhospitable shore for the mission at the River Yaqui, on the opposite coast, where he makes himself useful as an agent and purveyor-general for California.

But let us follow the Padre Juan Manuel Bassaldua to the River Mulege. He starts in 1705, and with great difficulty surmounts the crags as far north as Concepcion Bay. Here his progress is arrested by hills to all appearances insurmountable. But "trial before despair" is the Padre's motto. He fills ravines with rocks, and cuts away the woods; and after incredible labor, passes his animals over to Mulege.

There is a valley near the mouth of this little stream ten leagues in length, suitable for tillage. In this, two miles from the Gulf, he locates his mission, and consecrates it to Santa Rosalia; builds his dwelling and church of adobies; remains four years; collects the Indians from all the neighboring settlements; instructs them in religion and the useful arts; and so endears himself to them, that when his health fails, and he is transferred to Guaymas, the poor savages find it difficult to discover in his successor, the excellent Padre Piccolo, his equal in kindness and active benevolence.

Padre Piccolo exerts in this new field all his well-tried energies. Besides his labors as a spiritual teacher, he travels into the interior several times in search of proper sites for new settlements, and discovers those places which are afterwards occupied by the missions of Guadaloupe, La Purissima Concepcion, and San Ignacio. In the year 1718 he surrenders his charge to Padre Sebastian de Sistiaga. This Padre digs trenches to convey the waters of the river over the fields, and in other ways improves the facilities for training those active and intelligent children of the desert to the habits of a better life.

On the sixth of November, 1706, Padre Piccolo, three soldiers, and some Mulege Indians, with two asses bearing their provisions, journey westward towards the country of the North Cochimes, which is called Cada Kaaman, or Sedge Brook. It lies on the skirts of the mountains, thirty-five leagues, by the vales, from Santa Rosalia. On the third day he is met by a whole settlement of Indians, in a valley which, on a former visit, he has named Santa Aguida. These poor people express great joy at seeing the Padre again, and follow him to the neighboring rancherias, called Santa Lucia and Santa Nympha. In these places also he is greeted most kindly, and desired to remain. On the nineteenth of November he arrives at the head springs of the brook which waters the vale. Here he finds three considerable neighborhoods of savages, who welcome his coming with feastings, dances, and songs, in which those from Santa Lucia and Santa Nympha join with exceeding delight. He remains at this place until December, comforting and teaching them. A large arbor is built by the willing Indians, in which mass is celebrated. The neighboring villagers forsake their homes to attend upon the Padre's instructions. Fifty mothers eagerly offer their children in baptism. And now he departs, followed by a large crowd of people, who mourn that he leaves them; and preceded by others who shout their gladness among the parched hills, that he journeys towards their villages. They clear the path before him of stones and other obstacles; present him with strings of wild fruit to eat; and bring him water from the stream to drink.

While these new missions are in progress, the old ones, at Loretto, San Xavier, and Londo, are slowly advancing in comfort and usefulness. Nor are the Padres in charge of them idle in making explorations for other establishments.

In 1706 Jayme Bravo, in company with the Captain, seven soldiers, and some Indians, goes to San Juan Baptista Ligui, and having felicitated Padre Pedro Ugarte upon the happy beginning of his mission, passes along the shore towards the south. He has travelled a day and a half, when an Indian brings word that four of his soldiers are dying! Jayme Bravo and the Captain return, and find that one of them has found a fire where some Indian fishermen have been roasting a species of fish called Botates, the liver of which contains a very active poison. This soldier communicates the news of food at hand to his fellows, and they hasten to devour it. A friendly Indian warns them not to eat. But the soldier who first discovered the fire replying, "None of your noise, Indian; a Spaniard never dies," eats plentifully and gives to his companions. One of them chews and swallows a little; another chews, but does not swallow; the other merely handles and views the fish. Well would it have been if they had regarded the caution of the Indian: for in a very short time they are all seized with convulsive pains more or less violent, according to the use they have made of the fish. The first expires in half an hour. He is soon followed by the second! The third, who merely chewed the fish, remains insensible till the following morning! The man who only handled them is in a very bad condition for several days. This misfortune obliges the explorers to abandon their enterprise. They return to Ligui to bury the dead in the consecrated grounds of the mission, and send their sick to Loretto.

CHAPTER XI.

Padre Juan Ugarte and Jayme Bravo explore the Pacific Coast—Dearth—Thirst—Padre Salva Tierra—A Tempest—Landing at Loretto—San Josef—Wrecked—Padre Salva Tierra goes to the Rescue—Energy—Suffering—Die by Thousands—Wrecked—At Sea in a Long-boat—The Limit of Despair—They toil on—The Guaycuros—Massacre—San Ignacio—Padre Salva Tierra leaves California—Death of a Hero at Guadalaxara.

Meantime Padre Juan Ugarte prepares to reconnoitre the coast of the Pacific. The chief of the Yaqui nation waits on him with forty of his warriors. The Captain, with twelve soldiers and some converts, is at his command for the same duty; the beasts and provisions for the journey are ready; and Padre Juan Ugarte and the layman Bravo, on the twenty-sixth of November, 1706, leave Loretto, with their troops and pack animals divided into three companies, on their wearisome way over the western mountains. Their march lies through the Mission of San Xavier and the Indian village called Santa Rosalia, and from that point passes over the dry and herbless waste of heights and vales to the sea. Here they meet several hundred Guaycuros, who are friendly to them. Thence they march southward many leagues, and find no water in all the distance except in little wells dug by the Indians. They then turn their course to the north. They march all day over burning sands, famishing with thirst, and halt at night near the channel of a dry rivulet. Thence they send men a few leagues farther up the shore, and others up and down the thirsty channel, in quest of water. They all return to camp without success. Next they disperse themselves in every direction to find a plat of low ground where they may dig wells, but find none. As a last resource, they now let loose their animals, that they may, by their powerful instincts, find means of quenching their thirst; but all these contrivances are vain. They kindle a fire to keep themselves warm, and, weary and famishing, stretch themselves on the sand for the night.

In the morning Padre Ugarte greets the rising sun with the services of Mass; and while they sing the "Litany de Senora de Loretto," an Indian calls out in the language of his people that he has found water! With solemn gratitude they dig into the oozing soil; they obtain a supply for themselves and their animals; and having filled several vessels to serve them on their return, offer a service of thanksgiving to the Virgin, and commence their journey to Loretto.

While the Padres are thus employed in establishing missions and exploring California, Padre Salva Tierra is earnestly petitioning the Pope to discharge him from the office of Provincial Bishop of New Spain. He desires to spend his declining years among the Indians of California. In 1706 his discharge comes; and with inexpressible pleasure does the good old man collect supplies of clothing, provisions and ammunition, for the mission. He is joined by two other Padres, Julian de Mayorga and Rolandegui. To their care he commits the stores, with directions to repair to the harbor of Matanchel and await the arrival of the bark which is to take them to the peninsula. The Padre himself goes by land four hundred leagues along the coast to the harbor of Akomi in Senora, for the purpose of collecting free contributions from the missions in the regions through which he journeys.

About the first of January he sails for Loretto. He has a long tempestuous voyage. "This night," says he, "the thirty-first of January, was extremely dark. We were with the mast lashed, and without a rudder; and amidst rocks and islands; the sea continually making a free passage over us; the sailors spent with toil and hunger, having been without food for a day and a half, were prostrate, giving up all for lost. The least damage we could expect was to be driven into the sea of Gallicia or Acapulco. '*Tristissima noctis imago.*' The Californians got about me like chickens, and they were not my least confidants, as being new-born sons of the Great Madonna, and had run this risk in her service. After all my journeyings and voyages, I never knew what dangers or distresses by land or sea were, until now." They are driven by this horrible tempest into the bay of San Josef, thirty miles south of Loretto. On the third of February, the storm abating, they run up to the desired haven, and are received with universal gladness.

In 1708, Padres SALVA TIERRA and Juan Ugarte go with Padre Mayorga into the midst of the mountains to an Indian settlement called Comondu, and invest him with a mission there under the name of San Josef; and after having aided him in gathering the Indians, building a chapel, and some bough huts, they return to Loretto. Padre Mayorga forms some neighboring Indians into two towns which he calls San Juan and San Ignacio; builds a fine church at the former place; opens a school for boys at his own house; erects a seminary for girls; builds a hospital for the sick; prepares maize fields at San Josef, and plants vineyards at San Juan and San Ignacio.

Many other fertile spots are discovered among the deserts of California, soon after SALVA TIERRA's arrival, suitable for the establishment of missions. But misfortunes by sea and land retard their occupancy. The following is an instance of this kind. The bark San Xavier sails from Loretto in August, 1709, with $3,000 in specie, to purchase a supply of provisions in Senora. A storm of three days' continuance drives it on a barren coast, north of Guaymas, where it is stranded among the sands and rocks. Some are drowned; others save themselves in the boat. Hostile Indians, called Seris and Tepocas, fall upon those who escape and drive them to sea in the open boat; dig up the $3,000 which they have hidden in the sands; take the helm from the bark, and partly break it in pieces for the nails. The crew in the boat encounter very many dangers in their perilous voyage to the south. Storms overtake them. Their boat becomes leaky. They have no water. They live, however, to reach the river Yaqui, sixty leagues from the wreck. From this place a pearl-fisher's bark is sent to Loretto with an account of these disasters: PADRE SALVA TIERRA hastens over in the Rosalia to Guaymas; sends her to a port near the scene of the shipwreck; dispatches the bark San Xavier to the vessel, while he himself, attended by fourteen Yaqui Indians, passes up the rugged coast by land; is two days without a drop of water; and at last arrives at the wreck. The San Xavier's men are merely sustaining life on boiled herbs. He sends to the nearest mission for food by an Indian, who succeeds in passing through the hostile Seris and Tepocas, with a small supply. This does not suffice. Death is near them, when the indefatigable PADRE determines to journey through bands of murderous savages to the harbor of San Juan Baptista for help!

He has not travelled far along the coast when he arrives at a settlement of Indians, who come out against him under arms. They are led by an old man, who urges them on with terrible vociferations. Nothing less fearful than death seems promised in their present situation. But the PADRE, with his usual intrepidity, advancing alone towards them, makes some small presents to the old man and his son, which, accompanied by signs and kind gestures, soften their ferocity a little, when to their surprise and joy they hear the guns of the Rosalia! The explosion of these cannon is new to the Indians they think it the voice of avenging gods—they immediately run away and bring to the PADRE food, and $3,000 which had been taken from its place near the wreck. The PADRE thus unexpectedly recovers his lost money, and the means of continuing the lives of himself and men.

The Rosalia anchors near the disabled San Xavier; and the provisions on board for a time relieve the distressed workmen, seamen and Padres. But as two months are consumed in refitting the wreck, they are again often in want. The

Father Salva Tierra goes alone to meet the Indians.—P. 192.

missions of the region afford them occasional aid; but the dearth which has pervaded the country during this year, so far disables these establishments from furnishing adequate supplies, that PADRE SALVA TIERRA sends a messenger to the distant mission garrison, ninety miles up the country, called Nuestra Sennora de Gaudalupe, begging the Captain Don Francisco Xavier Valenzuela to send them food. This excellent man immediately despatches what succors he can command; and soon after comes in person with some of his men and a more liberal supply.

When he arrives, such is the distressed condition of the PADRE and those with him, that this commander and his veterans seat themselves on the beach and weep. After a continual repetition of trials like these, during two sultry months, the San Xavier is afloat, and the brave PADRE sails his vessel to the Californian coast; visits the Padre Piccolo at Santa Rosalia Mulege, and encouraging that lonely priest in the prosecution of his holy labors, drops down to Loretto. Soon after his arrival the small pox, that exterminator of the Indian race, sweeps away the greater part of the children and many adults, in all the missions. The garrison also suffers very much from irregularity of diet consequent upon the precarious means of supply, and the necessity of living in that sultry climate, on salt meat and maize. All these sicknesses and deaths the Indians attribute to the Padres. Their children, say they, are killed by baptism; the adults with the extreme unction; and the soldiers are made sick by continual exposure to the malign influence of prayers, masses and the exaltation of the Host. These suggestions are raised by their old sorcerers, and threaten to embitter the Indians fatally against the Padres. But the neophytes stand by their Priests, and convince their countrymen of their error.

From 1709 to 1711, a famine spreads over the entire Mexican Territories, and California consequently obtains no supplies from that source. The distress of these years is so exceedingly great, that the Indian neophytes betake themselves to the mountains, and live on roots and wild fruits; while the soldiers of the garrison eat herbs with the self-denying Padres: and to complete the misfortunes of this devoted country, two barks used in bringing a little food from Senora, are cast away.

In 1711, PADRE SALVA TIERRA sends Padre Francisco Peralta, who arrived in California two years before, to Matanchel to repair the old Rosario. But the frauds practised by the workmen consume many thousands of dollars, and make the bark so miserable a thing, that in its first effort at sailing it runs ashore in spite of the helm, and is utterly lost. They now build a new one, at an expense of $22,000. In this, then, laden with supplies, they put to sea. But a storm rising, the ill-built craft proves to be unmanageable, the sport of the waves and winds. She is driven to Cape San Lucas and back again to the isles of Mazatlan. Here some of the sailors forsake her; others remain on board, and after many difficulties, take her in sight of the coast of Loretto. A storm now drives her ashore on the opposite coast. It is the eighth of December. The night is terribly dark and tempestuous. Four seamen clear away the small boat, and regardless of the lives of the others, shove off. Those who are left hang to the main and mizen masts surging in the seas! Padre Bensto Guisi and six seamen are drowned. Padres Guillen and Doye, and twenty others, with the greatest difficulty, unlash the long-boat, bail out the water with two calabashes, and throwing aboard a piece of an old sail and some bits of boards for oars, commit themselves to the mercy of the waves In the morning they find themselves several leagues from land. They row down the coast a day and a half, and after a boisterous night land three hundred miles south of Guaymas. Eighteen persons, naked, wet, pierced with cold, exhausted with rowing, without food or water, with the single comfort of having escaped death in the sea, land on a barren waste interspersed with fertile tracts overrun with briars and brambles They gather oysters, wilks and herbs to eat, and march into the interior to find inhabitants. As they break their way, the brambles and briars lacerate their naked bodies. Two days of agony from this cause and from hunger and thirst, bring them into an open plain, where they are found by Indians. These they induce to give information of their presence and sufferings, to the commander of the town Tamasula, who visits them with horses, water and maize cakes, for their relief.

From this town they go to Guazave, the nearest mission in Cinaloa, where they fortunately find Padre Francisco Mazaregos. This Jesuit Missionary entertains them in the most liberal manner. The briars of the rugged path over which they travelled, have torn their clothing from their backs; and this holy man calls upon his Indian converts to contribute of their means, while he himself bestows his own wardrobe, to clothe the naked sufferers.

Having been refreshed by rest and food, and once more clad, they leave the hospitable Padre of Guazave for the town of Cinaloa. Here also they are generously entertained by Padre Juan Yrazoqui, until each departs to his appointed station. Padre Guillen is roused, instead of discouraged, by these hardships. Like all those great spirits who are sowing the gospel on the deserts of California, his sinews become the stronger as they are worn by hardship. He travels over the deserts to the missions at Yaqui, and in the month of January, 1714, sails to California in the good old San Xavier.

The missions are again entirely dependent upon this bark for the transport of supplies; the loss in New Rosario, of the commodities and clothing, on which the Padres, seamen, and soldiers depend to sustain life, no money left, no clothing, no food, the only sea-craft in their possession unseaworthy, and no means of repairing her, on a desert land and among hostile Indians kept in subjection chiefly by the supply of their physical wants, now impossible to be done, are the discouraging circumstances which weigh on the heavy hearts of the Padres But who shall set bounds to the power of moral motive, when linked with zeal drawn from faith in God? These Padres look for death, but they desire to die, sickle in hand, reaping the harvests of redemption! They toil on; they gather wandering Indians into towns; instruct them, thirsting and starving a part of each day, and spending the remainder among the mountains and forests, gathering here and there a dried root, or a bunch of wild fruit, to eat.

Padre Ugarte is even not content with these labors, but makes exploring tours among the Indian settlements south of San Xavier. Wherever he goes they throng his way, ask for the baptism of their children and the establishment of missions among them. It is 1712, and Padre Piccolo, though in bad health, imitates the zeal of Padre Ugarte. With the Captain, a few soldiers and Indians, he travels westward from Santa Rosalia Mulege, crosses the mountains of Vajademin, finds beyond them a small clear brook; follows it to the sea, examines the barren coast about its mouth, ascends a little stream about twenty miles; erects a cross and devotes the neighboring grounds to a contemplated mission. While he remains here many hundred Indians come in from the neighboring settlements, beseeching the Padre to remain with them, and as an inducement to do so, promise to give him their best wild fruits and feathers, and devote their children to the Catholic faith. He agrees to send them a Padre to instruct them more fully in religion, and returns to his station.

The vessels used by the people of the opposite coast in fishing for pearls bring a scanty supply of provisions. The Padre and people clothe themselves in the skins of wild beasts, and continue their labors. In the year 1716, Padre Salva Tierra sails south in a brigantine called Guadalupe, to La Paz, in order to make peace with the Guaycuros, who still retain an unfavorable remembrance of Admiral Otondo's ill-advised conduct, and the constantly repeated injuries of the pearl fishermen. He is accompanied by three Guaycuri prisoners taken from the pearl fishers, whom he is carrying back to their homes.

When he enters La Paz bay the Loretto Indians leap overboard and swim ashore; the Padre, Captain and soldiers follow hastily in their boats; but do not arrive in time to prevent the Loretto tribe from such warlike demonstrations as put the Guaycuros to flight. They flee, leaving their wives and children to follow after at a slower pace. The Loretto Indians do not regard the orders of PADRE SALVA TIERRA but led by savage impulse, fall upon the hapless women and children. These attempt to defend themselves with stones. But they must have perished had not the Captain and the nimblest of the soldiers arrived at the commencement of the infamous encounter. The unoffending creatures are saved; and wailing horribly, follow their cowardly fathers and husbands.

This unfortunate event tries exceedingly the good PADRE SALVA TIERRA. He sorrows that his benevolent designs should terminate in an outrage upon those whom he comes to cherish. But it is apparent that this rashness of the Loretto Indians renders useless any attempts at friendly connections with the Guaycuros. He therefore distributes to the prisoners from the pearlfishers' vessels, some agreeable presents, explains to them, that his object in visiting their countrymen was to restore themselves to their homes, and enter into friendly relations with the Guaycuros nation, and dismisses them with such other marks of his good intentions as will open a probability of successful negotiation with their countrymen on another occasion. He returns to Loretto with a heavy heart: and sends the brigantine to Matanchel for goods and provisions. A furious storm strands it; the vessel and cargo are a total loss; and nine persons are drowned. Thus death again thins the ranks of the Californian missions; want and nakedness stalk among them; and the old San Xavier, after eighteen years' service, is the only sea craft connecting them with the continent and with life. Amidst all these difficulties, however, the untiring Padres found the mission of San Ignacio in the Cada Kaaman, or the vale of the Sedge Brook.

It is now eighteen years since PADRE SALVA TIERRA landed in California and erected the cross at Loretto. His labors have been arduous and unremitted. His trials by shipwreck and tempests, by progresses over mountains and deserts, by hunger and thirst, by arrows and Indian knives, by endurances of all kinds, have whitened his hair, withered his bones and muscles, made his steps unstable and his head tremble at the throbs of his heart. He feels that the holy water must soon fall on his coffin lid, and California be deprived of his services. It is the year 1717. He is at Loretto, with little to eat, and badly clad, and scarcely able to walk or stand. But he teaches the children—exhorts the adults to the service of God, and superintends every particular movement of the garrison and the mission. In March, Padre Nicholas Tamaral, appointed to the proposed mission of La Purissima, arrives at Loretto, bringing letters from the reigning Viceroy of Mexico, in which among other matters it is stated that the King has forwarded important instructions relative to advancing most efficiently the spiritual conquest of California, together with a summons that PADRE SALVA TIERRA shall immediately repair to Mexico to aid in devising the best means of effecting that object. Disease, pain, want and danger present no obstacles to this aged Patriarch, when the interest of his missions calls upon him for action. He immediately determines to go to Mexico. Accordingly the government of California is committed to the wisdom of Padre Ugarte, and on the 31st of the same month of March, the good PADRE and Jayme Bravo sail for Matanchel.

Nine days' passage brings them to the desired port; they take mules for Tepic; the good Padre suffers greatly at every misstep of his animal; they arrive at Tepic; the Pa dre is in extreme torture; but tortures cannot deter him fron his holy labors; he is too weak and too much racked witl pain to mount a horse or mule, and is therefore borne in litter on the shoulders of Indians, to Guadalaxara. Here his illness increases so that he can proceed no farther. He is lodged in the college of Jesuits. The Padres are in attendance upon him. Two months of agony wear toward a close; and death begins to chill his limbs, glaze his eyes, and chain his utterance: and when he can no longer stir, he calls to him his faithful companion, Jayme Bravo, and in the most earnest manner, giving him instruction and powers for acting in his stead at Mexico, commends him and his beloved missions to the guardianship of Heaven. And now a hero dies! Not one who has swung the brand of war over the villages and cities of nations; not one who has crushed the hearts of men, yoked them in bondage, and severed every tendril of mercy and justice from the governing powers; not such a hero as men will worship; but a great and good man, offering life and every capacity of happiness within him to the well-being of savages in a barren waste of mountains; a hero in the heavenly armor of righteousness, enduring fatigue, hunger, thirst, and constant danger among the flinty, unwatered wastes of unthinking and uninstructed human nature; a missionary of a Californian wilderness! All the people of the city and neighboring villages crowd to the college, and kneel through the streets and alleys, on the balconies and roofs of the houses, and pray for the repose of the departed soul of Padre Salva Tierra. There is no noise in Guadalaxara, nor business; it is a city of prayer: they come one after another and kneel and pray, and silently retire; thirty thousands of people beseech Heaven with one earnest desire—that he whom they have loved, he who has labored so ardently in propagating the faith, may find a mansion of repose and reward in the upper world! Some Californian Indians, whom he has brought with him, exhibit extraordinary grief; the whole city assists at the interment; they bury him in the chapel he has erected many years ago to the Virgin of Loretto. And thus end the mortal part and mortal deeds of Padre Salva Tierra. But his remembrance is written in the imperishable record of those great minds who have conquered nations with the sabre of truth, and led them to a more intelligent and happy condition.

Jayme Bravo, after the burial of PADRE SALVA TIERRA, proceeds to Mexico, lays the condition of the Californian missions before the Vice-Royal Council, obtains an appropriation of four thousand dollars for the building and equipment of a vessel for the mission service, three thousand and twenty-two dollars for discharging the debts due at the death of PADRE SALVA TIERRA, and eighteen thousand two hundred and seventy-five dollars for the pay of the soldiers and sailors. While these things are transpiring in Mexico, a terrible hurricane, accompanied by violent rains, sweeps over California. Padre Ugarte's house, and the church at Loretto, are levelled to the ground; and the Padre himself stands by the side of a rock exposed to the tempest for twenty-four hours. At San Xavier, the channels used for irrigating the lands are filled with stones, and the water thrown in torrents over the fields. Both soil and sprouting crops are carried away. The same misfortune occurs at Mulege. The blasts of the tempests are so terrific at the garrison, that a Spanish boy named Matheo, is taken up in one of their gyrations and never seen more! Tornadoes of this kind are frequent in California But the Padres have seen none equal to this for violence and continuance. What little soil has been found in the country has been dislodged and swept into the sea; the country is laid waste; its rocks are bare; its plains and vales are covered with heaps of stones.

CHAPTER XII.

Padre Bravo in Mexico—Return to California—First ship built in North-west America—Expedition to the Guaycuros—Nuestra Sennora del Pilar de la Paz—Founding Nuestra Sennora de Gaudalupe—Burning of Idols—A Famine—Locusts—A Pestilence—The Dying—Explorations by Land and Sea—Indian Country—Dreadful Sufferings—Tempests—Water-Spouts—Return of the Explorers.

THUS stands the condition of the Californian missions in 1711. More than five hundred thousand dollars of private benefactions have been expended upon them; and the twenty-five thousand more lately granted by the government, have been invested, and chiefly lost in disasters by sea and land. Now the crops are destroyed, and the utter annihilation of these establishments is anticipated in the course of the year.

But Jayme Bravo is in Mexico. He collects a few provisions and goods, and accompanied by Padre Sebastian de Sistiaga in a Peruvian vessel presented to the missions by the Viceroy, arrives at Loretto in July, 1718, and gives new energy to the missions. The founding of the San Miguel by Padre Tamaral, in 29° and odd minutes N. among the mountains near the Gulf, is one of the features of returning hope. Soon after this Padre's arrival at his station, two neighboring settlements of Indians are baptised. After this he, with innumerable hardships, crosses the mountains to the settlement of the Cadigomo tribe. Here he meets with the Indians from the settlements of La Purissima Concepcion, and accompanies them home. He finds the soil of their fields washed away by the late tempest, but determines to establish the mission La Purissima among them. And after years of toil, the zealous man builds a parsonage and church, brings several maize fields under cultivation, opens a mule track over the mountains to the mission of Santa Rosalia, and extends his jurisdiction over forty settlements, situated within a circuit of ninety miles around him.

Many years ago the Philippine Islands were discovered and settled by Spain. Soon a considerable trade sprung up between them and the Spanish possessions in Mexico. Indeed the products of the Philippine Islands destined for old Spain, are landed at Accapulco, carried across the country on mules, and reshipped for Old Spain at the port of Vera Cruz. The passage from these islands to the Mexican coast is made, for the greater part, through the Chinese seas, to latitude 30° N. Here voyagers fall in with the variable winds, which take them to the American coast, between latitudes 30° and 40° N. At this point, during the spring, summer and autumn, they meet the northwesterly winds, which drive them down the coast to Accapulco. In these early times navigation is imperfectly understood. That ocean too is chiefly unknown. Navigators are not familiar with its currents, and consequently every voyage across its trackless waters is hazardous and prolonged. And when they reach the American coast, the crews are sick with the scurvy; and they should land for a supply of fresh provisions. But while no harbor is known, from Cape San Lucas to the remote north, at which wood, water and other necessary relief can be had, the ships are obliged to keep down the coast to Mazatlan, Accapulco, or some other port, before they make their first landing, after leaving the East Indies; a distance of more than eleven thousand miles. And when they arrive at these ports, it frequently happens that nearly all the crew are irrecoverably diseased, or dead. In order to avoid this dreadful evil, the Spanish crown has often ordered the missionaries to explore the coasts for a bay surrounded by a country suitable for the settlement of a colony. This they have often attempted, but the want of proper animals in their progresses, and the miserable character of the craft used in their voyages, have thus far prevented the attainment of their wishes. But Padre Ugarte now determines to survey both the Pacific and

Gulf coasts of the peninsula. His means are so small, however, in every respect, that his brethren do not perceive how he will do it. He wants provisions, men and a ship. And such is the condition of public feeling in Mexico, and such the difficulty of journeying there, that he cannot hope for aid from his friends in that quarter. But who knows the wealth of exhaustless energy! Padre Ugarte will build a ship in California!! He has, however, neither plank, timber, sails, nor rigging, tar, nor any other necessary materials for such a work; nor has he either a builder or shipwright, sawyer, or other naval artificers; and if he had, there is no food for their support; and worse than all, he has no money wherewith to supply any of these deficiencies. But the Padre says the King's orders must be obeyed; that this cannot be done without the ship; and therefore the ship must be built irrespective of means. The sufferings of his fellow beings also demand it. The people of the garrison and some of the Padres smile at Padre Ugarte's resolution against what seems to them an impossibility. But they do not estimate the creative powers of a mind bent on the accomplishment of its desires. He obtains a builder from Senora, and makes preparations for bringing timber from the opposite coast, as he has done for the erection of his churches. But hearing of a grove of large trees two hundred miles north of Loretto, he changes his determination, and in September, 1719, goes with his builders, two soldiers and some Indians to Mulege. Here he remains a day with Padre Sistiaga, and then strikes out for that line of mountains which overhangs the mission of Gaudalupe. They climb the heights and scour the barren plains; endure inexpressible difficulties and toils; and at last discover a considerable number of Guarivos trees of suitable size; standing, however, in such bottoms and sloughs, that the builder declares it impossible to get them to the sea. The Padre, disregarding this suggestion, goes to Loretto; makes preparations for a vigorous effort to build a ship of Californian timber; returns to the north; levels rocks, cuts away brush; and making a road ninety miles in length from Mulege to the timber, fells it, saws it into planks, transports them to Mulege, and in four months builds a vessel and launches with his own hands, in September, 1720, the first ship ever built on the northwest coast of North America!!

In this herculean labor the Padre has employed his entire means. The little valuables sent him by his friends in Mexico and elsewhere, have not been spared. Even his wardrobe has been freely distributed among the laborers. He himself has swung the axe, has used the whip-saw, the chisel and the hammer; he has risen with the dawn, and invoking the smiles of Heaven and the aid of ministering spirits in his toil of soul and body, kindly called his men to their tasks. They famish, and so does he. And when the fatigues of each day are over, the jutting rocks are their resting-place; a few hides their bed. Yet the ship is built. High on her stern, firmly affixed to her bulwarks, is raised the symbol of their faith. Her name, how appropriate, is, the "Triumph of the Cross." During the progress of the work, Jayme Bravo, as purveyor of the missions, goes to the coast of Cinaloa to procure goods and provisions. On his arrival there he is surprised to find letters from the Provincial of Mexico, ordering him to Guadalaxara for ordination. He accordingly ships his supplies and travels with all speed to that city; is admitted to holy orders; and by direction of his superior, proceeds to Mexico to procure aid for the missions.

His energetic labors are crowned with success. On the fifteenth of March, 1720, the council orders a bark built, to sail between Accapulco and Peru, to be delivered to Padre Jayme Bravo, together with the arms and stores which he desires. The means of founding a new mission at La Paz, are also furnished by the Marquis de Villa Puente; and Padre Bravo is designated as its priest and founder. With a new ship, therefore, well laden with supplies, and with new hopes for all the missions, and especially well furnished for his new work at La Paz, the Padre Jayme Bravo sails from Accapulco in July, 1720, and in August of the same year enters the harbor of Loretto, amidst a general burst of joy and religious thanksgiving of the starving people on shore. Comfort and joy reign again throughout the missions. The Padres and the garrison are clothed again; and the means being furnished, their thoughts are again turned to the establishment of other missions. Padre Jayme Bravo leads the new undertaking. Two expeditions are therefore projected; one by land and another by water. The former is designed to open a land communication between Loretto and the site of the intended mission; the other for the conveyance of the men and provisions, and other necessaries of the enterprise. The forces intended for the expedition over land rendezvous at San Juan Baptista Ligui, under command of Padre Clemente Guillen. Padre Ugarte leads the other. He embarks on board the "Triumph of the Cross" with Padre Bravo, the soldiers and Indians, and a good stock of stores and utensils. They arrive in safety at the bay of La Paz. This is in the country of the Guaycuros, or Pericues, who have been grievously wronged by Admiral Otondo and the Spanish pearl fishermen. They are consequently inimical to the Spaniards, and will perhaps make deadly war upon them as they land. But it soon appears that those prisoners from the fishing barks, whom Padre Salva Tierra has returned to their homes, have given to their countrymen such an account of the Padre's kind treatment as disposes them to friendship. Some of them appear in arms; but as soon as they see the costume of the Padres, their arms are laid aside. Seated on the ground, they allow the Padres to approach, and accept with high demonstrations of pleasure, various presents. The object of the expedition is made known. They are assured by the Padres that it is for their benefit They have come to found a mission among them: to make peace between them and the Indians of the neighboring islands: to teach them agriculture and the useful arts, and to instruct them in the principles of the Christian religion. Thereupon the Indians receive them as friends, and give them permission to erect the cross and consecrate their shores to God. Huts are now erected for all the people; the stores and beasts are brought ashore; a piece of ground is cleared for a church and a village; and to the great surprise and delight of the Indians, a mission is founded among them.

The expedition by land, under Padre Guillen, has not yet arrived; and much disquietude is awhile felt for its fate. But it is soon changed to gladness. Three hundred miles have been travelled, over mountains, through woods and morasses; and as the sun is falling on the brown heights in the west, a salute of musketry is heard on the northern shore of the bay; it is returned by the ship; and the boats are immediately sent over for Padre Guillen and his company. They are worn, naked, hungry, and thirsty; and with joy only known to themselves, they bathe in the surf, drink the water from the spring, and eat the food of their brethren in the new mission at La Paz. Padre Ugarte labors three months at La Paz, in establishing Padre Bravo in his mission. And now having confirmed the league of peace with the Indians by numerous acts of benevolence and Christian love, he takes a most affectionate leave of Padre Bravo and the soldiers who remain with him, and embarks for Loretto. Padre Guillen is so much worn with his land expedition, that he also returns by sea. The Ligui Indians who accompanied him, follow back the path by which they came. Padre Bravo, as all others in charge of these missions have done before, learns the Indian language; builds a parsonage, church and huts; and with the greatest assiduity, applies himself to gain the affection of the natives, civilize and instruct them, and relieve them from want. As a reward of his labor, more than six hundred children and adults receive baptism: and more than eight hundred adults are assembled in three well regulated settlements, called Nuestra Sennora del Pilar de La Paz, Todos Santos, and Angel de la Guarda. He also, as he pursues his holy labors, discovers some tracts of arable land sixty miles distant, which he annually plants with maize. All this Padre Bravo accomplishes single handed in seven years.

In the year 1720, while the Padres are yet at La Paz, a mission is founded by Padre Everard Hellen, among mountains in latitude 27° N., thirty leagues northwest of San Ignacio, thirty from Concepcion, and from sixty to seventy north of Loretto. The climate of this location is cold and unhealthy. But the Indians repair to it from the neighboring settlements, and express the utmost joy that the Padre, after long solicitations, has come to give them the religion of the white man. This mission is dedicated to Nuestra Sennora de Gaudalupe. In the midst of the labor of erecting the edifices of the mission, the Padre visits the most distant of the surrounding settlements, to instruct the aged and sick, who are unable to come to him. During his absence for these works of charity, the captain, soldiers and Indians, forward the erection of the church, parsonage and other buildings of the mission; so that at the end of six weeks, it is in so good a condition that the captain, leaving a guard of four soldiers, returns to Loretto.

Such is the zealous industry of Padre Hellen, and the interesting attention of the Indians, that on Easter eve, 1721, he baptizes a few converts. And now from all the villages come applications for instruction and baptism. The good Padre finds it difficult to make the Indians understand, that some knowledge and the abandonment of their old practices are necessary, before they can receive the sacred rite. He exhorts them to give up the trumperies used in their heathenish ceremonies, and worship Jehovah. At length they bring him a large quantity of pieces of charmed wood, feathers, cloaks, deer's feet, &c., which he commits publicly to the flames, while he receives the transfer of their faith to the religion of the cross. Thus the Padres are making all desirable progress in the spiritual culture of the Indians, and everything promises well. But the following years, 1722 and '23, are very disastrous to their feeble settlements; and especially so to Gaudalupe. The whole country is overrun with locusts The fruits, the chief sustenance of the Indians, are entirely destroyed. The maize and other supplies in the granaries, are distributed to save them from famine. But in Gaudalupe, even these are insufficient. The Indians are therefore compelled to subsist on the locusts; and the consequence is a terrible epidemic, by which great numbers are destroyed. They are afflicted with painful ulcers of a most loathsome character. During this epidemic, Padre Hellen has to fill the offices of physician, nurse, confessor, priest, and father. He endures almost incredible fatigue; flies from one village to another; administers medicine, prepares food, and smoothes with a woman's tenderness, the rude couches of his suffering children. Thus he continues till the sickness ends; when worn out with the multiplicity and the character of his labors, he hails the approach of a season of rest with joy and thanksgiving. But scarcely does it come, when another still more fatal pestilence breaks out among them. A dysentery unusually fatal summons the fainting energies of the good Padre to another effort. He again enters upon his charitable offices, going from rancheria to rancheria, like an angel of mercy, consoling, comforting, praying and blessing. At last the consequences of his severe labor fall upon himself in a distressing hernia, and defluxion of the eyes, so extremely painful, that he is obliged to leave his flock and retire to Loretto. In a few months he is sufficiently restored, however, to return to his duties, and his afflicted Indians receive him with every demonstration of faithful love and veneration. The Padre avails himself of this attachment to draw them to his faith so effectually, that, in 1726, seventeen hundred and seven converts of all ages are the fruit of Padre Hellen's devout labors. Some, living at a distance, are attached to the more contiguous missions of Santa Rosalia and San Ignacio. But twenty rancherias remain to Padre Hellen. These he maintains in the most peaceful and gentle intercourse with each other and with himself. They are divided into villages of four rancherias.

with each a chapel. And in these humble sanctuaries, as often as the Padre visits them, the red men gather and pay their devotions to the true God! The progress made in spiritual improvement is equal to his most ardent desires. But the nature of the country forbids equal advancement in the arts of civilized life. They cannot raise the small grains; and their only resource is the cultivation of maize and the raising of cattle. These are procured by the Padre; and with the native fruits afford them a comfortable subsistence. The justice and kindness of the Padre win him the love and esteem of all the Indians; and he desires to live and die among them. But his health again failing, and his superior regarding him with more tenderness than he does himself, transfers him to an easier office in Mexico. And thus, having spent sixteen years in the most arduous and faithful discharge of his duties as a missionary in California, he, with grief and tears, in 1735, takes leave of the Indians of Santa Guadalupe.

While these labors are being prosecuted, a very strong desire is felt by the Padres to extend the commercial and civil advantages of California by the establishment of colonies, garrisons, and good harbors, for the accommodation of the Philippine and Chinese ships. In order to accomplish this, it is desirable to do three things; first, to take a minute survey by water, of the Pacific coast, from Cape San Lucas northward, in search of such harbors; second, to pursue the same search by a land expedition, skirting the coast between the same points; and third, to survey the Californian Gulf, in order to ascertain whether the peninsula be really such, or an island, cut off from the main land by a channel at the north end Great difficulties oppose the prosecution of all these enterprises by the feeble powers of the Padre. But after much deliberation, it is resolved to undertake the two last. The survey of the Gulf being deemed the most difficult and important, Padre Ugarte determines to take charge of it himself, and while he is making the necessary preparation, he desires Padre Guillen to attempt the land tour, on the Pacific Coast.

They learn from the narrative of Viscayno, who has surveyed the coast northward from Cape San Lucas, in the preceding century, that there is a spacious bay in latitude 23° or 24° N.; and to this point Padre Guillen directs his steps in 1719, accompanied by a party of soldiers, and three bodies of Californians, armed after the manner of the natives. They travel over a rough, barren, craggy country, and are obliged to use the greatest caution to prevent the natives from cutting them off. Twenty-five days they journey thus, and at last reach the bay of Magdalena; a beautiful sheet of water reposing in the embrace of lofty mountains. On one arm of it they find a rancheria of Indians, whom they gain over by a few presents, and enter into friendly intercourse with them. From them they learn that there is but one well of fresh water in the vicinity; but that on a neighboring island called Santa Rosa, there is an abundant supply. They have no means, however, of crossing to it. The whole region proves so rough and divided, between marshes and inaccessible piles of rock, as to be worthless. They therefore make a circuit of four leagues from the sea to the rancheria San Benito de Aruy. Here they receive from the Indians a very discouraging account of the scarcity of water, on the whole coast. Notwithstanding this, the Padre is anxious to survey the country from north to south, and uses all his eloquence to induce the soldiers and Californians to undertake it. But being fatigued and disheartened, they refuse to proceed. The Padre yields reluctantly to the necessity of the case, and taking some friendly Indians of the coast with him as guides, commences his return to Loretto. From the superior knowledge that the guides possess, they accomplish their backward journey in fifteen days; and once more congratulate themselves on their arrival at the garrison.

Their report does not much encourage the hope of Padre Ugarte in relation to his expedition by sea But having made the best preparations in his power, he sets sail from the bay of Loretto on the fifteenth of May, 1721, with the "Triumph of the Cross," and a boat called the Santa Barbara, to be used in sounding such waters as are too shallow for the larger vessel. The Santa Barbara has eleven feet keel and six feet beam. She carries eight persons. The bilander carries twenty; six of whom are Europeans, and the rest Indians. Of the former, two have passed the straits of Magellan, another has made a voyage to the Philippine Islands and Batavia, and another has been several times to Newfoundland. The pilot passes for a man of learning and experience; and thus supported, Padre Ugarte departs on his momentous enterprise. He takes but a small stock of provisions, expecting to receive a full supply from the mission on the opposite coast of Pimeria. The winds bear them safely to the bay of Concepcion, where Padre Ugarte visits the mission of Santa Rosalia, and spends some hours in social pleasure with Padre Sistiaga. Hence they pass the islands of Salsipuedes. From these they cross the Gulf to the harbor of Santa Sabina and the bay of San Juan Baptista. Here they observe Indians standing on the shore, who flee as the boat nears them. When the Padre lands, he sees a rude cross set up in the sand. The simple solitary sign speaks to the good man's heart. He bows before it, and the crews prostrate themselves in reverence at its foot. This is enough. The Indians, reassured by this act, shout a friendly welcome, and rush from their concealment. They have known the venerable Salva Tierra; and the strangers' reverence for the cross allays all their fears; so strong have been their love and respect for that great man, that they put all trust in his brethren; and are so impatient to be near the Padre Ugarte, that they swim to the ship, and manifest their joy by kissing his hands and face, and embracing his feet. The good Padre's heart is deeply touched by these tokens of confidence and love, and having sent two of them with a letter to the Padre of San Ignacio, and distributed some presents among the others, makes preparations to procure a supply of water. For this purpose all the casks are immediately put on shore. They have no interpreter, but the

Indians seem to enter into some dispute relative to the casks. By and by they all take leave, intimating by signs that they will return with the next sun. The Padre and the crew grow apprehensive. What do the Indians mean? It cannot be known. But being late, they go on board, and wait the event. Night comes on; but no hostile savages break its silence. With the early morning, however, the dreaded savages are seen returning in troops, with rush buckets filled with water; the men with two, and the women one each. The faithful creatures, understanding the want implied by the empty casks, have visited their mountain springs during the night, and now rejoice to pour their crystal treasures into the good Padre's vessels. Repaying their kindness as liberally as his small means will permit, he undertakes to visit their kinsmen on a neighboring island. The pinnace and bilander are piloted by two of these Indians. A small party in a canoe row in advance of the ships, during the night. At dawn they are in a narrow channel full of rocks and sand spits; and notwithstanding their precautions, the bilander grounds on a shoal and requires all the efforts of her crew for some hours to get her off.

This period of anxiety over, another begins; for now the canoe and pinnace have disappeared. The bilander therefore goes on, though dangers beset her on every side, and after three days of tacking and sounding, reaches a tortuous channel leading into a large bay. In this lie the pinnace and canoe near the island they are seeking. Thither they direct their course without more difficulties or delays. As they approach, the natives appear on the shore, armed and shouting with the intention of intimidating the strangers. But their countrymen swimming ashore in advance, inform them that Padre Salva Tierra's brother is come in the ship to see them. Hearing this, they lay down their arms and express the liveliest sentiments of joy. The bilander having dropped her anchor, the Padre is earnestly solicited to go on shore But being attacked with the most excruciating pains throughout his person, from the chest downward, he reluctantly foregoes the pleasure of complying with their invitation. These pains have followed him occasionally since the severe exposure which he endured in the harbor of Seris. The Indians, seeing that illness prevents his leaving the ship, construct a number of small light floats, and send aboard a deputation of forty or fifty persons, requesting that he will occupy, during his indisposition, a house which they have erected for him on the beach. The good Padre cannot refuse this proffer of sympathy, and though every motion is agony, gives directions to be placed in the boat and rowed ashore. On landing, he is treated with great consideration. The islanders have formed themselves in double file from the waterside to the house; the men on one side and the women on the other. Between these lines he is borne to the dwelling. It is a small wigwam constructed of green boughs, fronting pleasantly on the open bay. Here the suffering Padre being seated, the people who have lined his pathway, come in one by one, first the men, then the women, and passing along, bow their heads that he may lay his hand upon them, and bless them. The Padre conceals his bodily agonies with great heroism, and receives them with much pleasantness and regard.

This ceremony over, the islanders gather about for instruction. He cannot remain sufficient time to do this; and recommending them to go to the Mission del Populo, and bring thither an Indian teacher, who will answer their inquiries and teach them the precepts of the gospel, he re-embarks and continues his survey. He soon afterward discovers a small open bay, where his little fleet comes to anchor. His supplies are now nearly exhausted. It therefore becomes him to hasten his explorations. Accordingly he sends the pinnace to survey the coast by sea, and three men to examine it by land. The latter return on the second day. They have taken an outline of the neighboring land, and have seen a pool of stagnant water, and some mule tracks in the path leading from it. The Padre sees much in these tracks, and despatches two seamen with orders to follow them. These arrive on the third day at the Mission of Concepcion la Caborca. Here they find Padre Luis Gallardi, to whom they deliver Padre Ugarte's letters, addressed to himself and the Padre Missionary of San Ignacio. These being found to contain urgent petitions for the promised supplies, the Padre Gallardi immediately sets out with such small quantities as he can collect at so short notice.

Padre Ugarte is still suffering the most excruciating tortures. The only position which he can endure, is on his knees. He has been twelve days in these dreadful agonies, unable even to go on shore. But now hearing of the arrival of Padre Gallardi, and the expected visit of the Padre Missionary from San Ignacio, he determines, if possible, to receive them ashore. It is no easy thing for him to leave the ship. But at last it is accomplished; and he travels a league and a half to meet his visiters.

The meagre supplies which they bring him are a source of anxiety to the host and his guests. The pinnace, too, is still absent. She was sent to survey the coast at the same time that the men were despatched by land. The shores of the Gulf have been searched for a great distance north and south, but no trace of her being found, she is nearly given up for lost. The bilander, too, is in continual danger from the agitation of the sea. She has already parted one of her cables; and now a heavy sea carries away her bowsprit, on which is mounted the "Holy Cross!" This causes great consternation. Fortunately a returning wave throws most of her bowsprit back; but the cross is still at the mercy of the waves! and the fears of the crew increase. Heaven frowns on their labors, and has removed from them the symbol of its mercy. The next day, however, an Indian recovers the sacred emblem, and it is again planted in triumph on the prow. Attention is now turned to obtaining wood and water. The former is easily procured in the glen near the shore; but the latter they bring from a spring several miles distant. While thus engaged, they rejoice to see three of the pinnace's crew approaching them. They relate that after weathering a very rough sea, and being several times in imminent danger, they cast anchor at sunset in a large shallow bay, with two fathoms water, and went to rest. On the following morning they were in a singular predicament for seamen, out of sight—not of land—but of water!! The sea had retired. What should be done? No water, either fresh or salt, was in sight, and the supply of provisions was very scanty. Some of them resolved therefore, to leave the pinnace in search of water and food. Finding none, however, and seeing nothing but famine and death before them, they concluded to travel down the coast to Yaqui. The pinnace, however, was visited by another flood tide, which her exhausted crew improved to get her afloat. Her keel had been much damaged. This they repaired, and immediately laid their course for the bilander. Four days after leaving her unfortunate berth she rejoins her companion. They now determine to depart from this ungenerous region and its treacherous waters, where neither food, fresh water, fuel nor home for man are to be found, but a mere wilderness of lonely shores. Somewhat disheartened by these unpropitious circumstances, Padre Ugarte, on the second of July, turns his prow westward for California. On the third day afterward he drops the anchor of the bilander and sends the pinnace ashore to talk with some Indians, who, at the sight of the fleet, have lined the shore, all armed in their native style. Before the men leave the pinnace the Indians draw a line on the sand, and intimate by signs it will not be safe for their visiters to cross it. A few presents, however, and some pantomiming, establish affairs on a better footing. They conduct the Padres and people to their rancheria, at which is abundance of water.

After remaining a short time with these savages, they journey about nine leagues along the coast and find five watering places, with a rancheria at each. The Bilander continuing her survey, at length casts anchor in a large bay; but finding the current so strong as to prevent her riding head to the wind, Padre Ugarte sends the pinnace down the coast in search of a better harbor, while the pilot goes ashore in the boat seeking an anchorage farther up the bay, returns next day with the boat in so shattered a condition, that it is with difficulty the people are taken on board before she parts asunder. The pilot reports that he left her on the sand and went a short distance to a rancheria; that while there exchanging friendly intercourse with the Indians, the tide came in with tremendous force, and threw the boat so violently upon the rocks, that she separated from stem to stern; that the Indians offered them timber to build another; but as this was impossible, they drew the nails from the oars, fastened the two parts together, and using their sounding line and painter for oakum, and substituting clay for pitch, caulked the seam. All night they were thus employed, the Indians kindly rendering them whatever assistance was in their power; and the next day keeping near the shore with their crazy leaky boat, they reached the bilander as related. In a short time the pinnace arrives, having cruised forty leagues and discovered no harbor.

The bilander now again stands northward, and in a few days finds herself sailing in waters whose variable hue indicates her approach to the outlet of some great river. Padre Ugarte keeps the pinnace sounding ahead, and after standing across, and making some northing, comes to anchor on the Peninsula side, near the mouth of the Colorado of the west. It is disgorging a great volume of angry waters, laden with grass, weeds, trunks of trees, burned logs, timbers of wigwams, &c. There has evidently been ruthless work inland. Terrible storms, accompanied with thunder and lightning, have visited the voyagers during the night, and spread over the country, whence the river issues. The men are anxious, as soon as the flood subsides, to go up and survey this stream. But Padre Ugarte thinks the floods beneath, and the angry clouds above, will render the undertaking hazardous. Beside, himself and several of his crew are very ill. They therefore cross the western mouth of the Colorado, and anchor in four fathom water, opposite the island which divides the outlet. From this point they have a distant view of the union of the Peninsula with the main land. The Padre is desirous of exploring this region more particularly; but ill health and the great danger to which his vessel is exposed from the impetuosity and height of the tides, make him hesitate. The pilot is satisfied from the present height of the tides that they are at the head of a gulf; and that the waters beyond it are those of the Colorado. The danger of remaining in this place becoming more and more imminent, they at length hold a council, at which it is determined to return to California. Their decision is received by the men with a general acclamation of applause, and greatly to the satisfaction of all, they weigh anchor on the sixteenth of July, 1721, for the port of Loretto.

Their course lies down the middle of the Gulf; sometimes standing toward one shore and sometimes the other; in order to note more particularly the islands and shoals, which fill these waters. Meantime they are visited by tremendous tempests and storms of rain; and the Padre, fearing for the people in the pinnace, which is without a deck, urges the mate to leave her and come with her crew on board of the bilander. But that officer trusting to his own craft, informs the Padre, that if he will furnish him with provisions, he will sail directly to Loretto; and to secure safety in so doing, will keep so near the shore as to be able to run in, should any accident render such proceeding necessary. They therefore separate, and each pursues his own course. The bilander, after much trouble, arrives at the islands of Salsipuedes. She is here obliged, by the winds and strong currents, to lie at anchor for several nights. At last, however, she weathers the Islands of Tiburon. But such is the force of the currents, that in six hours they lose the labor of eight days. Meantime the tempests continue almost every night with frightful fury. The hungry waters roar around the frail bark, and the winds and storms scourge her as if she were some doomed thing, laboring under their curse. But the men take courage, for the "Triumph of the Cross" is a special object of Divine favor. Three successive nights the fires of Saint Elmo light the cross at the mast head, and no evil can befall them after such evidence of God's protection. They are encouraged, therefore, to make a third attempt to escape from this dangerous neighborhood. Eight days struggling are vain. The currents and storms will not suffer them to depart; and at last they resolve to come to anchor at a convenient place which they discover near one of the islands, and go on shore. This begins now to be a matter of necessity on account of the sickness which has disabled all the crew except five. Some have the scurvy, and others are suffering from the effects of the sea water, which, farther up the Gulf, in the vicinity of the Colorado, has been so poisonous, as to produce painful, obstinate sores, and sharp pains in many parts of the body. Padre Ugarte himself, besides his other indispositions, is afflicted with the scurvy; and it is essential that he take means to recover health. The Padre, notwithstanding his illness, is desirous to go in the boat to the Seris coast, and thence by land to Guaymas. But the bare mention of his departure causes such dejection among the crew, that he promises not to leave them if it cost his life to remain.

They lie at anchor in this place about four days; during which time they are visited by a tempest more violent than any that preceded it. At length to their inexpressible joy, on the eighteenth of August, they escape these vexations, and are once more in an open sea. On the Sunday morning following, they hail a most happy omen to their future voyage. Three beautiful rainbows hang over the islands they have just weathered; bright arches of promise rising above the clouds that have so long lowered over them. The sick too are now

Water spouts.—P. 219

all recovering, and everything promises fairly to the buffeted mariners. Their hopes are vain. Other misfortunes are in reserve, more frightful than any they have encountered. For just before they reach the bay of Concepcion, a storm comes up from the north-east so very suddenly, that they have barely time to furl the topsails and reef the foresail, before its fury reaches them. The lightning falls around them, as if it would scorch an ocean to ashes, and the thunder-peals shake the firmament; the rain falls like the pouring of an upper sea, and the wind ploughs the ocean into mountains! In the height of this raging war, the terrified mariners discover a water-spout not more than a league distant, travelling directly toward the ship, with the speed of the wind! They fall upon their knees before the cross, and implore the protection of "Our Lady," and their patron saints. They spare neither prayers, vows, nor entreaties! And suddenly when the foe is almost upon them, the wind shifts and drives it among the thirsty mountains of California. It discharges its devastating energies upon their barren sands and rocks! Padre Ugarte says, that among all the dangers of the voyage, this was the time of greatest consternation.

About the first of September, the vessel comes to anchor in the bay of Concepcion; and they repair in boats to Mulege, to partake the hospitality of Padre Sistiaga. After spending about two weeks in recruiting the sick, they return to their voyage, and soon after arrive at Loretto. To their great joy they find the pinnace has arrived four days in advance of them. Thus ends this eventful and important voyage. It serves to satisfy the Padres of many things which before were doubtful; namely, that on the coast of California are some few watering places near the shore; that the Indians are kind, gentle, and willing to be instructed; while those on the main coast, east of the Gulf, are sluggish, ungenerous, and unwilling to enter into any intercourse with the whites. They are also now convinced that California is no island, but a peninsula; and that all their plans for extending the missions so as to form a chain of connection with those in Pimeria are feasible. They have also obtained a much more accurate knowledge of the Gulf and its islands, shoals and currents, than they ever before possessed; so that the difficulties and dangers of any future voyage are much lessened. Great satisfaction is felt at these results; and yet the Padres grieve that they have not found a safe harbor, as their King has desired, in which the distressed seamen of the ships, bound from the Philippine Islands to Acapulco, may anchor and be spared by timely care, a dreadful death from the scurvy. The Padres still consider it their duty to pursue this object. They feel a moral, as well as national obligation to prevent this suffering. It can only be done by discovering a harbor on the Pacific coast, secure from seaward storms and convenient to fresh water. With a view to this, Padre Tamaral surveys nearly the whole coast from his mission to Cape San Lucas, and far northward also, from the same point; but all to no purpose. It is found inhospitable and barren near the sea; and destitute of a harbor in which ships may lie with any safety.

Padre Ugarte, on his return to Loretto, directs a new survey of the same coast as far north as possible. And in compliance with this order, a small detachment of soldiers under the captain of the garrison goes to the mission of Santa Rosalia de Mulege, and thence with Padre Sistiaga, to the mission of Guadalupe. On the nineteenth of November, 1721, it leaves for the coast, and advances northward to 28° N. In this excursion they find three pretty good harbors, with plenty of water and wood, but no arable land near them. The largest one is not far from the mission of San Xavier; and may therefore be supplied with provisions, timber, &c., from that post. Highly gratified with these discoveries, they return to Loretto and report to Padre Ugarte what they have found. The Padre sends a narrative of his own voyage, together with the map and journal of his pilot, and Padre Sistiaga's account of his discoveries, to the Viceroy of Mexico, to be transmitted to the Court, for the information and action of the Government. Meanwhile the Padres turn their attention to the spiritual conquest of this wild country.

CHAPTER XIII.

A Mission Founded—A Tornado—Death—Another Mission Founded—A Vineyard—A Harvest—Indications of Trouble—A Murder—Forbearance—Three Murders—Measures taken for Defence—The Insurgents Captured—A Trial—A Sentence—A Reprieve—Death of Padre Piccolo—A Visitor—Further Steps in the Conquest—A Voyage—Birds—Natives—Country—Islands—A Plunge—A Shark—Death.

The Padres have lost none of their religious zeal while prosecuting these civil enterprises; and they have gained much topographical and other knowledge, which will be of general service in their future missionary labors. They have learned the practicability of extending their missions farther north. The country there is more fertile and better supplied with wood and water. The moral aspect too is more promising. The natives in that quarter are much superior in intellect, more gentle and friendly, more honest and faithful; and in every way more inviting and promising than those in the south. There, is a rich field of labor opened to them. But at the same time the condition of the southern natives renders it more necessary that they should be formed into missions. They are treacherous, vindictive, bloody; and have many vices which are unknown among the northern people. The whole nation of Pericues with its several branches of Uchities, Guaycuros and Coras, are continually engaged in destructive wars, so that no security can be enjoyed by the missions or their converts, until this entire people are brought under the influence of the Padres. To this end, during the time that Padre Ugarte has been exploring the Gulf and coast, two new missions have been founded among Pericues.

The Marques de Villa Puente, having a deep interest in the spread of the gospel in California, has endowed two missions which shall be founded between Cape San Lucas and Loretto. On receiving tidings of this, it is resolved that Padre Guillen shall leave the mission San Lucas de Malibat, and found a new mission between the Uchities and Guaycuros. Accordingly in 1721, he settles among them and lays the foundation of a church and other buildings necessary to a mission, on the shore of Aparte, forty leagues by sea, and on account of impassable mountains, sixty by land, from Loretto. The mission is dedicated to Nuestra Sennora de los Dolores, and is styled Los Dolores del Sur. The country around it is barren and desolate. The inhabitants are the most vindictive, treacherous and stupid of all the Californians. Padre Guillen has therefore no easy or pleasant task to execute. But he enters upon it with so much zeal and love, is so unsparing of his efforts, and so universally kind and gentle toward those whom he would win to his flock, that his labors are rewarded even more largely than his fondest hopes anticipate.

It is found advisable after the good Padre has been laboring here for some time, to remove his mission farther into the interior, to a place called Tanuetia, about ten leagues from the Gulf and twenty-five from the Pacific. In this region the Indians live in the wildest state. They have no villages; and the Padre is obliged to seek them in caves and woods, and among the almost inaccessible rocks of the mountains. With great labor and the most indefatigable perseverance he draws them from their retreats and forms them into six villages, called Nuestra Sennora de los Dolores, La Concepcion de Nuestra Sennora, La Incarnacion, La Trinidad, La Redempcion, and La Resurreccion. He also assembles many other wandering Indians, and erects for them the new mission of

San Luis Gonzaga. Lastly, he turns his attention to the conversion of the Indians on the Pacific coast, from the mission of San Xavier southward to the Coras; and founds among them a new mission. The Padre has now spread his labors over an immense tract of country, extending forty leagues up the Peninsula from Cape San Lucas, and embracing the whole territory from one coast to the other.

The soil of this region is extremely poor. A small tract at Aparte on which the Indians are enabled to raise sufficient maize for sustenance, is all that can be cultivated. And besides the physical difficulties incident to these desolate wastes, the Padre has savage poverty and its inseparable mental degradation, to weaken his hands and try his faith. This is peculiarly distressing to the good Padre. It appears to him impossible to bring these Indians into civilized habits of living, without the industry acquired by the cultivation of the soil. Notwithstanding all these momentous obstacles, however, (and few can appreciate them who have not seen the poor starving Indian in his native wilderness), the good Padre's labors here are so efficient and deeply grounded in the true philosophy of love, that these savages, once so vindictive and turbulent, are so changed as to stand firm during all the subsequent rebellions of the south, and offer the Padres and Christian Indians, flying from the treacherous and cruel Pericues and Coras, an affectionate and safe asylum in the mission de los Dolores del Sur. During the year 1721, another mission endowed by the Marques de la Puente, has been founded in the nation of the Coras, near Cape San Lucas, under Padre Ignacia Maria Napoli. Padre Ugarte, before embarking on his survey of the gulf, gave direction to Padre Napoli to wait the arrival of the bark with supplies from Mexico, and taking whatever he stood in need of for his new station, to proceed in the bark to La Paz, and thence by land to the Bay of Islands, the place chosen for his mission. This vessel arrives in the middle of July; and on the twenty-first, Padre Napoli embarks with four soldiers and Captain Don Estevan Rodriguez; and on the second of August, anchors at La Paz. Padre Napoli is met by the Indians with great veneration. They conduct him in procession to the church where Padre Jayme Bravo, then missionary, is waiting to receive him.

Having rested from the toil of the voyage, the Padre sends the supplies to Palmas Bay in a boat, while himself and the soldiers proceed by land for the twofold purpose of establishing some communication between the contemplated mission and La Paz, and also of inviting such Indians as they may meet on the way, to settle near him and receive instruction During the eight days of travelling through this wilderness, however, they meet no natives. The news of their approach has aroused their suspicions to such a degree, that they desert their rancherias and fly before the Padres, as if they were come to curse instead of bless them. On the twenty-fourth of August they reach their place of destination. Padre Napoli is suffering extreme pain in consequence of a fall from his mule. No Indians appear; the boat does not arrive; and the Padre therefore is troubled. One evening Padre Napoli is walking alone at some distance from the tent, when suddenly his ears are saluted by the most frightful howlings, and on looking up he sees a company of naked Indians approaching him with the most furious gestures. They are led by one of gigantic stature, painted for battle, in black and red, and partially covered by a kind of hair cloak. In one hand he has a fan of feathers, and in the other a bow and arrow. Several deer's feet and other unseemly objects dangle from a band around his waist. The Padre, concluding that his time is now come to die, commends his soul to mercy, and advances to meet the Indians. He remembers the instructions of Padre Ugarte, and concealing his fears, looks them boldly in the face, and even makes signs of contempt for their savage arts Their apparent fury is a little checked by his demeanor; and the Padre gaining courage, approaches nearer and signifies by signs that he is grieved, but not frightened by their intentions. He then proceeds with great kindness to distribute among them some trifling presents which he has about his person, and invites them to come to the tent and receive others. This treatment produces its desired effect. They follow him to the tent, where they are kindly entertained; and at length depart, bearing tokens of peace to their friends at home. They seem much pleased; but intimate as they depart that they are afraid of the mules and the Padre's dog; and that they cannot return, unless these are concealed from sight. This the Padre signifies shall be done. The next day the tent is thronged with little parties, to the number of five hundred, bringing such presents as the country affords, and receiving in return frocks of sackcloth, razors, and beads. This demonstration cheers the hearts of the Padre and soldiers. Still the boat does not arrive—and they are oppressed with fears lest she may be lost with all their supplies; for they have been here now five days. No tidings of her have reached them. They are, however, looking out on the sea at the close of the fifth day, when she makes her appearance. She has mistaken the place of rendezvous, and lain four days in a small bay a few leagues to the south.

Being relieved thus from these several troubles, they begin to clear the ground and erect the village. The Indians continue friendly and aid the work. But on a sudden they all disappear for a whole day. Now again the heart of the Padre beats with anxiety. When and how will the Indians return are questions which will arise, but which no one can answer. Toward evening he determines to go in quest of them with only one soldier and an interpreter. He finds a few, and expresses his regret that they should forsake him; when they frankly state the cause of their movement, as follows:—They are at war with the Guaycuros; the Padre is friendly to the latter, and has soldiers and Indians of that nation with him. They have watched their labors and see the walls of the church go up. For what other purpose could these be intended to answer, than a warlike one? Moreover, the Padre has that morning despatched three Guaycuros on the open road to La Paz; and the ostensible object is peaceful enough, being simply to drive in a mule laden with maize. Yet they are suspicious that some more important business lies under this affair. In short, they believe the Guaycuros are coming to massacre the whole nation. The Padre has much difficulty in removing this suspicion from their minds. At length, however, he so far recovers their confidence that a large number return to the tent. Others, still apprehensive, light large fires and keep strict watch, that the supposed enemy may not fall on them unawares. The night, however, operates unfavorably on their feelings. They are all missing again fcr two days. They look upon Padre Bravo, who speaks the Guaycuri tongue, as the head and front of their foes. His presence keeps their fears and suspicions continually inflamed. And though, when the mule and the Guaycuros return from La Paz, they see that Padre Napoli has told them truth, still they cannot so far quiet their fears as to return to their dwellings. Thus they continue between hope and fear for several days. Meantime the Padre continues his labors at the mission; and by and by the Indians, finding their fears unfounded, begin to come in. The women bring their children for baptism, and the men offer perpetual friendship. Peace is also concluded between the Guaycuros and Coras and celebrated with the usual festivities.

On the fourth of November Padre Napoli baptizes twenty-nine of their children, and everything seems to promise well for their intercourse with the Indians. But as almost everything which was brought from La Paz, even to the furniture of the altar, has been distributed among them, and as the supply of provisions is growing short, Padre Napoli finds it necessary to evacuate his post. He accordingly leaves the little furniture and the few remaining utensils in the care of some of the oldest and most faithful of the savages, and promising a speedy return, goes with Padre Bravo and his men to La Paz.

In January he returns to his mission, and finds that during

his absence, a band of forty depredators, from a neighboring island, called Cerralvo, has visited the mission, and finding neither Padre nor guard in possession, killed six baptized children, two women and one man; and taking another prisoner, returned to their homes. The Padre is sad at this unprovoked barbarity upon his neophytes. But the Captain of the guard is so enraged, that accompanied by a small party of soldiers, he crosses to the island to chastise the savages. They flee at his approach and hide themselves among the rocks. He, however, kills a sufficient number to intimidate the living from a like attempt in future, and returns to the mission.

The confidence of the Indian converts in the Padre, is greatly increased by this punishment of their enemies. Yet the Padre does not think best to continue his mission so far from La Paz, whence all its supplies must come. Accordingly, he selects a spot called Santa Anna, situated thirty leagues from La Paz, and five from the Gulf. Here he builds a chapel and small house, and labors with much success for the establishment of Christianity. In 1723 he builds a church farther in the interior, with the intention of making it the seat of his mission. But an unavoidable accident puts an end to this design. For when the church is so far finished that the beams and rafters are laid for the roof, the Padre is summoned one day to attend the deathbed of one of his Indians. During his absence one of the terrible tempests, so common in Lower California, comes up, and the Indians take shelter in the unfinished church. The storm increases, the church is prostrated, and several Indians are buried under it! Padre Napoli hastens to the spot, and does everything in his power for the relief of the sufferers. But his benevolent acts are misunderstood. The living are thoroughly incensed at the death of their friends, and begin to concert schemes to destroy the Padre. From this they are at length dissuaded by the repeated assurances of the survivors, that they retired to the church of their own choice, so that in time all becomes quiet again. The church is built and dedicated to San Jago;

some ground cleared and sown with maize; and comfort is slowly increasing among them. He spends three years among this slothful and stupid people, during which time he baptizes ninety adults, and about four hundred children.

The Padres have now for many years sustained a limited intercourse with the Cochimies of Tierra de San Vincente. They have frequently expressed a strong desire to have a Padre among them who would teach them to become Christians. But no opportunity has offered of founding a mission in their territory, till the year 1727, when Padre Juan Baptiste Luyando, a Mexican Jesuit of fortune, arrives at Loretto, and offers not only to endow, but to be the founder of a mission. His offers are gratefully accepted by the Padres. The seat of the mission has been selected by Padre Sistiaga of Santa Rosalia Mulege, during his frequent visits among the Indians of that vicinity. To this spot, therefore, Padre Luyando travels, accompanied by nine soldiers, in January, 1728, and arrives on the twentieth of the same month. The natives having been expecting a Padre for some time, hail his arrival with much joy, and flock to his tent in great numbers. Many of them are already acquainted with the catechism, and nearly all have received some instruction from Padre Sistiaga. Padre Luyando, therefore, finds his task comparatively easy. The Indians are very readily persuaded to destroy all their implements of sorcery and abandon the foolish and superstitious arts in which they have placed their faith. Some of the Catechumens return to their rancherias after receiving baptism, but many remain. The Padre has about five hundred at the mission during the first six months. At the end of this time his provisions beginning to fail, he despatches seven of his soldiers with letters to Loretto, asking supplies; meanwhile the two that remain together with the Indians, commence building a church, which is finished and dedicated on Christmas day. The Padre's heart is so encouraged by his success that he not only undertakes the instruction of all who come to him, but likewise makes excursions in search of new objects on which to expend his labors.

He finds all his people docile, kind, vivacious, and active. Their district is well adapted to agriculture. Padre Sistiaga had some time before sown maize on some of it, which yielded well; and Padre Helen had introduced the culture of garden vegetables; for all of which the Indians have acquired a relish. So that Padre Luyando has little difficulty in leading them into agricultural pursuits. He plants with his own hands five hundred vines, besides olive and fig trees, sugar canes, and many other exotic plants. He induces the Indians to sow considerable quantities of wheat and maize annually; so that on the fourth year of his residence among them, the whole harvest amounts to a thousand bushels of wheat, and a fine quantity of maize and fruits. He also persuades them to form themselves into villages, and to erect adobie and bough-houses. He introduces cattle, and makes every effort to create among them the desires of civilized life. And there is no doubt in the Padre's mind, that the adaptation of their country to the pursuits of husbandry, will greatly facilitate his wishes for their spiritual improvement. But in the meantime all is not as fair as it seems.

The old jugglers and priests of their former religion, so lately held in great respect, see their power and wealth fading under the new order of things, and themselves becoming objects of contempt to the younger members of the tribe. It is not in the nature of civilized or uncivilized man, to bear such a change with indifference; and these men resolve to use what influence they have left, to recover their rank. Accordingly they instigate some unconverted Indians to oppose the Padre's labors by every available means. On a dark night, therefore, eight of them fall upon a catechumen, near the Padre's cottage, and murder him. After this outrage, they persuade a whole rancheria, at some distance from the mission, to refuse all intercourse with the Padre. In this neighborhood, for two years, bands of malcontents shelter themselves, and dissuade the people from yielding to any advances from the Christians. And when at length three of its people are baptized, they are obliged to take refuge in the house of the Padre, from the fury of their disaffected relatives.

To all these outrages, the Padre makes no resistance, and for the evil, returns love, patience, and uniform kindness. Indeed, were he disposed to chastise them, he has not the power. His feeble force would be useless against an active, vigilant and fearless band of savages. He therefore betrays no disposition to punish these wrongs. He has not yet learned from experience, that undue forbearance is neither wisdom nor virtue. Some of the wild unconverted Indians, therefore, restrained by no fear of chastisement, falling upon a Christian rancheria, murder two men and a little girl. The remainder succeed in escaping to the mission. The Padre's people wish to avenge this outrage, but he restrains them, in the hope that forbearance may yet be effectual with these bad men. In this he is mistaken. The savages concluding, from the quiet manner in which he submits to their treatment, and also from some kind messages and presents which the Padre has sent them, that he is helpless and fearful, are emboldened to attack other rancherias, and plunder the Christians wherever they meet them. These last outrages awaken in the Padre a determination to prevent their recurrence. He assembles his converts, and with them retires to Guadaloupe for safety. Effective measures are now taken. Three hundred and fifty converted Indians are armed; and having, by the Padre's permission, elected their own leader, they march against their foes with great spirit and determination. They find them encamped near a watering place at the base of a mountain. During the night they succeed in surrounding them, and at day-break, raising the war shouts, advance on all sides upon the sleeping enemy. Finding themselves thus completely hemmed in by a force greatly superior to their own, they lay down their arms. Only two escape. The others, thirty-four in number, are taken to the mission as prisoners.

When thanks have been duly returned for this signal and easy victory, a court is organized from the soldiers and Indian Alcaldes, for the trial of the prisoners. They are convicted of the capital crimes of rebellion, robbery, and murder, and sentenced to be removed to Loretto for punishment. They are very much dejected at the prospect of death. The Indians of the mission are elated with the hope of being permitted to execute them. But the Padres assure the prisoners that they shall not die; and reprove the unchristian exultation of their people; instructing them that as Christians they should exercise charity and forgiveness toward all men. Meantime some of the converts are so gently disposed toward the prisoners that they beseech the Padres to convene the court the next day, that the sentence may be reconsidered. The Indian converts now come before the soldiers and Indian Alcaldes, begging them to make the sentence of their enemies lighter. After some deliberation it is commuted to a certain number of lashes. The punishment is first inflicted on the principal murderer. The Padres then pray that it may be confined to him. This is most unwillingly complied with. They are therefore deprived of their arms and liberated.

The prayers of the Padres are answered in the effect which this treatment has upon their enemies. In a few months all these prisoners have become catechumens. The victory and lenity are of great service to the missionaries. The former intimidates the unconverted Indians, the latter shows the excellence of the precepts of Christianity. Padre Luyando, however, now finds his health so much impaired that he must leave the mission to recruit his exhausted energies. The Indians are deeply pained at parting with him. But his place is well filled by the kind and active Padre Sistiaga.

The years 1729 and '30 bring heavy misfortunes on the missions of California, in the death of two of the oldest and most valued laborers among them; Padre Piccolo and Padre Ugarte. Both these men have by long years of the most arduous and faithful service, woven their names inseparably with the history of California, and left in their characters and lives, an example to all who would rear the cross in the solitary wilderness. Bold, indefatigable, self-denying, just, and true men, they were, who never shrank from any duty, however severe, and were never swerved by passion or love of ease, from the line of action marked out by judgment, truth and religious faith.

Padre Piccolo expires in the garrison at Loretto, on the twenty-second of February, 1729, having lived seventy-nine years, twenty-two of which he has spent among the missions of California. Padre Ugarte follows him the next year, having been thirty years a laborer on the same ground. The deaths of these excellent men are momentous events in the missions. Their great experience, their uniform kindness, their zeal, tempered by wisdom and sagacity, their unblemished integrity, and the veneration in which their very names are held by the Indians, make them powerful co-operators with the young and active missionaries, even though age and debility forbid them a personal participation in their labors. At this time, too, their presence is particularly desired, for the southern nations, never much relied on, are growing turbulent. The unconverted among them, and there are many of these notwithstanding the efforts of Padre Bravo at La Paz, Padre Napoli at San Jago, and Padre Guillen at Dolores, lose no occasion to insult and annoy those who have embraced the cross. They become so troublesome that in 1723, Captain Rodriguez, with a company of soldiers, marched into their districts, to intimidate them, and, if possible, put an end to their outbreaks. In 1725, also, he finds it necessary to go with an armed force against some rancherias of Uchities and Guaycuros, who have been stimulated into rebellion, by a few mulattoes and mestizoes, renegades of foreign privateers, that have touched at Cape San Lucas. These difficulties will ripen into fearful scenes. Another attempt is now made to found an establishment at Palmas bay, the original seat of the mission San Jago de los Coras. It is endowed by the Donna Rosa de la Penna, cousin of the Marquis de Ville Puente. This individual also offers to endow a third, in the neighborhood of Cape San Lucas. About this time, Padre Josef de Echeveria, the Mexican agent for California, is appointed by the papal court, Visitor General of the Jesuit missions; and he resolves to commence his visitation in California. Purchasing in Cinaloa, therefore, a bark to supply the place of one that, with a year's provisions, a few weeks before has been lost, he embarks at Ahome, and on the twenty-seventh day of October, arrives safely in Loretto bay, where he is received with great respect and affection by the Padres, and their Indians. Soon after his arrival, he is attacked with a most malignant fever. For many days his life is despaired of, but he recovers; and while yet very feeble, leaves the garrison for the northern missions, with only the ensign, one soldier, and a few Indians.

The Visitor finds great cause of rejoicing in the condition of the missions. The economy, neatness and order of everything connected with them, the quiet and regular conduct of the Indian converts, and their progress in knowledge of temporal things, the patience, kindness and industry of the Padres, the good understanding between them and their people, and most of all, the progress Christianity has made in the bosom of the wilderness, touch the Padre's heart with the liveliest joy. In a letter dated the tenth of February, he says, "I was well rewarded for the fatigue and cold, were it only in seeing the fervor of these new Christian establishments. And the least I could do was to shed tears of joy at so frequently hearing God praised from the mouths of poor creatures, who very lately did not so much as know whether there was such a being."

After examining the missions of the north, Padre Echeveria prepares to visit those of the south, and establish the two missions which have been endowed at Palmas bay and Cape San Lucas. But death and ill-health among the Padres render it impossible to carry both these plans into execution. Padre Segismund Taraval has been appointed to the charge of the former, called Santa Rosa, in honor of the foundress; but does not arrive. And it is determined, therefore, to commence that at San Lucas, called San Jose del Cabo. This is a post which requires great integrity, zeal and address. Padre Tamaral, founder of the mission La Purissima, is therefore chosen to fill it. This Padre and the Visitor General embark on the tenth of March, and visiting on their way at the missions of La Paz and San Jago de los Coras, proceed to San Lucas, and finding an agreeable spot a short distance from the Cape, erect a chapel and houses; and though only about twenty families present themselves, the Padre founder enters upon his labors. As soon, however, as the Padre Visitor with his two soldiers leave the spot, they come in great numbers to Padre Tamaral, assigning as a reason for not appearing sooner, that they feared the Padres had come with the soldiers, to punish their assaults on the missions of San Jago and La Paz. Padre Tamaral makes a journey in search of the rancherias and the people whom he is to teach, and also of a better site for his mission. The present one is infested with musquitoes and other insects; the dampness and extreme heat also render it intolerable. On becoming acquainted with the country, he determines to remove the mission to a spot about five leagues from the sea; and proceeds at once to erect a chapel and houses on the new site. He labors incessantly to induce the natives who have hitherto led wandering lives, to settle in fixed habitations; and so successful is he, that in one year he has instructed and baptized one thousand and thirty-six souls; and so far as their indolent roving character will permit, has bettered their temporal welfare.

In the year 1730, Padre Tamaral undertakes to survey the islands which lie near the Pacific coast. Accompanied by six Indians, he sets out on the festival of San Xavier, and after travelling six days by land, reaches one of the capes or headlands of a large bay, which he calls San Xavier. From this point they see two islands, lying some seven or eight leagues from the coast, which they determine to visit. Accordingly having constructed a raft of timber, they pass over to the nearest one, and find it a small desert, not more than half a mile in length, and less in width. It is a bank of dry sand, with neither a drop of water, nor a leaf of verdure upon it. It is called by the Indians Asegua, on account of the immense flocks of birds which frequent it. Among these is a small jet black bird, something larger than a sparrow, which burrows in the sand, and makes its nest some four feet below the surface, retiring to it at night only, and living all day in the sea. There is another bird quite unlike any known to the Padre. It is about the size of a goose, with black wings, a snowy breast, and light-colored feet, and a beak like the carnivora. This also makes its nest three or four feet below the surface It is a lover of storm and tempest, and never retires to its nest except when the sea is calm. These birds are hunted by the Indians for food. About four or five leagues distant from this island, lies another, called by the Indians Amalgua, or fog island. It is several leagues in circumference, and of a triangular form. In its midst rises a conical mountain of considerable height. It has several fresh-water springs; but no anchorage protected from the sea. Deer and rabbits live upon it. Among the latter is a small black species with fur finer than that of the beaver. It is frequented by a variety of birds, and sea-wolves, on which its inhabitants chiefly subsist. They find also a fruit here called *mexcales*, which is juicy and very pleasant. A variety of beautiful shells lie on the shore; some of an exquisite azure hue. From the top of the mountain on this island, the explorers have a view of two other small ones, eight or ten leagues to the westward There are also in the bay of San Xavier three other small islands, which are frequented by the sea-wolf and beaver Farther northward they discover others, which they conjecture to be those that form the channel of Santa Barbara. They can obtain no information respecting these latter from the people of Amalgua. For they inform the Padre that their sorcerers have prohibited them all intercourse with their inhabitants, and even the privilege of looking toward them. The Padre finds no difficulty in persuading the people of Amalgua to accompany him to the mission. The only opposition arises from an old sorcerer. But his influence effects nothing. Even his own wife proposes to leave him if he will not go with them. And he also finally consents. They embark, therefore, on their raft for the coast; but are obliged to seek shelter from a storm, on the desert island of Asegua, and remain there several days. With the return of fair weather, they put off again for the continent. As they are floating along close in shore, they discover some sea-wolves disporting themselves on a sand bank; and the sorcerer, anxious to vent his ill-humor upon something, and being a dexterous swimmer, plunges into the water for the purpose of killing one of the animals. They all flee at his approach; but in attempting to return to the raft he is seized, in sight of the whole company, by an enormous shark! By some extraordinary feat, however, he clears himself; and, not satisfied with this, throws the blood, which issues from his wounds, at the hungry fish! He is seized a second time with a hold not so shaken off. The exasperated fish goes down with him; and no trace of his existence is left, except a faint red tinge which slowly rises, and fades into the deep green of the sea!

Padre Taraval now receives orders from the Visitor General to proceed at once to the erection of his new mission among the Coras, at Palmas bay. It is particularly desirable that it shall go into early operation. For the continual presence of the Padres is indispensable to keep these turbulent and deceitful people in subordination. All preparation being therefore speedily made, Padre Taraval travels from Loretto to the bay of La Paz, thence to the mission of San Jago, at Palmas bay, and founds his mission on the old site of San Jago. He finds his people somewhat advanced by the former efforts of Padre Napoli, and the visits which they have received from Padres Carranco and Tamaral.

Nevertheless, he meets with so much violent opposition, that it requires all his address to advance his objects in such manner as not to arouse these Indians' malevolence. But he succeeds, not only in bringing a great part of the unconverted to seek baptism, but also in winning their confidence and affection to such a degree, that at a future period they save his life at the risk of their own.

CHAPTER XIV.

A Rebellion attempted—Arrival from the Seas—The Sick—Departure—Disaffection among the Indians—Insurrection—Fearful Times—Martyrdom of Padres Carranco and Tamaral—All the Missions in a State of Revolt—The Padres retire to Loretto—Aid denied by the Viceroy—It comes from the Indians themselves—The Missions in the North send Delegates to the Padres—Peace made and Padres resume their Labors—Southern Missions Recovered—Indians reduced to Subjection—Condition of the Conquest in 1745.

MEANTIME, in the winter of 1733–4, some signs of revolt have appeared in the missions San Jago and San Josef. The chief, called Boton, the offspring of an Indian and a negro, a most profligate mulatto, who has been reproved by the Padre Carranco, for some of his excesses, and afterward continuing in the same practices, has been punished publicly, allies himself with another mulatto, named Chicori, belonging to the mission San Josef, whom the Padre has also chidden on account of similar vices. These miserable men seek revenge. Accordingly they excite the unfriendly Indians in every possible way to an outbreak at San Jago. Padre Tamaral hearing of this, and unsuspicious that the like is growing in his own mission, hastens to San Jago to assist Padre Carranco in quelling the difficulties. Boton being absent when he arrives, little disposition exists among the Indians to persist; and Padre Tamaral proposes to return to his own mission. But he is informed by a friendly Indian that Boton and Chicori, with two bodies of men, are stationed on his route, to kill him. Being satisfied of the truth of this report by men dispatched to reconnoitre, the Padre sends to his catechumens at San Josef, to arm themselves and go in quest of the enemy. These, faithful to their teacher, put them to flight, burn their dwellings, and escort the Padre home in peace and triumph. The leaders of the rebellion now come in, and beg for peace. It is concluded in 1734, with the great rejoicings of both parties. When all is settled, the Indians confess their intention to have murdered all the missionaries in the country. A few days after this, some Indians who have been fishing off Cape San Lucas, come running to the mission with much joy and wonder expressed in their countenances, and inform the Padre that a large ship is near the Cape, standing directly toward the bay San Barnabe. The Padre sends a young man of Loretto to ascertain what this report means, and soon learns that a Philippine galleon has come to anchor in the bay, and has sent a party of armed men ashore for water. The mariners of this vessel are much rejoiced to hear that a mission has been erected in the neighborhood; and inform the good Padre that, besides their want of water, they are so dreadfully afflicted with the scurvy that they require his kindest attentions. The Padre, therefore, orders his Indians to collect fresh acid fruits and convey them on board. At the same time he directs the greatest part of the cattle to be driven down for the use of the afflicted mariners, encourages the Indians to assist them in filling their water vessels, and otherwise shows them every attention within his power to bestow. Under such treatment, all the sick speedily recover, except three. These are more diseased than the others; and accordingly, when the ship is ready to sail, they are invited to remain at the mission. Their names are, Don Josef Francisco de Baytos, Captain of Marines, Don Antonio de Herrera, boatswain, and the Most Rev.

Domingo de Horbigoso, of the order of San Augustine. They are commended to Padre Tamaral, by Captain Don Geronimo Montero, and the Padre Commissary, Matthias de Ibarra. The Captain informs Padre Tamaral that the galleon will always put in here for water and the recovery of the sick; and desires that a supply of cattle may be kept on hand for them. This the Padre promises, and the galleon weighs anchor for Acapulco.

The Padre takes his three patients to the mission, and devotes his tenderest skill and assiduity to their recovery. Every luxury or delicacy the region affords is kept exclusively for their comfort. He sends to the neighboring missions for the best of their stores, and gives them his own food to eat. In a word, he spares no self-denial or care for their benefit; and has the pleasure of seeing them all recover. But the boatswain is attacked by another disease, which proves fatal, and is buried with proper solemnity, in the little church. In the following April, Captain Baytos and Padre Horbigoso, being entirely recovered, leave San Josef for Mexico, in a vessel which has come up from La Paz for that purpose.

The Padre missionaries continue their labors; patiently hoping that these miserable Indians will, in time, come to such a state of comfort as shall, in some measure, compensate them for their efforts. In the summer of 1734, Padre Gordon, of La Paz, goes to Loretto to hasten the supplies for his own and the other missions of the south. Don Manuel Andres Romero, who superintends the mission during his absence, discovers some disaffection among the Indians. It seems, however, easily allayed. They appear happy and tranquil. But under this appearance, a most sanguinary spirit is at work! The Indians are becoming weary of the restraint imposed on their beastly propensities by the presence and rule of the Padres. The greatest trial, is the abrogation of their old laws, permitting polygamy. They are also prevented from entering into those bloody wars which have so long been their principal pastime; and from seeking revenge on those who injure them. Altogether, the restraint of Christianity, the personal malignity of Boton and Chicori, and the defenceless state of the missions, encourage these ignorant savages to attempt a revolt and the butchery of those whom they esteem their oppressors. It must not be understood that there are none among the converted to oppose so wicked a step, and abide by their spiritual fathers through all the troubles which follow. On the contrary, large numbers feel the deepest grief and shame at the conduct of their countrymen. But only a small portion of all the natives have ever professed Christianity. So that if none of these are unfaithful, the majority will be greatly in favor of the rebels.

The insurgents find some difficulty in concocting their plains. Their only fear is lest the arms of the soldiers shall do better execution than their own. And although among the four missions of Santa Rosa, La Paz, San Jago and San Josef, there are but seven, two of whom are invalids, they turn their first attention to disposing of them. The first act of violence, therefore, is the murder of one of Padre Taraval's soldiers, whom they fall upon when alone and unarmed, at some distance from the mission. They next repair to the Padre, and inform him that the man is suddenly taken very ill in the woods, and desires him to come to his relief. The Padre, having received some vague hints of the rising difficulties, suspects all is not right; and on questioning them closely, concludes from their confused manner, that they have murdered the man, and intend to draw him from the house alone for the same bloody purpose. He therefore declines going or sending a second soldier; but does not in any other way show suspicion or fear. In a few days this murder is followed by that of Don Andres Romero, at La Paz. This remains some time a secret among the perpetrators; so that they are encouraged by these successes to more open demonstrations in the district of San Jago; all which the Padre, from his defenceless condition and his desire to avoid provoking the Indians, suffers to pass without notice.

About this time Padre Tamaral is attacked with a dangerous disease; and being alone with the Indians of his mission, he sends for a soldier from Loretto to act as guard, nurse and physician. This soldier, after his arrival at San Jago, becomes convinced that danger broods among the savages. He communicates his thoughts to Padre Tamaral, and offers to carry him to La Paz. But the latter thinks his fear magnifies the danger, and refuses to go. The soldier declares he will not stay there to die at the hands of bloodthirsty Indians; but he cannot prevail upon the Padre to accompany him. He leaves him, therefore, and goes directly to La Paz. As usual, on his arrival, he fires his musket at a certain distance from the mission, to give notice of his approach. But no answer is made. He walks up to the house. All is silent and solitary as the tomb! A rifled portmanteau, some broken utensils and furniture, and some drops of blood on the floor, tell a story which thrills the breast of the solitary man! He hastens on to Dolores, a distance of sixty leagues, through a wilderness; a long road for a single man, when death lurks under every bush and tree!

He arrives safely, however, and immediately acquaints Padre Guillen with the state of affairs below. The Padre immediately sends instructions to his brother to withdraw to Dolores. But close upon the heels of the previous tidings, follow letters from Padre Carranco, informing him of an insurrection among the Pericues, and requesting instructions how to proceed.—Orders are therefore dispatched for all to repair to La Paz, whither he sends a canoe and seventeen faithful Indians, to bring them to Dolores. But the letters never reach the hands for which they are written! At the same time Padre Carranco sends a body of Christian Indians to Padre Tamaral at San Josef, entreating that he will permit them to escort him to his mission for safety and counsel. The Padre replies, that no signs of danger have appeared in his mission; that he thinks fear augments small things to great; that he trusts in God, whom he desires to serve in life and death; and does not think his condition such as to justify him in forsaking his mission.

The Indians who have been sent for him, on their return fall in with a party of rebels, and inform them that Padre Carranco is made acquainted with all their plans by the boy who lives in his house. They therefore change their design of falling upon Padre Tamaral. It is deemed more important to cut off Padre Carranco, in order to prevent his giving information of their purposes, or calling aid from other missions. They communicate their plans to some of the converted Indians of San Jago, and with menaces and warnings, invite them to join their party. After some wavering they do so; and the whole body moves toward the mission to take the life of their best friend and benefactor. They reach it between six and seven in the morning, on Friday, the first of October 1734.

The good Padre has just left the chapel after Mass, and is engaged at his private devotions in his own chamber. They first inquire for the two mestizos, or half-breeds, who act as the Padre's guard; and are informed that they have gone, by his order, to drive in two animals for the use of the mission. These then are not in the house to fire upon them. Nevertheless, conscious of criminal intentions, they keep at a safe distance and send in messengers, with the letter of Padre Tamaral. Padre Carranco is on his knees praying, when they enter. But he rises and receives them affectionately; expresses his surprise that Padre Tamaral is not come with them; and asks if they bring no letter? They say "Yes," and give it to him. The Padre begins to read; and when absorbed in its contents, the whole body of conspirators rush tumultuously into the house. Two of them seize and drag him out between the house and the church, and there hold him by the gown, while others stab him through the body with arrows! And while his blood flows from the wounds, the dying Padre offers most earnest prayer to God that He will accept this sacrifice of his life for his own sins and those of his deluded Indians!

After the wretches see that the Padre's life is far spent, they whip him with sticks, and bruise him with stones! His last word is a prayer for his murderers! Meantime one of them sees the boy who waited on the Padre, crying bitterly at the death of the good man, and says to him, "Why do you cry? Go now, and tell the Padre what is doing in the rancherias!" Another adds scornfully, "as he loved the Padre, it is but reasonable he should go and keep him company;" and taking him by the feet, they dash out his brains upon the floor and walls of the house, and cast him into the place where others are beating and stoning the cold body of the good old Carranco.

The uproar of these infernal proceedings brings together Indians of all ages and sexes. Some are indignant at such inhumanity; but dare not interpose to stop its progress. For among the murderers are some of the principal converts, even those who have been sent to escort Padre Tamaral from San Josef; the very men who joined the Padre in his morning devotions, are now sharing the rancor and fury of others against him. Some are heaping wood together to burn him; others are dragging his bloody and disfigured body, bristling with arrows, and still manifesting signs of life, toward the flaming pile! Here they strip him, not so much for the sake of his raiment, as to heap their execrable insults upon the naked body of him who dared to reprove their infamous bestialities! The shocking enormities practised upon his corpse, their revolting scurrility and lewdness while tramping, shouting, and jeering over his remains, must not be written. These, and all other parts of this terrible tragedy, show that the new doctrine of chastity and other Christian laws connected with the wedded state, particularly that which forbids a plurality of wives, are the chief causes of this malignity and murder!

And now, amid savage shouts, outrages and dancings, lasciviousness, shocking pollutions and execrations, they raise upon their shoulders the body of the venerable Lorenzo Carranco and his little servant, and tumble them together upon the funeral pile! They next proceed to pillage the house and church! The clothing and such furniture as they can use they keep. The crucifixes, the statues of saints, the altars, the chalice, the missal, and other things used in worship, they heap upon the burning body of the Padre. Amidst the wild exultations which accompany this act of contempt toward the religion of their murdered friend, the two domestics of the Padre come with the mules. Around these, as fresh objects of a fury not yet exhausted, they gather, and bid them kill the animals. No sooner have they done it, than the demon crowd pour a shower of arrows into them, and while still shrieking in the agonies of death, throw them upon the burning pile.

After perpetrating these cruelties at San Jago, the murderers go toward the mission of San Josef. Their number is now greatly increased. The disaffected from all the southern parts of the peninsula, with many of the well-disposed who have joined them to save their own lives, are gathered together. This company now approach San Josef. It is the Sabbath. Padre Tamaral's prayers for his poor benighted flock have been offered at dawn. It is now eight o'clock. He is sitting in his house, meditating on the means of extending his usefulness to these wretched Californians, when a party of the seditious, consisting chiefly of the Indians of his own mission, break in upon him, all demanding something, in order that, being refused, they may have a cause of quarrel with him. Perceiving their design, however, the Padre replies mildly, "Stay, my children, there is enough in the house to content you all." Being thus disappointed in getting a pretense for resentment, and not waiting even to contrive any other excuse, the very men who killed the Padre at San Jago, beat Padre Tamaral to the ground, drag him by the feet out of the house, and shoot arrows into his body. After this, the multitude rush up and demand that his throat shall be cut with the knife which he was accustomed to use in giving them food. This good man, like his brother martyr, prays for his murderers!

A villain approaches him with the knife. He implores God to save the soul of him who is about to slay him! The fatal blow is struck! The dying man commends himself and his sinning flock to the Great Shepherd of the human race, and while uttering the name of the Saviour, expires! They practice more abominable insults upon the body of Padre Tamaral than they have upon that of Padre Carranco. And now being relieved from the fear of their victims, a great multitude of all ages assemble, and, for many days, celebrate their villanies with that most brutish licentiousness with which, in the time of their infidelity, they used to solemnize their victories!

The delay occasioned by these infernal orgies saves the life of Padre Taraval at Todos Santos. A boy belonging to this village happens to be in San Jago on the day of Padre Carranco's murder; and while the rebels go to San Josef, he hastens home and relates what he has seen to an old man of his rancheria, who immediately induces him to tell the Padre. The old man offers to convey the Padre to a neighboring island, and with his friends, die, if need be, in his defence; but thinks it out of their power to protect him at the mission. While they are counselling, the boy's narrative is confirmed by the arrival of some Indians belonging to Santa Rosa, who have witnessed Padre Tamaral's martyrdom. There is now no more hesitation. To stay will be madness; nay, a suicide, which can answer no good purpose, since the Padre's presence can protect no one else. Indeed, there is little if any danger to others. For they only desire to destroy the Padres, that they may enjoy all the savage liberty of butchery and vice, which they exercised before these men came among them.

On the night of the fourth of October, therefore, Padre Taraval taking with him, from Todos Santos, the furniture of the altar, repairs to the bay of La Paz, and taking all the ornaments and consecrated utensils of the mission at this place, goes on board the boat which Padre Guillen has sent in compliance with Padre Carranco's request, and sails for the Island del Spiritu Santo, where he fortunately meets another boat with provisions and guards from Loretto. With these the good man hastens to Dolores, in order to prevent the savages from executing their bloody intentions against Padre Guillen. He arrives safely, and finds the good Padre overwhelmed with sorrow at the fate of the beloved Carranco. But his grief knows no bound when he learns that Padre Tamaral has fallen in the same manner, and that the four missions of San Jago, San Josef, Santa Rosa, and El Pilar de la Paz, are utterly ruined.

While this melancholy conference is being held, the insurgents, flushed with success, repair to the village of Todos Santos, whence Padre Taraval has just fled. Their rage is extreme when they find their intended victim escaped; they vent their disappointment on the Christian Indians in the neighborhood. Twenty-seven of these are killed. The rest flee!

Having now no common enemy against whom to direct their hatred, they fall into quarrels among themselves, and practice against each other the same treachery and cruelty they have shown the Padres and Christian Indians!

Meantime, Padre Guillen, as superior of California, on the first knowledge of these outrages, writes to the Viceroy of Mexico, informing him of their losses, and the danger which threatens them, and begging immediate measures may be taken to repair the one and remove the other. But his Excellency estimates life and missionary effort in California too lightly, to trouble himself much with the good Padre's complaints. He writes that he is sensible of the dangers to which they are exposed, and also of the great importance of the missions to religion and the King; and that he will, with pleasure, concur with the Padres in any statement which they shall judge proper to be made to their sovereign in respect to them; and will use his utmost interest with his Majesty, for the adoption of such measures as shall tend to promote their prosperity. He adds, that if he can obtain a warrant from his majesty to aid them, he will execute it in its full extent. In short, the Viceroy, like many modern politicians and placemen, says much that is extremely flattering to the general cause of missions, and of the faithfulness and assiduity of these missionaries in particular, but does not raise a hand to turn the assassin's knife from their throats.

In the meantime, as the rebellion increases, and some signs of violence appear at Dolores, the captain of the garrison at Loretto repairs thither with some soldiers. He finds Padre Taraval, from whom he learns the cruel murders that have been committed at San Jago and Josef. But as the Indians are emboldened by their successes, and his band is very small, he thinks it prudent to remain at Dolores, and by preserving order there, prevent, if possible, the flame from spreading to the northern tribes. But notwithstanding all his precautions, the evil tidings go forth. As if the winds of heaven served the wicked purposes of the enemy, they spread in an incredibly short space of time from Cape San Lucas to San Ignacio, a distance of more than two hundred leagues, and infect the common Indians to an alarming extent. But the chiefs of the tribes remain firm, and keep the Padres informed of the designs entertained by the people. They also beg to be participants of any measures for protection which may be devised.

Padre Guillen finding affairs grow more and more desperate, and no assistance adequate to the emergency offering itself, issues orders early in the year 1735, for all the missionaries to repair to Loretto, and put themselves under the protection of the garrison. These orders happily are acted on without the knowledge of the rebels, till the Padres are beyond their reach. Padre Guillen once more addresses the Viceroy, informing him that all the missions are forsaken, and that they are still in imminent danger, even at Loretto—for the garrison is too weak to contend successfully with such a body of savages as may be brought against it, should there, as they anticipate, be a general rising among the tribes.

These dispatches are sent to the river Yaqui, in Senora, and thence by Indian converts to Mexico. They arrive on the thirteenth of April, 1735, and the Provincial of New Spain immediately delivers them to the Viceroy. But though he urges attention to them in two memorials, praying him to consider the immediate danger of the Padres, the man of authority refuses to do anything in the premises. The Provincial has recourse to his Majesty. A ship being then ready to sail for Madrid, he forwards to Padre Gaspar Rodero, agent general at court of the Society of Jesus for the Indian Provinces, who lays it before his Majestry, and prays his earliest action upon it. But long before the Royal pleasure can be known in the New World, help has come to the little band at Loretto from the seed their own hands have sown.

It appears that as soon as it became known to the more reflecting of the converts, that the Padres had gathered up the consecrated utensils of the churches, and departed to Loretto, a sense of shame at their ingratitude, and a conception of the value of the Padres' services, forced themselves upon their stupid minds, and made them repent their want of fidelity. Accordingly they now begin to act. Reciprocal messages are sent through the country inviting each other to rendezvous and follow the Padres to Loretto. They come in bands from each mission, and form themselves into a long procession, the head men of San Ignacio bearing on their shoulders the crucifixes of their mission, those of Nuestra Senora de Gaudaloupe, the crucifixes of their mission, and those of Santa Rosalia, the crucifixes of their mission; and in silent sadness move on to Loretto, enter the fort and stand weeping before the Padres' dwelling! They say, "You have baptized us; you have taught us the name and worship of the true God; you have gathered us from the dry mountains to the watered vales; you have made us believe that good acts alone bring happiness; you have made us your children; will you now forsake us? We cannot live as we did before we saw you; we do not want to die in the crimes of our dark days!" Thus they reason with the Padres. "It is not just," they say, "that a whole nation should suffer for the sins of a few; especially when the mass are willing and able to deliver the criminal to the punishment their evil deeds merit." With one voice they promise to protect the Padres in every emergency. They implore them to return; and declare that if they refuse to do so, they also will remain at Loretto, for they will not live without them and their religion! The Padres and garrison are affected to tears by these evidences of contrition and attachment to the faith. They delay a few days in order to test the sincerity of the Indians. But noticing no defection they repair to their respective districts and are received with tumultuous joy by their people. The conspirators are surrendered: some of them are slightly flogged; and four of the most guilty of the band at San Ignacio are banished a short time from all the mission premises.

This submission and fidelity on the part of the Californians is followed by a most gratifying manifestation of sympathy by the Yaquis across the Gulf. These Indians, always noted for their honesty and bravery, assemble immediately upon the receipt of Padre Bravo's letter detailing the condition of California, to the number of five hundred warriors, and offer to go and put down the insurgents. But as the bilander, which is to convey them, can take only a fraction of that number, they select from among themselves sixty of their best warriors, and send them, with five hundred bows and arrows to arm the friendly Indians of the peninsula to fight in their stead.

With these the bilander sails and lands them near Loretto. Thence they march to Dolores. Here they meet the commander of the garrison, who greets them with the warmest expressions of gratitude for their generous conduct; but informs them that tranquillity has been restored among the northern missions by the Indians themselves. It is therefore determined to divide their strength between Loretto and La Paz. Accordingly, a sufficient force having been left in the former place, the remainder start in two divisions, the one by the sea, the other by land, for La Paz.

On the landing of the sea party, the strictest military discipline is preserved. This precaution proves of no slight service. For the lawless and still bloodthirsty savages, attack them on several successive nights with much skill and fury. A few are killed and several wounded. At length the land party arrives. A portion of these being mounted on horses, which the Indians suppose to be the running gear of irresistible monsters topped with the trunks and heads of men, so intimidate them that they flee, and are no more seen by night or by day for some time. At length, however, a few re-appear and join the Padres' forces. These protest that they have always been faithful, and have consequently suffered much from the insurgents. They declare that the rebels have committed some recent atrocities upon the crew of a Philippine galleon. They report the affair in this wise. The ship arrived there from Manilla, with many of her crew sorely afflicted with scurvy; and as her signals were not answered from the mission, the captain sent the pinnace ashore with thirteen men to inform the Padre of his presence. As the boat neared the beach, the people were surprised to see neither any person nor sign of life. The greater part of them landed and walked toward the mission, but on their way the armed Indians rushed upon them and killed every man, or rendered him helpless, on the spot! Having murdered these, they hastened to the pinnace, and finding those who were left in charge of it no more guarded than the other party had been, dispatched them also. They then seized the pinnace and broke it up for the old iron, nails, spikes, &c. While all this was going on, the captain of the galleon began to feel some anxiety at the long delay of his pinnace, and sent a band of armed marines in the long boat to seek her.

A most unexpected and painful sight met the eyes of these seamen when they reached the shore. Their pinnace was surrounded by a swarm of leaping and furious savages. It was already reduced to fragments; and the dead bodies of several of their companions lay upon the beach, trodden on and mangled by their ruthless murderers. Dreadfully enraged at this sight, the mariners and soldiers leaped ashore into the thickest of their foes, and gave them battle. A few minutes with fire-arms settled the question of victory. Some of the villains were wounded, some killed, and four captured alive and taken on board the ship. The narrators saw the ship leave her anchorage and stand away for the Pacific. They know nothing more.

It soon appears, however, that the Captain left port without making any other attempt to procure water or provisions; and having put into Acapulco, sent his four prisoners and an account of the murder of his crew to Mexico.

The Viceroy now begins to appreciate the importance of protecting the missions of California. The lives of the Padres a short time before could not be preserved without a special warrant from Madrid. But as his own credit at Court would suffer from the representations of the officers of the galleon, it becomes a moral duty to quell the insurrection. Accordingly he sends orders to the governor of Cinaloa to go over to the peninsula with a sufficient body of men to restore peace, but directs him to act independently of the Padres and never in subordination to the Captain of the garrison. These measures of the Viceroy are made known in California, and Padre Guillen, in order to facilitate their execution, despatches the bilander for the governor and his forces, and at the same time directs the Captain of the garrison to repair to Dolores, and there remain on the defensive until further orders.

In due time the bilander returns. The governor is received with great respect and joy by the Padres, and with the customary honors by the garrison. He, however, soon shows that he intends to reject all advice from the former, and act in the reduction of the country as he shall think proper. He therefore spends two years in manœuvering, and attempted hostilities with a fugitive foe, whom he knows not how to bring into a general engagement. At the close of the year 1736, he is obliged to confess that he has effected nothing for the suppression of the rebellion.

At this time the Padres lose one of their number—Padre

Julian de Mayorga, founder of the mission San Josef de Commondo. He has ruled his mission ever since its origin, 1707, greatly to the improvement and happiness of his Indians, and in such manner as to win the respect and love of all who knew him. His death, therefore, is a cause of deep grief to his brethren and the Indians of his mission. But while they lament for themselves that he is gone, they rejoice for him that he rests from the turbulence and anxiety which have been the portion of all for the last three years.

The governor becoming convinced that he can accomplish nothing on his present plan of proceeding, resolves to adopt the Padre's advice, and take some steps which shall make him a terror to the Indians. Accordingly he sets out with his troops in earnest pursuit of them, and has the good fortune to compel them to an action in which they are utterly vanquished. They have, however, been too long successful to be subdued by one defeat. Instead, therefore, of making any overtures of peace, they defy the governor and provoke his wrath in a series of most annoying skirmishes. He accordingly forces them to a second engagement, in which they are again put to rout. Soon after, they submit and implore his pardon. But he rejects all their advances until they deliver up the leaders of the rebellion, especially those who have murdered the Padres.

It will be supposed that a severe punishment was inflicted on these men. But the policy of the governor and Padres in California is singularly unlike that which prevails in the parent country. Here blood is never shed by way of revenge or punishment. These rebels, therefore, who have perpetrated two of the most revolting murders on record, beside the more common butcheries of their own countrymen, and the crew of the galleon's pinnace, are tried and banished to the coast of Mexico.

On their way over, they rise and attempt to take the bark. This compels the mariners to fire on them and kill more than half their number. Among the few that escape, are the two whose hands shed the blood of the venerable Padres. One of these two is, the next year, killed in an affray; and the other falls from the top of a palm tree upon some rocks, and is so horribly mutilated and torn as to be hardly recognizable. The remainder never return to their country. Thus, after three years of trepidation and violence, peace is restored to California. And it is chiefly attributable to the prudence and forbearance of the Padres that the whole peninsula has not been deluged with blood.

The refusal of the Viceroy in the first instance to protect the missions without a special order from his sovereign, results in a commission from his Majesty requiring him to erect a new garrison at Cape San Lucas; and to take such other measures as may be required to support the missions and maintain the conquests of the Padres. This, like all other efforts of that nation in similar matters, is made when the utility and necessity of action is past.

The Governor of Cinaloa, however, proceeds to the execution of the order. The garrison is to be independent of the Padres, and of the commanding officer at Loretto, and subject only to orders from the Viceroy. The son of the venerable Captain Don Estevan Roderiguez Lorenzo is appointed to the command of the new post. He is a native of California, and having been brought up by his father under the care of the missionaries, and being pious, brave, prudent, and well acquainted with the country, is admirably qualified to fill the office. He has thirty soldiers under his command, ten of whom he stations at the new camp of San Josef del Cabo, ten at the mission of La Paz, and ten at that of San Jago de los Coras. The young Captain, however, is not thought to act with sufficient indifference to the advice and opinions of the Padres; and is therefore soon displaced by a new man from Mexico, Don Pedro Alvarez de Acevedo. At the same time the Viceroy orders an accession of five soldiers to the garrison of Loretto, and particularly directs that the whole force shall be independent of the missionaries. They shall act as an escort, indeed, during their journeyings, but while so doing, shall be under the command of their officer and in nowise amenable to the Padres for neglect or disobedience; nor shall their entrance, discharge, or payment be in any way supervised by them.

The disorder and inconvenience growing out of this regulation, very soon became apparent. The missions are frequently forsaken by the guards, the Padres have much difficulty in procuring them as escorts in their visits to their parishioners; the Indians are frequently oppressed by them when distant from their captain; and a system of trading and chaffering commences between the soldiers and Indians, which dissipates much that the Padres have labored to establish, and seriously neutralizes their instructions and counsels. So much evil, however, grows out of this new order of things, that at the end of eighteen months the Viceroy abandons it; puts the new garrison under a lieutenant, subject to the captain at Loretto, and makes these officers subordinate to the Padres.

As soon as affairs are thus established on a firm footing, the Society of Jesus appoints new missionaries to gather the dispersed members of the ruined missions. Meantime his Majesty, continuing to receive advices of the condition of California both from the Viceroy and the Society, is induced not only to order a new garrison, but to direct that the loss occasioned by the rebellion shall be repaired from the Royal treasury; and also, that the Council of the Indies shall lay before him the best plan for effectually reducing the Californias. Such means are deliberated upon, a plan for the accomplishment of these ends proposed, and orders for its execution signed by his Majesty sent to the Viceroy on the thirteenth of November, 1744. He is directed to proceed in the execution of them without delay, and also to send further information.

The reply to these dispatches reaches Madrid after the death of Philip V. and the accession of Ferdinand VI. His Majesty is even more ardent than his predecessor; and, upon the information sent him, issues a more particular and full set of instructions than any that have preceded them. He decrees that near all the safe harbors settlements shall be formed and garrisons

The Sorcerer seized by the Shark.—Page 236

established; that there shall also be a garrison and town in the centre of the peninsula, or as near it as may be practicable; that facilities shall be afforded for establishing missions at the north, in order to cut off intercourse between the Californian Indians and those of contiguous nations; that in each mission there shall be two Padres instead of one, as heretofore; that in all the frontier stations there shall be a guard under the command of the missionaries; that the expense of carrying all these orders into execution shall be defrayed from the Royal treasury; and finally, that the missionaries in California shall be allowed the same salaries as are paid to their order elsewhere. These measures give great satisfaction in Mexico and California. The hearts of the good Padres are cheered by the assurance thus afforded them, that they have in their monarch an earnest friend, who has come forward in his strength to their aid. They now proceed on their pilgrimage of holy labors, with hearts full of grateful praise to Him whom they serve.

With renewed energy and a patience and self-denial worthy of all praise, they move onward in the great work they have commenced. No difficulties can daunt—no obstacles shake their fortitude. They seem to rise above the selfish passions of human nature and fix their hearts and their eyes solely on the glory of God and the advancement of his cause among these benighted Indians.

In the following year a statement of the number and condition of the missions was drawn up by the Padres for the information of their sovereign. From this it appears that at that time they contained about twenty-five thousand converts, living comfortably under the paternal government of the Jesuit Padres. Padres Salva Tierra, King and Ugarte are dead; but the good deeds which they have done, like the grass and the flowers on their graves, grow greenly, bud and blossom, and shed on the deserts of the Californian peninsula, a perpetual harvest of temporal and religious joy. The handicrafts which they have taught them; the science of agriculture which they have given them; the animals which they have reared around their dwellings; the great idea of a God; and the awards which He has woven inseparably with the elements of life, mind, and every condition of being; the discomfort, debasement, and misery of vice; the quietness, elevation, and happiness of virtue; all these, the Padres have scattered—seeds, bearing the fruits of the social and religious relations, and the numberless comforts of the civilized state. These integral laws of immortal rationality, have germinated among the wastes of man, under the kind planting of the Padres, on the Californian Peninsula. A mighty deed of moral suasion! Not by the steel of conquest, which drinks the blood of the weak, and opens the red pathway to physical supremacy; slaying body and mind; enslaving and murdering. This conquest of the Padres is a victory of Love. Instead of the torpedo, they plant the rose of Sharon; instead of the starless night of bondage, they bring the full day of knowledge—filled with the industry, trust, faith, hope and energies, of a ripened freedom. Who can contemplate these Missionaries, enduring the hardships which have been partially related on these pages, and not venerate their memory? They have voluntarily come from the shrines of early remembrances, and torn from the heart its young and tender impulses. They have left on the cold fields of the past, every tie of kindred, and the natural hopes of humanity. They have taken the vows of God on their souls; separated their hands and thoughts from every selfish service; and with bosoms bared to every shaft of possible events, entered the abodes of savages, shielded only by their good deeds and holy purposes! They have conquered Lower California. It has become a part of the domain of the Spanish crown.

From 1745 to 1767, the Jesuit Padres continue their labors at these missions. The Spanish government, meanwhile, give them small relief from the famines occasioned by the failure of their crops. They mainly depend upon the products of the mission plantations, and the rude manufactures of the Indian artizans, for every comfort of life. And not only do they sustain themselves, but every year brings in the ships from the Philippine Islands, with crews rotting of the scurvy, for the Padres to feed, clothe, restore to health, or bury in their cemeteries.

Their labors of love, however, draw to a close. The society of Jesus or Jesuits, to which they belong, has existed about two hundred years. It has sent its missionaries into Persia, Hindostan, China and Japan. It has written more than one hundred volumes in the Chinese language alone, many hundreds more in the different dialects of the Eastern tongues; has chided and controlled the civil powers of Europe; has made the kingdoms of the whole earth feel its power. The Pope himself holds his throne at the sufferance of this mighty association. The most profound learning of the age is found in their colleges, and the most vigorous moral movements of the times receive their life from them.

Whenever the sword of Conquest is drawn over the head of the defenceless, the Jesuit's hand arrests its fall, or alleviates its wound. In fact, on the American continent they have spanned the whole breadth of human society, except that part of it existing between the Alleghany mountains and the Atlantic, and brought a large majority of the native population under their control. In Paraguay indeed, they have organized armies, and established an Empire of their own; and from California to the mouth of the Rio de la Plata, Spain holds sway only so far as these priests permit. They protect the savages against the ruthless cruelty of Spanish barbarity. England in 1604 has expelled them from her dominions; Venice in 1606, Portugal in 1757, France in 1764, Spain now in 1767, does the same.

That government would have the sole sway over the bones, sinews and intellects of the Indians. Its worthless officials would be unrestrained in the use of them, to dig for the precious metals, and work their plantations. The Jesuits have prevented this. They have uniformly befriended the Indians and elevated their bodily and mental condition. They have so organized and enlightened them, that they can annihilate the Spanish name from the continent, in a day. This state of things is well known.

A remedy is devised. Secret orders of government are issued from Madrid to every Alcalde and military commandant in Spanish territory, to prepare ships and other means of transport, and on a given day, nine months from the date of the edict, to seize and ship to Italy every Jesuit within in dominions. And so profoundly secret is this measure kept, and so complete in its execution, that on the day appointed, all the individuals of this order in Europe, America, and the Spanish islands, are on route, to the several ports from which they are to sail for their destination. The worthy Padres of California are now, therefore, taking leave of their weeping converts. The whole land is sad. The services of the churches are interrupted with their lamentations. The poor savages crowd about the departing Padres for a blessing. How shall they console their grief? Who shall love and labor for them? Who shall teach, pray for them, and rear them step by step onward, to the high estate of a virtuous, enlightened and religious people? Alas, poor Indians! from this day onward, you return to vice, and fade away.

This is the history of the conquest of Lower California, by the priests of the Catholic church. Religious men persuaded the Indians into submission to the civil authorities of Spain.

CHAPTER XV.

Padre Junipero Serra—An Expedition by Sea, for the Conquest of Upper California—Arrival at Loretto—Expedition by sea and land to the North—Arrival at San Diego—Ceremonies of Founding a Mission—A Battle—Going Northward—Naming the Bay of San Francisco—Return to San Diego—The Resolution of Padre Junipero—An Arrival—Departure for Monterey—Founding a Mission, &c.—Arrival of thirty Monks—Other Missions Established—Padre Junipero goes to Mexico—Great Scarcity of Food—Padre Junipero returns by Sea—A Land Party from Mexico—Exploration to 55° N.—A Diabolical Plot at San Diego—A Dreadful Battle at Night—Death—Mission Destroyed—San Juan Capistrano—Mission and Presidio of San Francisco Founded—Death of Padre Junipero—Number of Missions in Upper California—Dates of their Establishment—Progress, Wealth and Influence of Missions—Mexican Revolution—General Echeandra arrives in California—Measures taken to Destroy the Missions—A Revolution—California Independent—Declaration of Rights—Alvarado and Villejo—Jose Castro—Don Carlos Antonio Carrello—Domestic War among Californian Freemen—Operations of the Grand Armies of the North and South—A Victory of Noses—Return of Upper California to the Mexican Dominion.

As related in my account of Lower California, the Jesuits, who have brought the Indians of the territory into subjection to Spain, and induced them to embrace the Catholic faith, have, in 1767, been expelled from these scenes of their usefulness. And now, that the influence of this powerful society is prostrated, the Government turns its attention to the conquest of the country by the employment of another religious order, who are supposed to be more subservient to the dictates of the civil authority.

In 1768, Padre Junipero Serra, a Franciscan monk, is appointed Missionary President of the Californias, and arrives at San Blas in the month of February of this year, accompanied by a staff of sixteen brothers of his own order, from the Convent of San Fernando. Here he meets sixteen of the expelled Jesuits, in sorrow that their forsaken flocks must return to the misery of the savage state. These men have labored long to plant the tree of life in the rude soil of the savage heart; it has begun to put forth its branches to the sun, and shed its odors over the land; but while the fruits of their trials are being garnered, they have been compelled to retire from the harvest, and leave others to reap or despoil.

On the twelfth of March, 1768, Padre Junipero and his associates sail for Loretto in the same vessel which has brought Jesuits thence, and arrive there in safety about the middle of the following month. Padre Junipero is a worthy successor of those great and self-denying men who have preceded him in this field of martyrdom. His own peculiar faith in religious things is warm and far-reaching. He sees on the barren heights of the Californian peninsula, many a dwelling-place of righteousness for future generations; and hears in the solemn midnight, the voices of angels encouraging him to his work. The miracles wrought in the days of the primitive church, he believes may still be wrought by the saints militant; and that the mighty arm of faith will yet bring down Omnipotence, to mould anew the distorted world. He unites with his zeal various and extensive learning. The ancient and modern languages, with all their stores of philosophy and eloquence, are known to him. The life of courts—the sweets of the social ties—the vast and stirring acts of the world moving on to its civil and religious destinies, are familiar to him, for he has mingled with them, directed and enjoyed them. Yet Padre Junipero has landed in the wilderness of California, and begins the duties of a missionary among its Indians.

He dispatches his brethren to the several missions north and south, and remains at Loretto awaiting the arrival of

Josef Galvoz, the Visitador General, whose commands are to guide him in his labors. This dignitary arrives at La Paz in July, with orders from his superiors to visit the missions in Lower California, to superintend expeditions about to be dispatched to San Diego and Monterey in the upper province, for the establishment of missions and forts. Soon the three packet boats of this undertaking arrive. They are called the San Blas, San Carlos and San Antonio. In them are provisions, agricultural implements, and seeds of Spanish and Mexican grains, fruits and esculent roots, to be planted at the contemplated establishments. They will need cattle, horses and mules. A party therefore is organized to drive these over the country to Monterey. The San Carlos is ready for sea, and the Visitador General fixes the day for her departure. In this vessel is Don Vincent Vital, Commander, Don Pedro Prat, Lieutenant, twenty-five Catalonian volunteers, a good ship's crew, and Padre Fernando Parron.

Death has visited the Spanish vessels in these seas ever since Cortez' iron prow ruffled them. In all the north the freezing hand of the Great Destroyer is seen! No living men on board the San Carlos dare unfurl the canvass till heaven is appeased. The red cross is therefore raised to the peak, the orange flag of Spain floats beneath it; and the crew and the soldiers and officers, and priests with shaven crowns, are gathered on the deck; the holy sacrament is administered by Padre Junipero; and Mass is said to San Joself, the chosen patron of these expeditions; the vessel and colors are blessed; an absolution and benediction administered to the people; and the vessel San Carlos leaves the harbor of Loretto on the ninth of January, 1769, on her voyage to Upper California. The San Antonio sails from Cape San Lucas on the fifteenth of the following month. Her commander is Don Juan Perez. She has on board Padres Juan Biscayno and Francisco Gomez, and her crew. The San Josef leaves Loretto on the sixteenth of June of the same year.

Meanwhile the land expedition is being forwarded with all

possible dispatch. It is divided into two companies; so that if one of them shall be destroyed, the other may chance to be saved. Don Gasper de Portala is the commissioned Governor of the Californias and commander of this land expedition. He is a captain of dragoons in the Spanish army. Captain Fernando Rivera y Moncada is his second. The latter receives command of the first division of the landsmen; and in the month of September, 1768, takes up his line of march for the north. He soon arrives at a place now called Nuestra Senora de los Angelos, on the Indian frontier, and having found some supplies and baggage, sent in launches from the missions to this place, he proceeds eighteen leagues northward, to a valley of excellent pastures, wood and water, and halts. Here he remains until the first day of March, 1769, and again marches northward, until the twenty-fourth of the same month, when he arrives at the port of San Diego, in latitude 32° N. Here he finds the San Carlos and San Antonio at anchor. These vessels have suffered greatly from storms and contrary winds. The first arrived on the first of May, 1768. Her whole people, except the officers, cook, and one seaman, have died of the scurvy and thirst and hunger. The San Antonio arrived on the eleventh of April, having lost eight of her crew by the scurvy. The San Josef was not seen after she left Loretto. Don Rivera y Moncada, his twenty-five soldiers, his three muleteers and his converted Indians, Padre Crispi and a midshipman, now form a camp upon the green plain, and rest from the fatigues of a march of fifty-four days, over the dry crags of the Californian wilderness.

The second part of the land expedition, with its mules, horses, black cattle, muleteers and baggage, on the thirteenth of May, 1769, are at a place called Villacata; and Padre Junipero and the Governor are with them. They are waiting the arrival of the troops; and while thus unemployed, examine the surrounding country—find it valuable, and consecrate it to the use of the mission in the neighborhood called San Francisco de Borja· and hither this mission is to be removed. The ceremony of consecrating the location of this mission is worthy of being known. The soldiers and muleteers clear away the rubbish from the future site of the church—hang seven bells upon the trees, and form a grand cross. This is the work of the first day. On the second, Padre Junipero, invested in robes, blesses the holy water, and with it sprinkles the site of the church and the cross. The latter, adorned with flowers, is then erected in front of the consecrated area. This mission then receives its name, San Josef. The first Mass is now chanted—and Padre Junipero pronounces a discourse upon the coming of the Holy Ghost. The sacrifice of the Mass is now concluded, and Veni Creator is sung. In the progress of all this there is a constant discharge of musketry. The smoke of the burning powder is the only incense from the mountain altars of this day's worship.

They leave Vellacata on the 15th of May, 1769, and direct their course northwardly towards the mouth of the Colorado; but after traveling above thirty-five leagues, their progress is intercepted by a steep and rocky mountain, over which their cattle cannot pass. They therefore return southward as far as the frontier mission, San Borja. Having rested themselves and their animals a few days, they take a route in a north-westerly direction. Forty-six days do they travel. The southern half of their way passes through a sterile rocky country with occasional fruitful valleys skirted with timber. The northern half is plentifully supplied with streams of water running among rich savannas clothed with the wild grasses, roses, and vines bearing a large sour grape. The timber is not abundant—but on the hills the deep loamy soil frequently produces the live oak and other valuable trees, and the vales which run up from the seaside, are often clad with heavy forests. Many Indians meet them. The males, both old and young, are entirely naked, while the females of all ages are covered with rush mats and skins from their breasts downward. Their food consists of seeds, fruits, and fish. They are uniformly familiar and friendly. On the first day of July they pitch their camp on the

the beach among their countrymen, at the long-sought port of San Diego.

As the crews of the vessels have been thinned by death, till there are scarcely enough to man one of them, they cannot proceed farther north without recruits. Accordingly the remaining members of both crews are put on board the San Antonio, and the ship dispatched to San Blas for more seamen. It is also determined that the Governor shall lead the principal part of the landsmen along the shore to Monterey. The Padre's President and two missionaries and eight soldiers are therefore detached to remain at the newly consecrated mission of San Diego; and Don Gasper Portala, the Governor, with one servant, the Padres Juan Crispi and Francisco Gomez, with each a converted Indian to attend on him, and Don Fernando Rivera y Moncada with his sergeant and twenty-six soldiers, and his lieutenant Don Pedro Foxes, with seven Catalonian soldiers, and Don Miguel Constanzo, engineer, and seven muleteers and fifteen Indians from the southern missions, start over land to Monterey.

They search the coast for bays and harbors, examine the lands and their products, pass the harbor of Monterey without recognizing it, go north to the Bay now called San Francisco, and give it that name under the following circumstances:— When the Padre President, Junipero, received orders from the Visitador General respecting the names of the new missions which he was sent northward to found, perceiving that the name of the Patron Saint of his order of priests was not among them, said, "And is our Father San Francisco to have no mission assigned to him?" To which the Visitador replied, "If San Francisco wishes to have a mission, let him show you a good port, and then it shall bear his name." When the Monterey expedition, therefore, see this unequalled bay, they exclaim, "This is the port to which the Visitador referred, and to which the Saint has led us," and immediately called the bay Bajia del San Francisco. They now erect a cross on the western shore of the southern great arm of this bay, and having taken possession of the country in the name of their sovereign, celebrate the Mass, commence their return to San Diego, and arrive there on the twenty-fourth of January, 1770.

During the half year occupied by this expedition, the Padre President Junipero is not idle at San Diego. On the sixteenth day of July, 1769, he consecrates the foundation of a mission. This is the day of the year, when in 1212, the Spaniards, under the banner of the cross, prostrated the power of the Mahomedans in the south of Spain; and the good Padre Junipero hopes that the same banner shall yet wave over the Gentiles of Upper California. He chants the Mass, celebrates the triumph of the Holy Cross, sprinkles the ground with the baptismal water of the Church, and calls it San Diego, or Saint James. Afterwards he dedicates one of their huts to the use of a temporary church, and invites the Indians to attend service; presents them food which they reject; gives them small pieces of cloth with which they are greatly delighted; yet they cannot be persuaded to bow before the cross, and gladden the Padre's heart by embracing the Catholic faith; but on the contrary, they allow their desire for cloth to induce them in the night time to go on large rafts built of bulrushes to the ship San Carlos, and purloin a part of her sails. This act is followed by precautions to prevent its repetition; yet as no punishment is inflicted on the thieves, they arm themselves with bows and arrows, wooden swords of keen edge, and formidable clubs, and begin to steal so boldly that the Spaniards find it necessary to oppose them by force; and as soon as their determination to do so is manifested, the Indians resolve to accomplish their designs by war. On the thirteenth and fourteenth days of August, therefore, they force their way into the quarters of the people and carry off several garments and other valuables; but are driven away without an attempt to kill any of them. On the fifteenth, it becomes necessary for Padre Fernando to go on board the San Carlos to celebrate the Mass with two soldiers who guard the ship. Padres Junipero and Biscayno are left on shore with only two other persons able to do duty; and the Indians, perceiving the advantage to be derived from the absence of one of the boldest of those they would rob, gather in large numbers while the people are at Mass, and begin to carry away every thing they find, even the sheets that cover the sick! The corporal calls "to arms!" whereupon the Indians retire a short distance and shoot their arrows. And now the four soldiers, the carpenter and blacksmith commence firing their guns. The latter, although he had no armor to protect him from the arrows, charges upon the savages, crying out, "Long live the faith of Jesus Christ, and die the dogs his enemies!"

Meantime the Padre President Junipero is praying that none may be hurried to the world of spirits with their sins unforgiven.

The battle rages on, accompanied by the terrible war-cry of the savages. An arrow takes effect; a boy called Josef runs in great haste and prostrates himself at the Padre's feet, exclaiming, "Father, give me absolution, for the Indians have killed me." The Padre absolves him. The arrow has passed through his throat; and he immediately dies! His death is kept secret and the battle continues. Many of the savages fall. They drag away their dead and dying, till at length, panic-smitten by the destructive effects of fire-arms, they flee to the hills in great precipitation!

It cannot be known how many of these savages have perished by this mad act. Very many are known to be wounded; for in a few days their friends bring them into the mission and entreat the Padres to cure them: and the surgeon and the Padres treat them kindly till restored to health.

Padre Biscayno, one soldier, an Indian Christian, and the brave blacksmith are wounded; but in a short time all the whites, except the poor boy Josef, are well again. This unsuccessful attack has a salutary effect on the Indians. They come fearfully into the mission every day, and treat the Padres and the religion they teach with deference. A boy about fifteen years old is among the most frequent and devout. Him the Padre President teaches the Spanish language, in order that he may learn the prayers and catechism, and act as interpreter. He learns easily, and is soon able to inform his countrymen that the Padre desires to baptize their children, and instruct them in the Catholic faith. One is selected from the many which are offered, and the holy water is about to fall from the Padre's hand, when the parents of the child snatch it away, to the great grief of the Padre and the indignation of the soldiers. The latter in their zeal ask permission to destroy these blaspheming gentiles. The good Junipero denies them.

Distress follows these Franciscans as it has the Jesuits. The country is unploughed and yields little food. The San Antonio has gone to San Blas for supplies; but heaven only knows if the storms will spare her to save them from starvation. She has already been absent so long that they begin to fear she is lost. The Governor, therefore, orders an account to be taken of the provisions on hand, and notifies the Padre President that they can hold out no longer than March following; and that if the ship should not arrive by San Josef's day, the twenty-fifth of that month, he shall abandon the enterprise, and commence his return to Loretto. This announcement greatly afflicts the Padre Junipero. Leaving the country he feels will carry with it for a long time to come, the abandonment of the Indians to their heathenism; and he retires to his closet and implores aid from Heaven. God is his master; from Him he seeks light. San Josef is the Patron Saint of his holy enterprise; from him he seeks celestial intercessions with the Ruler of events. The conversion of the Gentiles is the work which burdens his heart; and he holds the cross toward Heaven and vows never to leave California till he has thrust the spiritual plough into the glebe of its moral wastes. He communicates his resolution to the Governor, and waits the approach of the eventful day with the greatest solicitude.

The twenty-fifth of March at last comes. The Padre greets

its dawning light with the chants of the Mass, and the celebration of the most sacred services of the church. The people are called together at mid-day, and prayers are most devoutly said and praises again sung to the Creator.

The good Padre speaks. He draws an exhortation from the Laws of God. He exhorts as one soon to be left alone in a land of martyrdom. He ceases; he blesses; and the tide of thought and emotion is now setting upon the busy movements of the departure for Loretto, when lo! in the offing is perceived the outline of a vessel standing towards the land! Was it an omen! shadowed on the rim of the sky to arouse faith in God? It disappears during the night! The sun rises and sets over the hot seas three times afterwards, and it does not re-appear! The fourth day dawns and waxes to the meridian, and wanes on the western waves! And when night shuts in, the cable of the San Antonio rattles its rude salutation to the silent shores around the Bay of San Diego!

On the arrival of this ship with provisions and a recruit of men, it is determined to make another expedition to Monterey. A party by land and another by sea, are detailed for the undertaking. Both leave San Diego about the middle of April, 1770.

Long and tedious are the voyages of these infant days of navigation. Forty-six days are spent by the San Antonio in making 4° of latitude. On the thirty-first of May, however, Padre Junipero with joy beholds from the ship the green hills around the bay of Monterey. The anchor is let into the waters, the boats are lowered, they shoot away to the shore; the land expedition having arrived eight days before, meet their countrymen on the rocks at the beach. The first and second of June are spent in that hearty social intercourse, which those alone ever feel who have thrown their hearts for months on the cold breast of the wilderness. Dangers incurred, sufferings endured on rock and surge, remembrances of the sacred past, the sensations cf dawning joy crowding on past misery like day on the heels of night, cluster around the mind and bid the affections increase the pulsations of life. On the third of June, they celebrate their landing. It is the Pentecost day. The officers and men of the sea and land expeditions assemble under a great oak tree near the shore. They erect an altar in its shade, hang bells on its branches, and proceed with their services. They chant *Veni Creator*, consecrate the water, erect and bless a grand cross, unfurl the royal standard, chant the Mass, and sing a *Salve* to the Virgin, whose image occupies the altar. And after the Padre Junipero has delivered a pathetic discourse, a solemn Te Deum is sung to the Great Creator. The officers now take formal possession of the country in the name of their king. These ceremonies being completed, they repair to a shady place on the beach and dine, as they have worshipped, amid salutes of small arms, and the cannon of the vessels. Thus is commenced the settlement of Monterey, in Upper California. All this done, the Padre President proceeds to found the mission of Monterey, in the same manner as he has done that at San Diego. But he finds it more difficult to induce the Indians to avail themselves of his teachings. The firing of the artillery and muskets at the celebration of the first Mass, has so terrified them, that the heart of the excellent Padre is not gladdened by a baptism, till the twenty-sixth of the following December.

Meanwhile the ship San Antonio being detained some time at Monterey, the Padre President is enabled to explore portions of the neighboring country. He finds the fertile soil so abundant and the natives so numerous, that he writes to the chief of the College of San Fernando in Mexico, that a hundred more missionaries may be well employed in the Californias. This favorable account of the country induces the Viceroy at Mexico to order thirty Franciscan monks to proceed to San Blas—twenty of whom are destined for Lower and ten for Upper California. The latter sail from San Blas in the San Antonio, on the seventh of January, 1771, and on the twelfth of March, put into San Diego, sorely afflicted with the scurvy. They go overland to Monterey.

The monks destined for Lower California are less fortunate.

Their ship, the San Carlos, is allowed by its unworthy commander to drift ashore, in the Port Mansanillo, a fine harbor lying some distance south from San Blas; and the poor friars, left to shift for themselves, are compelled to toil over three hundred leagues of rough, pathless, uninhabited coast along the ocean and gulf, till they find themselves on the coast of Senora opposite to Loretto. They cross the gulf to Loretto, thither the San Carlos follows them in the month of August, having been eight months at sea, between two ports which are now but five or six days' sail apart.

The reinforcement to Upper California enables the presiding Padre to found a new mission, which he dedicates to San Antonio de Padua. This station is built among the green hills of Santa Lucia, about eight leagues from the Pacific coast, and twenty from Monterey.

The grounds are broken and the seed sown; but a blighting and untimely frost comes, and the total loss of the wheat is threatened. The Indians are disheartened, and still more so the Padres, who anticipate with keen forebodings the loss of their bread. They send the Christian Indians to the woods to gather seeds, roots, fruits, &c., for their subsistence, as in former times has been their custom. The Padres strengthen their own and the Indians' faith, by a firm reliance on their patron saint; and to conciliate his highest favor, they resolve to celebrate his Novena with all their converts. At the same time they take the more business-like precaution of irrigating the blighted field; and in a few days, such is the efficacy of the water, and still more, as they believe, their prayers, that the resuscitated grain field is seen springing into new life. At the end of the Novena, the whole field is covered with beauty and promise, and at harvest yields more abundantly than was ever before known. This encourages the new converts, and kindles the gratitude of the Padres. Meanwhile new efforts are resolved on in San Diego; and on the tenth of August, Padre Pedro Cambon and Padre Angel Somera, with a detachment of ten soldiers and the requisite number of mules and drivers, set out and travel northwardly. When they arrive at the river Temblores, about forty leagues from San Diego, and while they are seeking a desirable site for their mission, the Indians, armed and led on by two commanders, rush from their lurking-places with dreadful yells and the most unequivocal demonstrations of hostility. The Padres dread bloodshed. They exalt the image of "Our Lady;" the subdued savages prostrate themselves in crowds around the standard; allow them without interruption to proceed with the solemn ceremonies of founding the mission of San Gabriel; and the swelling notes of the first Mass chanted in these solitudes, mount to the ear of the Omnipotent in the year 1771, from a little group consisting of the Padres, the rude soldiers, the careless muleteers and wandering Indians, gathered under the spreading boughs of a tree on the consecrated ground, just as the sun is rising to bring the anniversary of the nativity of the Virgin.

The Padres have now divided their forces as much as practicable. No more missions can be founded till help arrives from Mexico; and oppressed with care, labor, hunger, and anxiety, lest the Indians should relapse into their heathenish belief and practices, they remain with little to encourage their minds, or strengthen their fainting hearts, until the autumn of 1772, when Padre Junipero founds the mission San Luis Obispo de Tolozo, and in November embarks at San Diego for Mexico. There he struggles with the Viceroy Bucareli to prevent him, if possible, from abandoning the port of San Blas as a naval station; and so successfully presents the cause of the infant missions to him that he is induced to finish a frigate which has been begun at San Blas, for the purpose of exploring the coast of Upper California, and also to freight a packet boat with provisions for Monterey. But again these navigators, on whose skill so much depends for the comfort and sustaining of the missions, fail through ignorance, negligence, or misfortune, to reach the port of destination; and the packet enters the bay of Loretto without her rudder, and otherwise disabled from proceeding on her voyage So that the good Padres, with their ignorant, helpless dependents, are doomed to another tedious famine. For eight months they subsist almost exclusively on a scanty supply of milk. But in the meantime, food and aid and kind hearts are on their way to them from Mexico. The indefatigable Padre Junipero toils faithfully till September, 1773, when, with missionaries, officers, soldiers, and a large supply of necessaries, consisting of maize, beans, flour and clothing, to the value of $12,000, he joyfully embarks for California. He has also procured the despatch of an expedition, under the command of Captain Juan Bautista Anza, through the interior by the rivers Gila and Colorado, in order that the disasters by sea which have so often overwhelmed the missions with disappointment, famine and despair, may in future be averted The good Padre himself proceeds to San Blas, and freighting the packet San Antonio and the new frigate Santiago with his supplies, embarks on his return in January of 1774, and after forty-nine days' sail puts into San Diego.

Monterey is the place of destination; and Padre Junipero proceeds thither over land, that he may visit the various missions on his route. Anza's land expedition is there: and the Padre rejoices to learn that there is no obstacle to a land communication between Mexico and Monterey. But the pleasure arising from this discovery is greatly lessened by the announcement that there are no provisions among the people, and that famine is rapidly wasting the energies and hopes of his new establishments. The good man's heart is wrung by this tale of suffering, and he hastens on with a few supplies; but finds at his arrival on the eleventh of May, that the frigate he left in San Diego is two days in advance of him, and that the hungry are already fed. Joy and welcome everywhere meet the Padre President; the Friars hail him as a loved brother and strong companion; the poor Indians as a father and protector. Thus strengthened and encouraged, the laborers of the cross toil on. Meantime the frigate, which is under orders from the Viceroy to explore the northwest coast, departs from Monterey on the eleventh of June, proceeds as far as Lat. 55° N., and finds an inlet which they name Santa Margarita, and returns. In March of the next year, she makes another expedition, accompanied by a schooner under the command of Bodega, afterwards the friend of Vancouver. As these vessels, however, are separated in a gale on the thirtieth of July, the frigate proceeds to Lat. 49° N., and puts back in search of the lost schooner; arriving at Monterey on the twentieth of August, she finds her consort riding at anchor in the bay. The failure of these expeditions seems rather to stimulate than cool the enterprise of the Viceroy. He orders a new frigate to be built at San Blas, and sends a naval officer to Peru to purchase a vessel to accompany her over these vexed waters. These vessels sail from San Blas on the twelfth of February, 1779, under command of Don Ignatio Artiago. Two missionaries from the Convent of San Fernando accompany the expedition. The object of the voyage is to discover a water passage from the Pacific to the Atlantic. They reach Lat. 55° N. on the third of June, and discover a strait which they call Bucareli. Here they look in vain for a passage eastward; and about the first of July proceed still farther northward. On the first of August, in about Lat. 60° N., they discover a large and safe harbor, with abundance of wood, water, and fish. This they name Santiago; and after spending several days in searching an inconsiderable creek for the passage, the prudent commander, finding his crew infected with the scurvy to an alarming degree, and dreading the rigor of the advancing season, resolves to return. Accordingly he sails southward, and on the fifteenth of September, 1779, safely moors his little fleet in the harbor of San Fernando. The return of this expedition is hailed as a momentous event in the progress of the conquest.

While the civil arm is thus extending itself over the unexplored wilderness, the spiritual warriors lose none of their ardor The accession of laborers and the abundant supplies brought by the Padre President enable the missionaries to prosecute their holy enterprise with renewed energy. New missions are founded, the old ones zealously advanced. Converts are added to the flock, and everything encourages the hearts of the lonely self-sacrificing Padres. In the fall of the year, 1775, however, a most diabolical plot is laid and partly executed by the unconverted Indians aided by two apostates, for attacking San Diego, and murdering the missionaries and other white persons. The onset is made in the dead of night, by two strong bands of armed savages; and the good Padres, all unprepared for defence as they are, with their feeble force of a few soldiers and mechanics, have but a small chance of escape. One of them, the Padre Luis, is cruelly murdered and chopped in pieces, and Padre Vincente is dangerously wounded. A whole night is spent in this precarious defence, and at sunrise the Indians retire, carrying away their dead and wounded. All the whites are wounded, some of their buildings are burned, and their peaceful intercourse with the Indians is sadly interrupted.

The Padre President at Monterey hears of this calamity, and resolves to proceed at once to San Diego to repair, as he best may, the misfortunes of his brethren. He is prevented from reaching them until June of the following year; when with the aid of the crew of the Princesa, he re-builds the burned tenements, and by his influence renews the amicable intercourse of the mission with the natives. On his return, he founds the mission of San Juan Capistrano. Here he is attacked by hostile Indians. But he escapes all dangers, endures all trials, and on reaching Monterey, prepares to establish the mission of San Francisco, on the bay of that name. Great preparations are made for this event. Supplies are sent to the harbor of San Francisco in one of the packet boats, and the good Padre with a small detachment of soldiers, and a number of families with cattle and mules for the new mission, leaves Monterey on the seventeenth of June, 1776. Ten days

ness, and they arrive near the proposed site of their future home on the banks of a beautiful lake near one of the arms of the bay, select a situation for the Presidio, and cut the timber to erect it. The natives, meanwhile, throng around to witness their labors and make demonstrations of friendship. The vessel arrives on the eighteenth of August. The work progresses, and on the seventeenth of September, they take solemn possession of the new garrison. The holy cross is planted above the peaceful waters of the bay, and the silent hills re-echo the chanting of the Mass, the sublime Te Deum and the roar of artillery and musketry, announcing to the untamed tenants of the wilderness, the dominion at once of the cross and the sword. The same ceremonies attend the taking possession of the mission on the ninth of the following November. These objects accomplished, the vessel returns to San Blas.

The faithful Padre Junipero continues his labors without ceasing, founding in addition to the missions already named, those of Santa Clara, Santa Barbara, and San Buenaventura. But his efforts draw to a close. He has thrown the gushing energies of a warm and kind heart upon the arid wilderness. Solitude, famine, heat and cold, thirst and hunger, have been welcome as the sole conditions under which he could perform his errand of mercy and love to the red man. And now that the holy cross which his hands have planted, gleams heavenward from the dark bosom of these wastes, and devotion blends its gentle tones with the harsher pœans of the winds and waves, and the voices of human industry, the good Padre, worn out with the fatigues and anxieties of his arduous post, must prepare to rest from his labors. The hand of age is upon him; his head whitens; his frame bends and trembles; his steps falter; he leans upon his younger and more vigorous brethren for support; and at last his grateful and beloved spiritual children, the sons of the forest, see him no more He retires to die. His heart clings to those who have so long lived under the protection of his fostering hand, and the last beating of life mingles with a prayer for blessings on his infant missions. The bereaved Friars watch his last breath and close his eyes on the day of San Augustine, in the year 1782. His life has been nearly seventy-one years long; fifty-three of which have been spent in holy orders, thirty-five in the stern and trying duties of a missionary in the New World. Thus closed the life and earthly labors of Padre Junipero

NAMES OF MISSIONS, AND DATES OF THEIR FOUNDATION

Date of Foundation.	Missions.
1769, - - - -	San Diego.
1770, - - - -	San Carmelo, or San Carlos [de Monterey.
1771, - - -	San Gabriel.
" - - -	San Antonio de Padua.
1772, - - - -	San Luis Obispo.
1776, - - - -	San Juan Capistrano.
1777, - - - -	Santa Clara.
1779, - - - -	San Francisco
1782, - - - -	Santa Buenaventura.
1786, - - - -	Santa Barbara.
1787, - - - -	La Purissima Concepcion.
1791, - - - -	Na Sa de la Soledad.
1794, - - - -	Santa Cruz.
1797, - - - -	San Miguel.
" - - - -	San Jose.
" - - - -	San Juan Bantista.
" - - - -	San Fernando.
1798, - - - -	San Luis Rey de Francia
1817, - - - -	San Rafael.
1822, - - - -	San Francisco Solano.

These missions at length became very rich, and from 1793 to 1820 sold an immense quantity of hides and tallow to American and British ships which visited the coast. An anecdote related to me by an intelligent man in California is in point. Previous to 1793 the Padres killed the surplus bulls of their herds, saving the hides, and leaving the tallow to rot on the plains; because it was an article difficult to preserve until foreign ships should begin to visit them and furnish a market; and thus untold quantities of it were lost. One of the Padres, however, who had a little more chemistry and other worldly wisdom than his brethren, caused his Indians to dig a very large and deep vat in the earth on a shaded spot, and line it well with brick and a durable cement, in which from year to year, as his bulls were killed, he stored his tallow; and thus continued to do, till the trading ships called for the deposit; when it was found that his vat contained three large cargoes of excellent tallow.

The cattle in the missions at this period were very numerous. Most of them had from eighty to one hundred thousand each. They also had bands of horses and other kinds of stock proportionably large. The Padres of a single mission not unfrequently purchased an entire cargo of goods from American merchants—and such were the known resources of their establishments, and their uniform punctuality and honesty, that these cargoes were frequently delivered to the priests with no other security than their verbal promise to pay. Indeed, these old Franciscan Friars, who entered this wilderness clad in their grey habits with sandals on their feet and the cross in their hands, were men for whose equals in mental power, in physical courage and moral intrepidity, we shall seek in vain in these days of vapid benevolence, of organizations which spend their money in sustaining a system of denunciation, instead of applying it with day-laboring energy for the extirpation of the evils against which they inveigh. These men had not made addresses before the assemblies of anniversary occasions, but had wielded the pruning hook of holy truth and of the principles of the social state, and of the refining and exalting virtues, upon the unpruned territories of degraded human nature. They had not bewailed the woes of men at the point of a goose-quill, and from the dark walls of a complaining heart shut up in an indolent body, sent forth a sack of theories for alleviation, which the world must adopt befo a freezing hand can be warmed or a hungry mouth filled But they had bared their hearts to the arrow of the savage and gone out to the theatre of personal labor, driving before them domestic animals bearing seed-grain, the plough, the axe, the spinning-wheel and the loom, gathering the stupid wandering Indians into communities, rearing the edifices of Christianity and the family condition on the shore of that great ocean girded with heathenism and wretchedness, opening its unploughed plains and training them to yield their increase tc nourish the body—and from the garner of Heaven drawing manna for the soul. They did not teach religion only and at all times, and rely on that as a nutriment for the rearing and comfort of the whole man. On the contrary, they recognized in the human being a nature allied to matter as well as spirit; with faculties which connect him as a material existence with his material abode, and powers of mind which were made to teach him his relations to the material world, as well as those which raise the hand of religious faith to the skies, to seize the hope of the after world. Like knowing and reasoning, as well as pious men, they cared for the bodies as well as the souls of those whom they went to convert to Christianity. And in bringing the Californian savages into that industry which must always accompany true virtue and piety, the labor of the converts produced in that climate, where so little is required to sustain them during unproductive seasons, a vast amount of surplus wealth. This the Padres alone were capable of throwing into the market; and consequently, at the period just spoken of, the business of the Californias received its origin, its character and impulses from them. Society from them took its form and its tone; and the Government of the country was as mild, wise and just, as these unpretending men who directed its action. The golden age was this of the Californias. The Indians in the whole of Lower, and that part of Upper California which lies between the first range of mountains and the sea, and extending from San Diego t.:

the north till it embraces the shores of the Bay of San Francisco, were gathered into missions; not less than seventy-five thousand of them were living, laboring and worshipping God with the Padres on those immense plantations! Their granaries were filled with grain, their orchards were laden with oranges, plums, pears, citrons, lemons, apples and figs. Their vineyards covered the hill-sides, and their flocks and herds the plains! If a stranger arrives in the Californias, and approaches a mission, the Indians and Padres go out to meet him! He receives the welcome of sincere hearts. The wine from the vineyards—the bread and beef and frixoles are placed before him, and the Padre's best bed given him. He is pressed to remain, not a cold hour of freezing ceremony and suspicion, but months—during life if he will—in their hospitable abode. But if he will travel on, he is furnished with horses and attendants to the next mission, where he is again welcomed and treated in a similar manner, and thus he journeys through the entire country if he desires, and leaves it with regret. But the history of this delightful realm shows a change in the features of this scene.

In 1821, New Spain had achieved an independent national existence, and adopted a partially republican form of government. The Californias, removed by their geographical situation, as well as the feelings of their people, from the wars and victories of that eventful crisis, had retained their loyalty to old Spain until as late as the year 1825, when General Echuandra arrived in Monterey with full powers to receive the submission of California to the authorities of the Mexican Republic.

The first act of this functionary was to require of the Padres to take the oath of allegiance to the new Government. This they could not do according to the rules of their Order, without the consent of their Prefecto—the Padre President. This priest declared himself unwilling to give his consent until his King had abandoned the sovereignty of the Californias; whereupon General Echuandra arrested him, conveyed him to Monterey, and banished him to Manilla.

Immediately after the Padre Prefecto's banishment, Echeandra made a tour of the missions, assembled the Indians in each, and by an interpreter, explained to them that the Mexican Government had directed him to declare the Indian converts of the Californias to be free citizens of the Mexican Republic—released thereafter from what he termed slavery to the Padres, and subject only to the laws of the nation and his commands as its official agent; aud that all those who bore good characters, and had learned agriculture, or any of the useful arts by which they could gain a livelihood for themselves and families, he was instructed to say were entitled to have lands assigned them on the mission premises, and a proportionate quantity of the animals, as cattle, horses, &c., and be gathered into parishes with Padres to superintend them who should be subject to the missions; that those of them, who had not learned agriculture, or other useful art, or had not sustained reputable characters, must remain at the missions and earn by their increasing knowledge and virtue a title to freedom and the rights of property. The Padres were required to aid in carrying out these mandates of the Republic, and at the same time to continue their work of converting and training the Indians for the civil and social state contemplated by the Government. Meantime the General informed the Padres that their yearly stipend of four hundred dollars would be indefinitely withheld; ordered them to have bells rung whenever he approached the missions; and to instruct the converts that they, as well as themselves, were subject to his authority.

This course of the Mexican Government appears on its face to be one of those high moral acts which a single age seldom sees twice performed. The Creator has sent down to us, through the train of ages, the evidence that in the beginning He created as great a variety of the human genus as He did of any other race of living beings. From the New Hollander, who is connected to our kind by a physical form but little superior to that of the ape, and by the instinct and capacity to build a fire to warm his frame when beset with cold—to the Negro—the Hottentot—the Indian—the Asiatic and the European species, there is a gradual development of beauty and capacity of body and mind, which forces us to think that the same harmonious variety was introduced into the creation of the human family, which is so manifest in other orders of the animal world. Among celestial intelligences, toc, there are greater and lesser stars of existence; and the Great Maker burns above them all. Such variety is a palpable fact on earth. The highest obedience to God is the recognition of Him in His own character, and of creation as it fell from His hands; and having done these things dutifully, to place ourselves in the ordained relation to the external world, to other men, to ourselves and to Him. One of the noblest acts in this line of obedience is to say to those who are for wise purposes made inferior to us, be free—be men. And if we had no other sources of information from which to learn the real nature and intent of the course of the Mexican Government towards these Mission Indians, we should place it among the noblest deeds of men. But unfortunately it deserves equal distinction of an opposite character. Let succeeding events be heard in evidence.

These declarations of Echuandra and the banishment of their Prefecto, diminished the Padres' hopes of perfecting what they had so gloriously begun—the rearing the Indian population by degrees to the labors, the thoughts, the religion and happiness of civilisation. They well understood what all men will eventually come to know, that an ignorant, stupid species of the human kind, never was and never can be free before their stupidity and ignorance are removed; that the introduction of such people as civil agents among a body of citizens of the higher species, who sustain the responsibilities of advanced society, is attended with no good to any party; but on the contrary, attaches to the acts and thoughts of the higher, advancing and thinking species, the antagonism of the unthinking, the indolent and degrading inferior, whose influence can only be to weaken the moral power of their superiors, and draw them off with all the force of physical indulgence to the confines of barbarism. They perceived, indeed, that freedom to their converts, from their paternal restraints, was only an illusive synonyme of annihilation; that they would, when removed from the action of a superior intelligence, return to the savage state, or use their liberty in following their strongest instincts, which, after all their labors, were towards vices alike ruinous to bodily and moral health. The Padres, for all these causes, became discouraged, and made less effort for the temporal enlargement of their missions. The departure of their best neophytes to the lands assigned them by the Government, left them only the refractory and the ignorant to work the lands, guard ne herds and flocks, and manufacture the cloth, leather and wine, and these being encouraged by Echuandra, neglected their labor, and insulted the Padres when punished for so doing. They even went in bodies to Echuandra and complained that the Padres insisted that they, the free citizens of the Mexican Republic, ought to cultivate the mission farms; and the General encouraged them in their folly. They informed him that the Padres withheld their rations, unless they cultivated the land to raise a new supply; and Echuandra assured them they had reason for dissatisfaction. And on one occasion, when a Padre was insisting on obedience to these wholesome regulations by which they had been elevated from the most abject barbarism to the comforts of a partially civilized state, the deluded creatures threw him violently upon the ground, and otherwise abused him. This, Echuandra assured them, was an act worthy of a citizen of the Mexican Republic.

While the Padres were thus seeing the mission plantations becoming covered with weeds, the buildings going to ruin, their influence over the converts lessening, and these, their spiritual children, given to drunkenness, gambling, theft, and lasciviousness, a party of young Friars from the Convent of San Fernando, in Mexico, were distributed among some of the missions, and the Padres resident commanded to instruct them in the Indian languages and other matters which would prepare them to supplant their teachers. The influence and usefulness of these excellent men was, by these measures, rapidly undermined, till the year 1827, when two of them, Padres Repol and Altemira, of the mission Santa Barbara, fearing for their personal safety, secretly left the country in an American vessel bound to Boston, and sailed from that city to Spain. In the year 1835, others left with passports from Government, and went through Mexico to Spain; and others, worn out with labor and sorrow, died in the country and were buried under the churches of their missions.

In the same year a body of Franciscan monks from the College at Zacatecas, were sent into the Californias by the Government. To these were assigned the rich missions lying north of San Antonio. The old Padres retained the poorer ones lying to the South. Thither these good old priests retired, banished from the missions they had reared, and deprived of the means of comfort which they had procured; and now, in those inhospitable places, they continue to perform their spiritual functions, deprived in their old age not only of the comforts, but of the very necessaries of life. Aged men, tottering grey-headed men; men who had in youth left the abodes of civilized life; who had forsaken father, mother, kindred, and for forty years toiled in the Californian wilderness; ploughed the soil, built churches and dwellings; brought into life, justice and hope and music and prayer to the God of the Universe; under whose hands the trees of virtue and civilisation flourished, adorning the hitherto barren wastes of matter and soul; such were the men condemned by a selfish anarchy to wretchedness and want. But a policy so blind brings evil as its legitimate result.

In 1835, the whole power of the priests over the temporal affairs of these establishments, in both the Californias, was transferred to officers of government called Administradores.

One of these was located at each mission. Their duties ostensibly were to farm them for the benefit of the converts, in order to allow the Padres their whole time for their spiritual labors. But the actual object of this measure was to bring the income and property of the missions within the grasp of the hungry leaches of the Californian Government. For, immediately after the appointment of these officers their wants became pressing, and they began to send orders for hides, &c., to the Administradores, which were uniformly honored and passed to the credit of the missions.

Thirty thousand hides and as many *arobas* of tallow, had been the annual export of this country; but now, a slaughter of the animals commenced, which surpassed the annual increase; and the Padres encouraged the defrauded Indians at the yearly branding, to let many go unmarked and run wild, in anticipation of the approaching period, when tyranny would drive them from their homes to the wilderness. The effects of these measures were to decrease the number of cattle and the amount of the products of the missions, paralyze the industry, deteriorate the morals of the whole community, and introduce in the place of the mild and paternal government of the Padres, the oppressive anarchy of a weak and cruel military despotism; the more despicable in itself, as it proceeded from a source where liberty and equality was the theory, and slavery and robbery the practice of the governing class.

In the year 1836, a quarrel arose between the Mexican Governor at Monterey, and a custom-house officer by the name of Juan Baptiste Alvarado, in regard to the division of certain bribes which had been paid to the officers by the supercargo of a foreign ship, as a remuneration for entering upon the government books only half of the cargo, and admitting the remainder for a certain sum in specie and goods, paid to themselves; and the first result of the difficulty was a revolutionary movement under Alvarado and Graham, as I have heretofore related. But it is necessary here to add that, after the surrender of the Mexican authorities, the foreigners and Californian Spaniards assembled at Monterey and passed these resolutions as the basis of a provisional government.

1st. Upper California is declared to be independent of Mexico during the non-re-establishment of the Federal system, which was adopted in 1824.

2d. The said California shall be erected into a free and governing state, establishing a congress which shall dictate all the particular laws of the country, and elect the other supreme powers necessary, declaring the "Actual Most Excellent Deputation Constituent."

3d. The Religion shall be the Roman Catholic Apostolic, without admitting the exercise of any other; but the government will not molest any persons for their particular religious opinions.

4th. A Constitution shall regulate all the branches of the Administration "provisionally," in conformity as much as possible with the expressed declaration.

5th. Until what is contained in the foregoing articles be put in execution, Señor Don Guadalupe Vallejo shall be called to act as Commandante General.

6th. The President of the "Most Excellent Deputation" shall pass the necessary communications to the municipalities of the Territory.

These proceedings were followed by the banishment of the Mexican Governor, officers and soldiers from the country; the proclamation of Juan Baptiste Alvarado, Civil Governor, and his uncle, Señor Don Mariano Guadalupe Vallejo, Military Governor, or Commandante of the "Republic of Upper California."

Meantime this new Government had placed the seal of final ruin upon the missions. The official corps which had formerly drawn salaries from the Central Government at Mexico was now dependent upon the resources of the country. The Revolutionists and Lawgivers owned large plantations, many of which grazed ten or fifteen thousand head of cattle, besides horses, mules, sheep, &c. But these were private property, not to be taxed for public purposes by these self-denying patriots. The missions, therefore, were resorted to for the means of supporting the Californian Government during the years 1836, 1837, and 1838; and sad was the havoc made upon them by those base descendants of the Chivalry of Spain.

As soon as information of this Revolution in Upper California reached Mexico, the Central Government, with Bustamente at its head, and a kennel of worthless cowards to bark, but never to bite at approaching danger, raised, as is the custom of that hybrid nation of Indian and Spanish Don Quixote-Sancho-Panza-Rosinante-Windmill-Furiosos, on such occasions, an army of fulminating proclamations to the citizens of La Republica Mexicana, and the remainder of the universe, to arm themselves and proceed in terrible array, dealing death elbow-deep in annihilation, against these audacious and unnatural sons of the great, brave, free, glorious, and never-to-be-insulted or conquered nation of Mexico. But these Californians were true, at least, to the weakness and follies of their Spanish blood. Nowhere on the vast plains and mountains of one-half of this continent is there anything Spanish, whether negro, Indian, mulatto, or mestizo, in which may be found anything stable and bloodless. The character of these people may be summed up in these few words: volatility, ignorance, stupidity and pride, coupled with the basest and most cowardly cruelty. Their very language is a furious hyperbole, and their entire nature as a people, is the superlative degree of the adjective frothy, without a substantive of any sort to qualify. The lofty chivalry of Spain was buried in the tombs of the American discoverers and conquerors. Its corslet and spear have fallen into the hands of their Indio-Spanish descendants; and a more worthless rabble of bastards never assumed the name of nation.

See these Californians. No sooner had they declared their independence and rid themselves of the officers from Mexico, than they divided into two parties; the one in the North under Alvarado of Monterey asserting complete inde-

Bustamente.—P. 288:

pendence of Mexico; and the one in the South under Don Carlos Antonio Carrillo, seeking to unite the country again to the parent State. And a blight of idiocy must have fallen on that mind which cannot perceive in the events that ensued, the terrific tread of oppressed human nature, when, clad in the armor of its own avenging power, it goes forth to the conquest of its rights. The Ides of March! How ominous! Cæsar quailed in March! And how much more ought all the enemies of the great Alvarado's supremacy to have shaken from heel to crown, when, on the fifth of that dreadful month of March, he announced to his troops that Don Pedro, the Russian Governor at Bodega, had received letters from St. Petersburg, containing news that France and England had resolved to place Iturbide II., son of the Emperor Iturbide I., upon the throne of Mexico!! The reader may almost see His Excellency's wrath kindling at this proposed encroachment on the liberties of nations. "What, France and England pretend to foist a monarch upon the people of Mexico, and even upon His Excellency of California!"—and that too while he was Governor? Such impudence, if it were not "ridiculously impotent as against Mexico, would be found so in regard to California!!" And to this effort at patriotism and self-complacency, see his heroic Californians emitting some fumes of bravery, accompanied with a series of consolatory threats, stamping their feet on the Lord's footstool, and strongly grasping their swords, looking things unutterable enough to put a notable end to the hopes of Iturbide II. During this daring demonstration for freedom, Alvarado is universally believed to have stood firmly at his post, and unshrinkingly done his duty. The Don in the South also is reported not to have lost a meal of beans on account of this startling intelligence. Courage in California, as elsewhere, is a fine tonic for weak nerves. The event too which succeeded this in the history of the Californias found both these worthies in the field of glory. So that if some ignorant reader should presume to say, at this point of our narration, that the

Don was less brave, patriotic, or in any other sense less a Californian cavallero, than Alvarado, he is desired to suspend the expression of such an unworthy opinion until he shall have read the following account of a campaign which, I am credibly informed, is considered by the warriors of that country the most remarkably glorious on record.

In the spring of 1838, a courier arrived from Santa Barbara, bearing a message of mighty import from the illustrious Don Carlos Antonio Carrillo to Alvarado the Conqueror. Its purport was that the high—mighty—invincible—and ever-to-be-dreaded Central Government at Mexico, had bared its puissant arm, stretched it out, raised it up, brought it down, and at a single blow, made and put together a gentleman Don, to wit, Don Carlos Antonio Carrillo, and constituted him the Goubernador del Alta California: and with the exercise of the like resistless power had ordered the said Alvarado—villain—robber—slave—to surrender, lay down, and for ever after eschew the sceptre of Goubernador del Alta California; unto which message His Excellency, in the true Castilian spirit, and with as much good sense as any one had a right to expect of him, Alvarado the Conqueror, replied. "On seeing the commission of my successor, and on finding it conformable to the usages of the Nation; and on obtaining from him my said successor, a guaranty of safety to my person and property, and also to the persons and property of those who acted with me in the Revolution of 1836, I will resign the reins of government into the hands of my illustrious uncle. Otherwise not—never!" This response of the lofty Alvarado was soon *en route* towards the dwelling-place of the Don. But the mountainous character of the country over which its bearer passed retarded its speed so much that the sixth day had well nigh closed before the indignation of that exalted man was fired at the story of Alvarado's insolence. It was fortunate, undoubtedly, that so much time was allowed to elapse between the development of the courage necessary to enable the Don to send the messenger to Alva-

Mexican Cavalry.—Page 290. *Mexican Infantry.*—Page 290.

rado, and that effort of sublime forbearance required to receive his answer. For it is deemed an established principle in the physiology of courage as well as of steamboats, that too great a pressure upon the internal surface of an enclosing boiler will cause a bursting, disastrous, in a certain sense, to those in the vicinity. Soldiers going into battle for the first time are said to give the happiest illustrations of this law. Be this as it may, however, true it is, that when the courier related to him all that the Governor had said, the exalted Don exhibited a capacity in the manufacture of fury at short notice, which made the floor tremble on which he stood; and it is currently believed that if there had not been a hiatus between the demand of the Don and the said refusal of Alvarado, greater danger to the integrity of the Don's physical system would have been the unwholesome consequence. As it was, however, that immense personage merely took a glass of native wine, and summoned his friends to arms for doing battle in behalf of La Republica Mexicana.

Alarm, that protecting genius of all cowards, is declared to have a swift wing. At all events, no sooner did the banner of the glorious old Don begin to flap on the breezes of wakeful night, than she presented her fluttering form at Monterey, and whispered in the ear of Alvarado, of power, of camps, of carnage fields, of fame's bold clarion, and the terror of his uncle Don. All these things put together made one other thing quite clear to Alvarado's vast comprehension; namely, that he must again take to the field—the field in which in 1836 he had earned bright laurels, and again fight as he then did, for country and freedom, or bow submissively before the overpowering valor of his great rival. Nor was his genius at fault in this trying exigency. He took his resolution; and having done so, what else could the world have expected, than that his Excellency and the never-to-be-equalled Captain Jose Castro, of villainous memory, should call the troops to arms and march for the seat of war. And this they certainly did as nearly as circumstances permitted;

that is to say, Alvarado remained in Monterey, three hundred miles from powder and ball, and Jose Castro marched towards Santa Barbara with an army of six men.

The Don meanwhile was not inactive. He wisely determined, as a first step, to take military possession of Santa Barbara. Accordingly, from the balcony of his habitation, which the foreign residents had fitted up for him at El Pueblo de los Angelos, he gave notice to his veteran army assembled one hundred strong, that he should march immediately upon that devoted town and sack it according to the rules of war. After a long and tedious forced march on horseback, of thirty miles, in a single day, over a grassy and undulating country, during which they endured more, if possible, than their forefathers did in all their wars with the Moors, they arrived on the 20th of March, 1838, upon a hill about two miles from that village, encamped, held a council of war, and hnmanely determined to send in a flag, and an expression of their unwillingness to shed blood; but the messenger was especially instructed to announce, that the town of Santa Barbara must be surrendered, or the veteran army would take possession of it, if, in so doing, they "trode at every step upon the pulseless hearts of the dying inhabitants!"

The Commandant of the place was not so much frightened by this announcement as he ought to have been. But, on the contrary, knowing probably that the old Don was a man of his word and not of deed, sent back the following reply. "Señor Carlos Antonio Carrillo had better not be in haste to enter Santa Barbara. Alvarado will soon make his grand entrance. If, however, the Don should deem it his duty to sack Santa Barbara, it will be mine to yield to the disagreeable necessity of preventing such a catastrophe, by firing on his ranks and destroying the lives of fellow-countrymen. God and Liberty!" This message was more terrific than satisfactory to the commander of the invading army. But as night soon cast its protecting mantle over the fierce brows of the immortal one hundred, it was never known to the fullest extent how much heroism they exhibited when ordered into quarters for the night, with the injunction to hold themselves ready for the dreadful work of death at a moment's warning. It is however known that a mounted picket guard was stationed on the hills, and a strong patrol along the ravines, between the camp and the town, and that all, Napoleon-like, slept upon the eve of vast events; that the next morning dawned; the earth turned on its axis, showed the sun and hid it again; and that the army of the Don neither left its encampment, nor took possession of Santa Barbara; and that night came again; that patrols and pickets were stationed as before. But such apparent inaction was not to continue

On the morning of the 23d, a movement clearly showed that irresolution was no part of the Don's nature. And well did he exclaim, as he addressed the soldiery on that most memorable day,—"The pent fires of Californian bravery, who can quench them? What one of us, whether plebeian born or a descendant of the Spanish Cavaliers, will flee before the servile minions of the ignoble Alvarado? What man with a heart quickened by Castilian blood, will not pour out that blood in defence of California, and the union of the Mexican States?" To this appeal a response arose and echoed among the hills, in that hearty and lusty manner so characteristic of Spanish Californians, and other animals distinguished for long ears. He next commended the courage displayed, and the valorous exploits performed in the siege they were prosecuting. "They had crowned their names with deeds of immortal renown." And then the officers' swords flamed from their scabbards, and the privates stood shoulder to shoulder in the most threatening attitudes of the genuine warrior, as the Don took breath, and with emphasis remarked, that the army of Santa Barbara was approaching!!! It approached!!! All saw it!!! Halted!! The Don reconnoitred!! and horrible to tell—the opposing forces numbered one hundred and four noses!! His own, himself included, one hundred and one only!!! A difference of three whole noses, against the Don!!! And who in California knew better than he, the power and effect of such superiority? Who understood more clearly than the Don, the execution which that number of noses might do in the approaching struggle for "LAW AND ORDER?" But who, among all living and dead heroes, could better rally the energies required to meet that horrible crisis, than the Don? None! His horse even partook of the overpowering magnitude of the energies that bestrode his back, and bore his rider along the line with unwonted speed and fire as the order boomed along, for the soldiers to prime anew their pans —shoulder their gleaming muskets, and retreat within the walls of the Mission Santa Buenaventura!!

Three days after this intrepid retreat of the invading army, the redoubtable Captain Jose Castro arrived at Santa Barbara, with the army of the North, six men strong, well appointed with muskets, powder, ball, and Californian patriotism. His entry was a triumph; rendered sweet to that warrior's heart by the consciousness of being looked upon, while his army defiled through the streets, as the saviour of all the mud walls, tiles, and babies of that famous town. He repaired to quarters in the barracks, dined with becoming dignity, and smoked a cigar. After this important business had been dispatched, he summoned before him the authorities, and made an exhibit of the luxuriant love of country, which had led Alvarado—that superlative adjative of the genus *homo*, to assume the government of Alta California, and assured the Commandante, and Alcaldes, that he was authorized and ready to receive the surrender of the place, and the fealty of the inhabitants to the Revolutionary Government. He added, that he hoped it might not be necessary for him to use force in the premises. This latter intimation, backed as it was by the standing presence of the army of six, was deemed of great service to humanity, for no hesitation was manifested by the population, amounting to some six hundred souls, about submitting to the new order of things so gallantly proposed to them by the renowned Captain.

Captain Castro.—Page 294.

The next act of Captain Castro which history will delight to record, was that of arresting certain persons at Santa Barbara supposed to be favorable to the pretensions of the Don; namely, Pedro C. Carrillo, the old Don's son, and a Don Angelo, former Administrador of the Port of Monterey, under the late Mexican authorities. The former he put on board the bark Kamamula, and sent to sea for safe keeping; the latter was transmitted to Monterey as a tropny of the glorious victory achieved by the Grand Army of six at Santa Barbara.

Captain Castro tarried only two days at Santa Barbara. But during that short space of time he was enabled, by using that indefatigable industry and intrepidity for which he was so remarkable, to make the two arrests which I have mentioned. And although it has been said by persons presumed to be envious of the Captain's right to call himself the Napoleon of California, that these prisoners made no attempt to escape, but, on the contrary, surrendered themselves without resistance, yet the impartial historian will undoubtedly find, on thorough investigation, that he who captured Graham and others with so much bravery and renown, could not, in the possibility of things, have done this act so tamely as the enemies of the Captain would maliciously represent. Captain Castro *was* a Napoleon, and by what specious sophistry can mankind be made to believe that he did not arrest Señores Pedro and Angelo, in a manner worthy of that immortal name?

On the third day, the Grand Army of the North being increased by the people of Santa Barbara to one hundred men, and supplied with three field-pieces, moved against the Grand Army of the South at San Buenaventura. They arrived in the night; and while the darkness shielded them from view, they planted the cannon on the heights overlooking the Mission, and otherwise prepared themselves for the horrors of the coming day. When the morning dawned, the Captain had the satisfaction to perceive that his position had been so well taken that the garrison of the opposing forces was completely at his mercy; and like all other great men, being shocked at the idea of shedding blood so profusely as he must do, if he opened upon the Mission the terrors of his cannon, he sent in a flag and demanded a surrender. But, strange to say, the Don, not having before his eyes the fear of Castro's ammunition, refused obedience to this reasonable request, and commenced a brisk discharge of musketry from the walls. This was answered by those outside with both muskets and cannon. The work of death thus commenced went on until the shutting in of night on the fourth day! How grateful were the shadows of that night to the besieged! The lighted taper that burned at the altar of the Chapel, sent a straggling ray over the area within the walls, and glimmered faintly on the arms of the Don's soldiery! But neither that light from the altar of hope, nor the beaming bayonets of the besieged veterans, could inspire their hearts with the firmness required to prolong so terrific and destructive a conflict. In the silent moment of midnight, therefore, more than half of the Don's remaining troops made a desperate sally from the gate, and not being opposed for awhile, believed that their intrepidity had saved them! But they were unfortunately mistaken! The Captain's sentinels had noticed their operations, and sounded the alarm so bravely that they surrendered themselves at discretion, without waiting for the unnecessary ceremony of being captured, or in anywise endangered.

After these men had thus daringly given themselves up to their foes, their companions, the glorious old Don and all, capitulated. And now came the calling of the rolls and the burial of the dead! Sad rites to those who survive such days of carnage! Forty-eight hours of cannonading on the one side, and of busy musket-shots on the other!! How many had ceased to breathe, was the anxious inquiry! The official returns read thus, "Of the army of the South one man killed. Of the army of the North one man wounded.—God and Liberty." It is proper to observe in this place, that it was afterwards a question often raised between the soldiers of the two armies, whether the Don or the Captain surrendered. But the most authentic accounts rather favor the opinion that the Captain had the better of the battle. And I have little doubt that when the Hume of that country shall write its annals, and some unborn Ossian shall sing of the mighty tread and thundering bucklers of the Castros and Carrillos of that streamy land, they will not only commemorate the bloody ramparts of San Buenaventura, but speak worthily of the Don, as great even in defeat, and of Captain Jose as gloriously triumphant. This idea is remarkably strengthened by the fact that as soon as the termination of the campaign was announced at Monterey, the puissant Alvarado journeyed to San Buenaventura, and thence in company with his Captain Castro to El Pueblo de los Angelos, where he took possession of the worthy old Don's house, and acted the Governor upon the wines and brandies therein contained, with all the taste and suavity so well known to be his peculiar excellences, and possessed himself of whatever else he listed of the Don's personal estate. But—how unjust not to name it—after having robbed his uncle, he gave in return a promise to pay, which I was told still stands good against him, a sum equal to his own estimate of the value he had taken.

From El Pueblo de los Angelos, Governor Alvarado proceeded to San Diego, the southernmost port of Alta California; and received there and elsewhere the submission of the inhabitants, till the whole country recognized the said Juan Baptiste Alvarado, El Goubernador del Alta California. Even the glorious old Don Carlos Antonio Carrillo is said to have paid court to the young conqueror, and not altogether unwillingly, after so much blood shed in defence of his dignity and the high honors of his office, to have laid aside his pretensions with much grace and apparent satisfaction; thus demonstrating that noble and rare principle which leads the truly great man,—after the exercise of every energy, after wading through seas of gore, after baring his bosom to the knife of fate, after having met, defied, endured, every hazard, every hardship, for the attainment of his just rights,— to prove himself not only "par secundis," but "major adversis," by seeking repose, and calling on the shades of forgetfulness to fall around the memory of heroic exploits, which such a man blushes to hear coupled with his name. So little need has true worth of noise and praise. But I should do great injustice to the worthy Don, if I neglected to state his manner of obtaining the commission of Governor of Upper California, in support of which he struggled so manfully.

About two years after the Revolution which raised Alvarado to power, the excellent old Don sent an account of that event to his friend Sa Excellentissimo, El Presidente Bustamente, in which among other matters it was stated that, in case Mexico would make an appointment of a Californian of the Governorship of the country (suggesting at the same time that he the worthy Don was at the service of the State,)—he, the Don, and his *amīgos* would reconquer the country, and return it to the allegiance of Mexico. The Don's brother, a man of great patriotism—*id est*, Mexican patriotism, or the most devoted disposition to take care of himself,—bore this dispatch. In due time he returned with a commission—empowering his brother Don to assume the Government of Alta California. The only irregularity in the instrument which arrested attention was the absence of the proper signatures and the Seal of State. But as the Don was called El Goubernador in the body of the instrument, that irregularity was deemed by his friends of trifling importance. But it was this that the wily Alvarado seized upon as a pretext for not delivering up the helm of Government to the most excellent and stately old Don, and allowing himself and his partisans to be shot according to the law, for having rebelled against La Republica Mexicana.

From the year 1838 to the year 1840, the time when the author entered California, Alvarado continued to be the Governor of that lovely land. And during that period no events occurred worthy of being detailed.

CHAPTER XVI.

A New Era in California—War with the United States—Various Battles—Heroism of the Americans—Conquest—Discovery of Gold — Brilliant Hopes — On the Pacific again — Long Tom Finishes his Yarn—Speculations on the Future of California—The Prisoners—Poor Graham—Home and my Wife—Reflections.

Soon after this commenced a new era in the history of California. In 1845 a rupture occurred between the United States and Mexico. Commodore Sloat of the Pacific Squadron, hearing of the commencement of hostilities on the Rio Grande, immediately seized Monterey, hoisted the Star Spangled Banner from the Custom House, and issued a proclamation of war to the people of the Californias.

It would be foreign from our purpose to give a detailed history of this war. The principal incidents are doubtless still fresh in the memory of most of our readers. Suffice it to say, that Commodore Stockton, General Kearney, Colonel Fremont, Captains Barrows and Thompson, and hosts of others, did honor to the flag of their country by their gallant achievements. At the Rio San Gabriel, and on the plains of Meza, decisive battles were fought against overwhelming odds, when victory, as usual, perched upon the American banner, with a loss of only one killed and thirteen wounded in the two fights. Various other engagements occurred, the history of all of which will be found in other volumes.

One incident will illustrate the daring and heroic character of the men engaged in that glorious struggle. At

Santa Barbara, Lieutenant Talbot, with only nine men under his command, was besieged by a large body of the enemy and compelled to evacuate the place. He gallantly forced his way through the besiegers to the mountains in the vicinity, where, refusing to surrender on any terms, he kept the enemy at bay like a tiger in his lair, until they set fire to the groves and bushes around him, and actually burned him out. He then forced a march of five hundred miles through the enemy's country on foot to Monterey, where his arrival caused the utmost joy to all the Americans, with whom he was a great favorite, and who had given him up as lost.

By the terms of the treaty of peace, California came into possession of the United States. Next came the discovery of gold and the rush of emigrants to that country from all parts of the world. Exaggerated stories of the immense mineral wealth of the new El Dorado inflamed the minds of men, and thousands left the slow but sure pursuits of home for sudden wealth in a strange land. With a few the dream has been realized; and although in the aggregate vast sums of gold have been obtained, yet a large proportion of the miners have learned the to them sad lesson that man, in any country, to be truly happy, must earn his living by the sweat of his brow. Through much exposure and suffering, wearied and heart broken, the poor miner has not unfrequently returned from the scene of his brilliant hopes to spend his last hours among his early friends—a sadder but a wiser man.

But to return. On the fifth of May, 1840, we made our adieus to our acquaintance in Santa Barbara, preparatory to falling down the coast. The American visited the sick Englishman, found him breathing faintly, and apparently very near death. But it was necessary to embark, and leave the dying man in the kind care of his nurses, who, I have no

Battle of the Meza.—

doubt, administered to his last want, and made his grave-dress with willing hands. "Dead—starved to death! Death of a Briton from thirst and starvation, by direction of Juan Baptista Alvarado, Governor of Upper California," is the account which truth will give, on earth and at the judgment, of this man's death.

At twelve o'clock, the lusty fellows at the windlass had the anchor on the bow, and our good old ship was bearing down the coast under a fine northerly breeze. She, or rather he, for I believe all Dons are males, and particularly Don Quixotes, being in ballast, ran rapidly, cheeringly, and exultingly over the quiet sea. And right glad were we to be under weigh. We had been long enough among the jolly birds and flowering meadows of California, to rejoice to be again at sea. It was sad, however, to be borne away from the prisons and the moans of our fellow-countrymen. And now the deep blue sea—its mermaid song—its anthems of sublimity—its glories and beauties; really and in truth, what are they? What man in his senses loves the Ocean? The mermaids are all porpoises, and their songs all grunts! The deep sounds of the ocean's pealing organ, are the rude groans of the winds and the dashing rage of far-rolling surges, rapping madly at the bows! The tufts of dancing foam on the bitter wastes—desert, heaving, unsympathizing, cold, homeless! Love of Ocean!! Poetry of Ocean!! It is a pity I cannot love it—see in its deep still lower realm, or in its lonely tumults, or its surface when the air is still, its heat, thirst and death, its vast palpitating tomb, the shady hand and veiled smile of loveliness!—that I cannot believe Old Ocean has a heart, which sends its kindly beatings up and down all the shores of earth! Poetry! Loveliness! They may be there; but Ocean's odor and mien are not poetry to me! If I have ever said anything to the contrary, I beg the pardon of the sea poets. There is, however, a certain class of beings who hold a very different opinion: these are the regular old *Salts;* men who from boyhood have slept in the forecastle, eaten at the windlass, sung at the halyards, danced on the yards to the music of the tempest, and hailed the tumult of the seas as a frolic in which they had a joyful part. We respect these poets. Indeed, the Ocean to them is a world, the theatre of their being; and by inhabiting it all their days, these singular men become changed from participants in the delights of natural life on land, to creatures of memory. Memory! that mental action which sifts the past of its bitterest evils, and gives only the blossom and the fruit to after-time. These they enjoy in the midnight watch, at the dawn, in the storm, the calm, and in visions of sleep; but for ever upon the deep, on the great expanse of the Sea! Is it wonderful, then, that they should love it? that their affections become poetry? See them seated at their meal before the mast; their wide pants lap over their sprawled limbs; the red flannel shirt peers out at the wrists, and blazes over their broad chests between the ample dimensions of the heavy pea-jacket; and crowning all is the tarpaulin with its streaming band, cocked on one side of the head; and grouped in the most approved style of a thoroughly lazy independence, they eat their meal. At such times, if the weather be fine, studding-sails out, and top-gallants pulling, they speak of the ship as a lady, well decked, and of beautiful bearing, gliding like a nymph through the gurgling waters. If the breeze be strong, and drives her down on her beams, they speak of her as bowing to her Lord and Master, while she uses his might to bear her on to her own purposes. And if the tempest weighs on the sea, and the fierce winds howl down upon her dead ahead, and the storm-sail displays over the fore-chains its three-sided form, and the ship lays up to the raging elements, breasting every swoop of wave and blast, she still is a lady, coming forth from her empire of dependent loveliness to bow before an irresistible force, only to rise again, and present the sceptre of Hope to dismayed man. These *Salts* believe in the poetry of the sea, and of the noble structures in which they traverse its pathless immensity. And it may be that they are right, and I am wrong.

During the day we passed near to the coast. A fruitful strip of land running along the shore; broken by hills increasing in height from the water-side towards the interior, and bounded by high mountains partially covered with trees, but generally burnt and barren, is a true showing of that part of California. It was a bright day, with a cool wholesome air. Every sail was out and filled, as white as snow, the wind on the larboard quarter, the crew lounging, and the dolphins chasing, and the gulls screaming, and the spray dashing at the bows. Home, and the mother of my buried boy, if I may speak of myself, the heart's guiding star on those wastes of soul and of nature, were drawing near me, and in thought were there. Speed on, noble ship, speed on; it is the illusion of happy memories, speed on!

On the sixth and seventh the breeze continued favorable. The coast was generally in sight, and appeared to be more and more barren as we followed it down!

On the eighth we sailed along the east side of Guadeloupe. This island is about thirty miles in circumference, somewhat mountainous, evidently of volcanic origin, surrounded by immense reefs of black rocks, and destitute of coral formations There are two places of access, the one on the southwest, the other on the northwest side. It has no harbor for anything else than small boats; and though containing considerable quantities of arable land, is uninhabited except by sea birds, turtles and goats. The latter are the offspring of a few of these animals landed upon it by the early Spanish navigators. They have been in unmolested possession of the island for the last eighty years, and are now so very numerous, that they could be profitably hunted for their skins and tallow. In former times this island used to abound in sea elephants and hair seal; but the American hunters and whalers have nearly destroyed them. As we passed, a right whale spouted near the shore. The circumstance electrified Tom, and opened his word loom to the following yarn.

"The lubber, that whale! I would like to be in the bow of a staunch boat, with four stout oarsmen, and a bold fellow to steer upon him; I would soon make him spout blood instead of water!

'I was telling you the yarn of my becoming a sailor, when the old man coiled up my thoughts among the halyards. Now that whale brings them back again, and while he is taking his observation, and blowing his nose, I'll finish my yarn. I was about nineteen when I blundered against the capstan of a whaler, and shipped at New Bedford for a three years' cruise. We left port with as good an outfit of harpoons, lines, knives, trying-pans, stores, and ship's crew as ever swam the brine. I remember we had a studdin-sail breeze a longer time on our passage out, than I ever saw before or since, except in the trades. We put out all sail in sight of the New Bedford Light, and never took in a rag until we had crossed the equator; and then we struck a dead calm, which continued fifteen days. That was the worst siege at oakum and spun yarn that Tom ever saw. The sun seemed to pour down fire! It was so warm that the tar in the deck fried and bubbled; and the old long boat shrunk so much that you could stick your thumb through between the planks; and the decks were so hot that we were obliged to keep them constantly wet to enable us to stand on them. And as to breathing, we found that the hardest work of all. The great atmosphere seemed to have escaped, and left a perfect void! The ocean was smooth; not a rough spot upon it as big as a cent, except when the cook threw his slush overboard! It lay and rolled like a bending sea of glass! The vessel, with its sails hanging loose on the mast, rose and fell on it like a sheet upon the breast of the dying. The sky was awfully bare and deserted! Not a shred of a cloud dotted it for fifteen days! I never felt lonesome till that time. I had rather lay to under storm sail a twelvemonth, than be compelled to pick oakum and make spun yarn, and think through a calm like that. Well, at the end of fifteen days, just as the sun set, a little cloud about as large as John's tarpaulin, scud up in the nor'west, like an angel of mercy to tell us there was wind once more in the heavens; and about eight o'clock the old ocean began to stir; the air struck our parched bodies, and the sails flapped, the vessel moved, and we began to feel that we were climbing out of a great hot grave; I never shall forget that calm.

"Well, we had light breezes till we got off Montevideo, when a stiff norther came on, which bore us on under double-reefed topsails down to the Cape. Here it came on to blow a gale, and we were obliged to run into Magellan, and lay to under the lee of the highlands. After lying there two days, the wind chopped round northeast, and the old man thought we might as well run through the Straits. But the gale was renewed, and rushed overland upon us with such fury that we could carry for a number of days, only sail enough to make the ship lay her course. At last we hove in sight of the Pacific, and run afoul one of those villainous head winds which you know often set into the west end of the Straits. This detained us nine days. At the end of this time, it hauled into the northeast, and enabled us to get into the open sea. Our course from the Straits was NW. But the wind again chopped round dead ahead; consequently all we could do was to try to hold our own. We accordingly beat off and on, and lay too twelve days, when we found me must up helm and let her run. The gale was awful; and as we advanced south the raggedness of the sea was continually more and more frightful; the cold became intense; the water froze upon the deck six inches deep; and the spars, and masts, and rigging were covered with ice to such an extent, that the ship swayed under the gale, and was likely to swamp; the most like a death-call from the mermaids that Tom ever saw, was that gale. The ship lurching her spars into the waves, the sailors slipping, the rigging stiff, and the only sail set, covered with ice several inches thick; the masts like vast icicles, and the old man and every man expecting every moment to go down! After drifting, however, as far as 70° South, the gale abated, the wind changed, we cut away the studding-sail, rigged another, and stood away for the north, and in a few days got rid of our ice and other troubles. We now took our course for New Zealand, and about 300 miles east of that island fell in with the whales I thought of, as we"——. "Bear a hand there, you lubbers." "Aye, aye, sir." "Bring out the old trysail, and run your yarns into that." "Aye, aye, sir." And thus was Tom's yarn again severed, much to his chagrin, and my regret; for I longed to hear a whalesman's account of his bold and dangerous calling.

On the 10th of May we came in sight of Cape San Lucas, bearing thirty miles SE. It was about five o'clock, P. M. The wind had been dying away since noon, and now barely kept the ship moving. The western portion of the sea was all light and glorious; it lay panting, as a wearied giant just returned from the field of conflict. The sun, as he fell steadily down the great arc of heaven, was reflected more and more widely and intensely, until his reddest rays shot through the clear tops of the billows, and scattered a purple drapery of clouds sprinkled with gold up half the western sky. Gay-plumaged land birds gathered on the rigging, and twittered and sang to the approaching twilight. The land was eight miles from us; a rough red waste of mountains! those holy desolations where the Indians' God made his descent to bless them, their streams, their fruits, and give elasticity to their bows. Sturdy scenes! rocks on rocks, gloom on gloom, sand on sand, and dearth feeding dearth, and universal thirst preying on animal and herb! The living things in the sea frolicked around us. The dolphin, the bonitos, the flying fish, the porpoise, the right whale, were all employing their muscles in their own way among the sleeping waters; and about the sides of the almost motionless vessel swarmed shoals of bright and active little fish that seemed to beseech us for protection and food. As the sun's disc sank below the horizon, and he withdrew his last rays from the mists of the sea, and left the stars to their own twinkling, the mellow clear blue of a tropical sky came out over us; such a sky as hangs over Athens and the Egean tides and islands. This was reflected back from the waves, on which the stars danced and flickered, were extinguished and lighted up again, as swell after swell approached the ship, and rocked, as does the heart of the mother the child slumbering on her breast. The moon was in the first quarter, rounding to the full. And I remember never to have felt so strong a sympathy with it as on that glorious night. If dreams come when reason sleeps, and recollection serves only to feed the affections, and deepen the musings of the imagination and associating powers, I certainly dreamed with eyes on the moon and stars and the sea of that night. The day had gone; it was night; the stars were out, and the sea was dancing to the music of the far distant and ceased tempest, and the moon had come over my home, was shining through its windows upon the table at which we ate, on the chairs in which we sat, on the walls that had witnessed the high and unmarred pleasures of the domestic affections. It was lighting up the altar of my holiest hopes, and crowding upon it every gem of joy which had shone on the path of the past! A bird chirped among the rigging a note which resembled one that had gladdened evening walks, and often died in the ear as in the opening spring sleep was gathering us to rest; and that chosen star, that consecrated star, that star on which we hung our vows at parting, was looking down upon me! I walked forward among the watch, who were loitering about the forecastle in silence. "A fine night this, sir," said one of them, "a fine night, sir. This weather reminds one of our New England Indian summers, when I used to go out of an evening to a country dance, and throw clubs into the trees to get the finest apples for the neighboring girls. I recollect that I lost my heart on just such a night as this, when about twelve years old! I went over to neighbor Parker's to invite them to a husking, and the old gentleman insisted, after I had done my errand, that I should stay awhile and help John shell a grist of yellow corn; for he wanted to go to mill at sunrise next morning. So down I sat on a little wooden bench at one end of the warming-pan handle, which was put through the ears of a wash-tub, and shelled away bravely. But all the time I was at work, Rachel was pulling my ears, and throwing kernels of corn at me, and showing her white teeth and sweet lips and eyes around me, until my ears and cheeks burnt, my eyes were swimming with love, and my head and heart felt so mixed up together that they have never got unravelled since."

Another one said that these yarns about love were always coming up around the windlass, and he hoped they would be hauled in, and stowed away soon, for it was quite enough to remember one's girl and poor old mother thousands of miles away when obliged to; and that this way of bringing them into every watch, and harrowing up one's feelings, was worse than being strung up at the yardarm every twelve hours: as he said this, he turned away, and wiped his moist cheek on the sleeve of his pea-jacket.

On the 11th, we lay along the Cape. The contour of the land was distinctly visible. The mountains rise in arid grandeur, rough volcanic cinders, red and desolate. They are curiously piled. Huge mountains sprout from the main masses, and hang over wooded jungles a thousand feet below. Turrets rise on turrets like giant castles of an olden land They are an irregular, unstratified, ugly, desolate confusion of rocks and dust. On the 12th, we lay six miles SE. of the point of the Cape. We had a fine view of both shores of the Gulf of California for fifty miles. The scenery was extremely interesting. The eastern Cape shore was much like the western. The eastern shore of the Gulf, the edge of the Mexican main, was sublime. Not so much so on account of its massiveness or its altitude, as its resemblance to a continent of continuous cities, interspersed with groves. The general aspect was dreary.

On the 13th, a light breeze from the south bore us along about three knots the hour. The Gulf shores opened wider as we advanced. High mountains rose on the main in the NE. The coasts of the Gulf are said to be mountainous up to the mouth of the Colorado of the West.

In the evening the mountains on the Mexican side were lighted up with immense fires—some of them resembled those of volcanoes; others, the raging flames among the firs and pines of the Green Mountains; others, the deep glow of the log heaps of the American fallows.

On the fourteenth we sailed across the mouth of the Californian Gulf or sea of Cortes, and at night-fall lay in full view of the rocky islands around the anchorage of Mazatlan. Cape San Lucas had faded away in the northern horizon near sunset, and I confess I regretted to know that I should probably see its hills and plains no more; but a reflection upon the destiny of the Californias took the place of such sorrow. That country must become a constituent member in the great brotherhood of American Nations. As a maritime country it is unequalled on the western coast of America; indeed I should say, it is not approached in this respect by any country bordering on the Pacific seas.

The harbors of San Quintin in Latitude 30° 23′ N., San Diego in Latitude 33° N., and San Francisco in Latitude 37° N., afford secure anchorage for the navies of the civilized world, and every desirable facility for erecting wharves, docks and arsenals. These indenting a country capable of sustaining thirty-five millions of people, with the healthiest climate on the continent, affording abundance of live oak and other materials, without stint, for the construction and rigging of vessels, and a rich soil bearing on the same acre the fruits of the tropical and the temperate zones; with the greatest possible facilities for commercial intercourse with the eastern shores of the Russian Empire, China, India, Australia, and the Hawaiian, and other Islands of the Pacific, as well as the whole western coast of America, indicate the Californias as the seat of the ruling maritime power of that half of the world.

But there are other reasons for this opinion. A canal can easily be cut from the head of steamboat navigation on the San Joaquim to the head waters of the Gulf of California. This, for warlike and commercial purposes, would be invaluable.

Another circumstance, however, is of more value than any I have named in forming an estimate of the undeveloped greatness of this charming country. It is the intellectual and physical might of the people who are to inhabit it.

In order to indicate what race this is to be, we need only refer to the facts, that the navigable waters of the Missouri River are within six hundred miles of Puget's Sound: that a railroad of that length will send the commerce of the Indies, China, and the Californias into the Mississippi valley, and send the inhabitants of that valley to the Californias; and that Nature herself has connected that country with the States by an excellent natural road.

This route from the San Joaquim to the plains of the Missouri is not only feasible but easy. A Mr. Yunt, from Franklin, in the State of Missouri, and now a resident of Upper California, travelled from the Great Salt Lake to Monterey with loaded mules in thirty days. From this lake to the navigable waters of the San Joaquim is not more than three hundred and fifty miles, with plenty of wood, water and grass the whole distance. The high range of mountains between the San Joaquim and Mary's river can be passed in six hours. There is a low gap, pathway leading through it. The route from this gap leads up Mary's river to the forks; thence up the east fork, and over the plains, to the Pont Neuf branch of the Saptin; thence through a gap in the mountains to Big Bear river at the Soda Springs; thence up Bear river and over the plains to the Rendezvous on the Sheetskadee; thence over the plains to the Sweetwater branch of the north fork o

Great Platte; thence down that river to its entrance into the Missouri.

Along this track population must go westward. No one acquainted with the indolent, mixed race of California, will ever believe that they will populate, much less, for any length of time, govern the country. The law of Nature which curses the mulatto here with a constitution less robust than that of either race from which he sprang, lays a similar penalty upon the mingling of the Indian and white races in California and Mexico. They must fade away; while the mixing of different branches of the Caucasian family in the States will continue to produce a race of men, who will enlarge from period to period the field of their industry and civil domination, until not only the Northern States of Mexico, but the Californias also, will open their glebe to the pressure of its unconquered arm. The old Saxon blood must stride the continent, must command all its northern shores, must here press the grape and the olive, here eat the orange and fig, and in their own unaided might, erect the altar of civil and religious freedom on the plains of the Californias.

Mazatlan; we anchored in the roads, and having passed a day and two nights with Mr. Parrot, our worthy consul, and another American who was addicted to aristocracy and smuggling, we bade adieu to Captain Paty and his Don Quixote, to Messrs. Johnson and Chamberlain, and sailed for San Blas in the schooner Gertrudes, formerly the Honduras of the Hawaiian Isles. On the sixteenth we anchored along side the prison-ship in the roads of San Blas, and had the pleasure of knowing that none of our countrymen had perished on the passage. They had suffered greatly from thirst and hunger; but they lived; and that to us and to them was cause of the deepest gratitude. Forty-six Americans and Britons in chains!—in the chains of Californian Spaniards! Will not the day come when vengeance will be repaid?

During the afternoon and the night following day we rode sixty miles to the city of Tepic, and laid the case of these prisoners before the American and British consuls, who rendered them all the aid and protection which their situation required. Graham finally returned to California, a broken-spirited, ruined man. The others are dispersed elsewhere.

From here we mounted our mules, crossed the Republic of Mexico, and sailed to New Orleans.

THE END.

www.ingramcontent.com/pod-product-compliance
Lightning Source LLC
LaVergne TN
LVHW010200110826
845151LV00002B/565

* 9 7 8 1 4 2 5 5 3 6 7 7 0 *